COASTAL SE

MARITIME DIMENSIONS OF INDIA

Coastal Security

Maritime Dimensions of India's Homeland Security

Prof. K. R. Singh

(Established 1870)

United Service Institution of India
New Delhi

Vij Books India Pvt Ltd
Ansari Road, Daryaganj, New Delhi

Published   by

Vij Books India Pvt Ltd
(Publishers, Distributors & Importers)
2/19, Ansari Road, Darya Ganj
New Delhi - 110002
Phones: 91-11-43596460, 91-11- 65449971
Fax: 91-11-47340674
www.vijbooks.com
e-mail : vijbooks@rediffmail.com

ISBN: 978-93-81411-29-2

Contents

Preface

I have been studying multiple facets of maritime security for decades. Earlier, the focus was on naval strategy *vis-à-vis* state actors, at the level of super powers as also regional powers in South Asia. By the end of the eighties, I got interested in the increasing role being played by non-state actors like pirates and the opposition that used sea space to target state actors. That was represented by the hijacking of *Achille Laura* by a section of Palestinian radicals as also by the *Sea Tigers* of the LTTE. It was followed by the smuggling of RDX for bomb blasts in Mumbai in 1993.

Each of them threw light on different facets of the use of sea space by Non-State Actors (NSA) and terrorists, to target state actors. What was equally noteworthy was that there was no structured response from individual states to understand and take measures *vis-à-vis* the new challenges posed by NSA and terrorists. Undoubtedly, the hijacking of *Achille Laura* led to the Convention for the Suppression of Unlawful Acts Against the Safety of Maritime Navigation (SUA) Convention of 1988 that sought to equate acts of violence against ships and installations on the continental-shelf with acts of terrorism, but without specifically using that term. But, challenge posed by the *Sea Tigers* was seen as a domestic issue of Sri Lanka, with no international response, despite the fact that several foreign vessels were targeted by the *Sea Tigers*. It was Sri Lanka that strengthened its navy to confront the *Sea Tigers*.

Since the *Achille Laura* incident was not repeated and threats from *Sea Tigers* was seen as a domestic issue of Sri Lanka, the international community took no measures to confront the new challenge, primarily because their vessels had not been similarly targeted. There was no effort to coordinate action, even to suppress acts of piracy till 2004, when things went out of hand and a large number of ships, including oil tankers, began to be hijacked for ransom.

Maritime violence/terrorism was taken seriously only after the US destroyer, *USS Cole*, was attacked by a suicide boat near Aden in October 2000. After that US-led coalition began to deploy warships in that region to combat threat of maritime terrorism as also of proliferation of WMD material and its delivery system.

Even till 2002, no steps had been initiated at the level of individual state actors to meet the challenge posed by nsa and terrorists in the adjacent sea space. India was no exception even though it was facing the potential challenge of Tamil-based insurgency in Sri Lanka with its spill-over in South India since mid-eighties and from the nexus of smugglers and terrorists after 1993. No long-term strategy was formulated to secure India's various maritime frontiers *vis-à-vis* the emerging threat to homeland security. Whatever steps were taken, were confined to so-called patrolling by the Navy, the Coast Guard and the Customs with a notional presence of local police probably to facilitate court proceedings. No steps were envisaged to induct coastal states and UTs in the context of security of adjacent sea space.

Even after 2004, when some steps were initiated to involve coastal states and UTs, they were part of a larger package. Even in that context, the role of Marine Police was that of a beat constable along the shore line. The major role was still reserved for the Navy and the Coast Guard. Even Customs (Marine) were not strengthened in that context. Is that adequate or do we need a fresh review of three interrelated facets of India's maritime policy; maritime development, sea governance and maritime security, and, in that context, a review of the role of the Central Government, coastal states and UTs. Because of their geographical location, they are the primary actors in all matters related to maritime affairs.

While there is enough literature dealing with different facets of the topic related to maritime security, this book is probably the first effort in India to deal with multiple facets of the subject. It also attempts to offer guidelines for future action. Topics covered in the book include themes like multiple maritime zones as defined under UNCLOS-III and India's MZI Act of 1976 as also state's criminal jurisdiction in these zones under prevailing international norms and state practices as well as under India's legal norms and state practice. An attempt is made to assess the available capability of various maritime enforcement agencies like the Navy, the Coast Guard, the Customs (Marine) and the Marine Police as well as the possible role that CISF can play in basic point security of port and off-shore platforms.

Last two chapters deal with developments since 2004 and steps that were taken to evolve a framework for coastal security as well as steps initiated after 2008, to strengthen cooperation among various agencies involved in that context. Attempt has been made in the last chapter to suggest ways and means to improve not only the overall structures of maritime security but also to strengthen sea governance during Phase II (2011-16) of the Coastal Security Scheme. Much more, however, remains to be done in the context of maritime development, sea governance and maritime security.

It is often forgotten that maritime security is directly related to sea governance. Unfortunately, India has not evolved a mechanism to strengthen sea governance at the national level. Each ministry and even department acts almost as an autonomous unit while defining its policy and its implementation. In the absence of any coordination or synergy amongst them, the result is near anarchy. Some corrective steps are being initiated in that direction after 2008, but only in the context of coastal security.

What is needed is a fresh look at the entire maritime policy and to evolve a mechanism to bring about greater synergy among multiple agencies involved in maritime affairs. An apex body that can be entrusted with that role will be a welcome step. A robust system of governance automatically strengthens the framework of security, be it on land or the sea.

A coordinated framework of sea governance will also give a boost to maritime development. Though India has vast potential for exploiting its maritime assets, for enhancing its food security and energy security or improving its overseas and coastal traffic, ship-building and repair facilities, ports etc., that potential is not being fully exploited because of lack of maritime vision of decision makers as also a disjointed framework of sea governance.

The three factors, maritime development, sea governance and maritime/coastal security are interrelated. It is time that decision makers rise above the present narrow focus on so-called coastal security and chalk out a long term strategy that will link maritime security to sea governance and maritime development and, in that context, integrate the coastal states and UTs in the overall framework of maritime strategy for the 21st century. May be then the steps taken after 2004 will help India break its traditional continental mindset and evolve a maritime vision and, thus, give India its rightful place as a major maritime power, at least in the Indian Ocean region, in the years to come.

Though I have been interested in the theme for some time, the project was initiated and completed in one year. That was too short a period for a comprehensive study of the vast subject. It is possible that experts in international law or India's national legal norms might find gaps in the study. Similarly, experts might find loose ends and even inaccuracy in my analysis of capability of various maritime enforcement agencies like the Navy, the Coast Guard and the Customs (Marine). That is because I had access only to published data. I hope that critics will overlook these limitations. Since I have covered in my book, multiple facets of the issues involved, it was inevitable that I would have repeated some of the arguments so as to relate them to the main theme that was being discussed in the chapter. I may be excused for that.

I am thankful to the United Service Institution of India, New Delhi, for offering me institutional support to complete the project. I am also thankful to various other institutions and libraries for providing me with material related to this project. Above all, I must thank my family members who went out of their way to encourage me for this difficult challenge.

Prof. K.R. Singh

SEA GOVERNANCE AND MARITIME
1 | SECURITY FRONTIERS

Concept of Sea Governance

Though often ignored, the state's perception of its adjacent sea space has undergone a revolutionary change, especially after the Law of the Sea Conference held at Geneva, in 1958. Subsequently, the UN Convention of the Law of the Sea (UNCLOS-III) of 1982 gave a definite shape to that transformation. Though UNCLOS-III failed to address the question of maritime terrorism, it laid down broad guidelines defining coastal states' exclusive jurisdiction, over certain well defined subjects, upto an outer limit of 200 n. miles from the coast (baseline). While coastal states benefited from that, it also posed the new question of the need for appropriate sea governance over the adjacent sea space.

This sea governance is influenced by the nature of jurisdiction enjoyed by the coastal state in multiple maritime zones in the adjacent water space and the extent of state's enforcement rights in those zones. As is well known, the state has sovereign jurisdiction over the territorial waters that extends upto a maximum distance of 12 n. miles from the coast. Its criminal jurisdiction extends a further 12 n. miles, *i.e.* upto the outer limit of its contiguous zone, in matters like smuggling, immigration, pollution etc. It has only a limited jurisdiction over matters like exploitation of living resources like fishery as also of non-living resources on the continental-shelf and EEZ in water space that extends upto a maximum of 200 n. miles from the coast. This vast sea space is almost equal to two-thirds of the total land space of India. India, like all other coastal states, enjoys these rights. As will be seen, they have contributed to the maritime development of India. Sea governance, therefore, requires a framework for management of these resources as well as the question of maritime security that is closely linked to development and sea governance.

Sea Governance and Maritime Development

Over the past six decades, India has witnessed rapid growth in sectors related directly to maritime development. These sectors include port facilities, shipping, fisheries, off-shore oil and gas exploration etc. India has even gone further away and has staked its claims to deep sea nodules in mid-Indian Ocean. While Indian decision makers took cognizance of these developments, they have failed to evolve a suitable structure of sea governance to take maximum advantage of the new opportunities as also to ensure adequate security in its adjacent sea space. Reasons for that will be analysed in subsequent pages.

India had a long maritime tradition, be it in ship building, shipping both coastal and overseas, maritime trade and commerce etc. Several factors, largely due to the impact of colonial-metropolitan linkages since mid-nineteenth century if not earlier, reduced India almost to the level of a land-locked state and its maritime activities were deliberately stunted during the British imperial rule. It was only after independence that India began to expand its maritime activities. It took some time to overcome the technological constraints but it rapidly expanded its maritime related activities since the seventies. This was reflected in the field of port facilities, shipping both overseas and coastal, marine fishery, off-shore oil and gas exploration as also fast growth in industrial activities like refineries, ship building and repairing facilities, fishery-related industry and the inevitable urbanisation along the coastal belt, largely due to these maritime developments.

India had only four major ports in 1947. Their number rose to 11 by 2008. Besides, India has about 170 non-major ports spread all along India's long coastline and in its island territories. As seen from the accompanying table, quantity of cargo handled by these ports increased from less then 20 mn tonnes in 1950-51 to 61.8 mn tonnes in 1970 and 452 mn ton in 2003. It was estimated to increase to 1,273 mn tonnes by 2010. What is important to note is the major jump in the cargo handled by non-major ports from 11.0 mn tonnes in 1990 to 108 mn tonnes in 2003. This is due to the entry of private enterprises in the port sector and construction of large ports, like the Mundra port in Gujarat, under the broad spectrum of 'non-major ports'.

Table 1

Cargo handled by Indian ports (in mn tons)					
Cargo handled	1950	1970	1980	1990	2003
Total	19.2	61.8	87.1	163.3	452.0
Major ports	19.2	55.7	80.4	152.5	344.0
Other ports	n.a.	6.1	6.7	11.0	108.0

Sources: *Economic Survey,* 2003-04, New Delhi, 2004, pp. 188-89 and T*he Hindu,* June 2, 2006.

Under the Indian Constitution, major ports are administered under the Central Government, while non-major ports that were earlier classified as minor ports are administered at the level of the concerned state governments. Under the new scheme of promoting the role of private sector in ports, the capacity of cargo handled at the 'non-major' ports is likely to increase fast. Overseas trade is also significant for India's development. The value of that trade was Rs. 229 crores in 1995-96. It increased to Rs. 645.6 crores to 2003-04 (*India*, 2005, p. 135). By 2010, 96 percent of its foreign trade by volume and between 65 to 70 percent by value was to be routed *via* the sea (Sharma, 2005, 381).

Indian shipping too saw a rapid growth despite the fact that Indian shipping, especially in the private sector, was starved of government support. It was also heavily taxed. Yet, it survived and flourished. As seen from the accompanying table, its gross registered tonnage (GRT) was only 0.192 mn in 1947. It crossed the one million GRT mark in 1962 and two million GRT mark in 1970. It, however, stagnated at about 6 mn GRT between 1980 and 1995, before reaching the mark of 8.29 mn in 2005. By 2010, it was expected to cross the 10 mn GRT. What is worth noting in the table is the rapid expansion of coastal shipping from 0.119 mn GRT in 1947 to 0.8 mn GRT in 2005 and 1.01 mn GRT in 2010. It is a pity that despite the increase in Indian shipping, it could not share a large percentage of India's overseas

Table 2

Indian Shipping

Year	Total		Overseas		Coastal	
	No	GRT	No	GRT	No	GRT
August 1947	59	0.192	11	0.073	44	0.119
1961	174	0.901	70	0.539	104	0.362
1981	403	5.900	338	5.903	65	0.300
1995	460	6.840	na	na	na	na
2005	707	8.286	237	7.481	470	0.804
2010	na	10.170	na	9.160	693	1.01

Sources: Ministry of Surface Transport, *Annual Report 1999-2000* New Delhi, 2000, p. 197 and *India 2007,* p. 82 and *India 2010,* p. 934-35.

trade. Its share was 6.6 per cent in 1961. It rose to 19.8 per cent in 1970 and was 32.3 per cent in 1981. But its share declined to 15 percent by 2005 (Mukherjee, 2006, p. 218). It was largely because rapid increase in the volume of India's foreign trade far outpaced the growth of Indian shipping. It is most unfortunate that while India's overseas trade is expanding, foreign shipping is benefiting from it.

Another factor that is worth underlining is the rapid growth in the number of oil tankers. As seen from the table, their percentage share in Indian shipping increased from 11.7 to 48.35, between 1971 and 2003. This is a matter of significance in the context of maritime security, since tankers are often the preferred targets of terrorists.

Table 3

Indian Shipping and Oil Tankers

Year	Total shipping GRT mn	Oil tanker GRT mn	% share
1971	2.478	0.289	11.7
1991	5.938	1.798	30.5
2003	7.133	3.449	48.35

Over the years, India has done remarkably well in the field of imparting high quality training in shipping-related field. The quality of its training for the merchant marine is recognised world wide and Indian seamen are reportedly among the best in the world. This is reflected in the fact that though only about 20,000 Indians are employed by Indian shipping, about 40,000 are employed abroad. (*The Hindu,* May 2, 2002).

India has made good progress in the field of exploiting its marine resources like fisheries. There were hardly any mechanised fishing boat till 1947. By 2006, there were in all 280,000 fishing crafts. Of them, 181,000 were non-mechanised, 45,000 mechanized crafts and 54,000 mechanised boats. There were only 184 deep-sea fishing boats of whom only 60 were in operation (*Economic Survey, 2006-2007,* p. 165).

By 2006, India had constructed six large fishing harbours, 40 minor fishing harbours and about 38 approved fish landing sites (*India, 2007,* p. 108). Government also promoted marine fishery by subsidising high speed diesel for mechanised fishing boats and by granting loans for acquiring fishing crafts. India had 400 freezing units, 102 quick freezing plants and 477 cold storage units. While Indian fishermen had confined their activities near the shore in the past, now they are able to operate upto 100 miles away from the coast and stay at sea for 3-4 days. Efforts are on to promote deep water fishing so as to fully utilise the resources not only of Indian EEZ but also to go further away in adjacent ocean space.

As seen from the accompanying table, these efforts have paid rich returns both in terms of increased quantity of marine fish catch and also foreign exchange earned through their export. As will be analysed in the subsequent pages, though India's exclusive jurisdiction in terms of exploitation of living resources extends upto the outer limits of its 200 n. mile EEZ limit, very little effort has been made to regulate and govern marine fishery beyond the territorial waters, whose governance under the Constitution falls under the Central Government and is clubbed along with agriculture, animal husbandry, dairy, poultry and inland fishery. Governance of fishing in India's EEZ is thus downgraded under the Indian Constitution and the related distribution of administrative responsibilities at the level of the Central Government. It needs to be underlined that marine fishery, smuggling and maritime terrorism are interlinked. Hence, fishery management is an important component of maritime security.

Table 4

India: Marine Fishing

Year	Total fish catch (mn tons)	Marine fish catch (mn tons)	Export of Marine fish product (000 tons)	Value Rs. crores
1950-55	0.7	0.5	20	2
1970-71	1.8	1.1	40	35
1990-91	3.8	2.3	140	873
2005-06	6.57	2.8	551	7,019
2009-10	7.85	2.98	664	9,921

Sources: Economic Survey, 2001-02, p. 193.
Economic Survey, 2003-04, p. 151.
Economic Survey, 2005-06, p. 167.
Economic Survey, 2010-11, p. 206.

India has benefited from the provisions of UNCLOS-III that grants the coastal states, exclusive right to exploit non-living resources in its continental-shelf. This has enabled India to develop its offshore oil and gas field. As seen from the accompanying table, this has contributed greatly to India's domestic energy security. India has also proven oil reserves of 786 mn tonnes of which 410 mn tonnes are on the off-shore. Similarly, India's proven natural gas reserves are estimated to be 1,101 billion cubic metre (bcm). Of that, 761 bcm are in the offshore. It is expected that more oil and gas reserves may be discovered in the continental-shelf. Thus, the continental-shelf not only has development-related importance but also demands a mechanism for the security of large number of high value offshore oil and gas installations that are spread over thousands of square miles of sea space away from the coast. While a great deal of effort and investment was made by public and private sectors in developing these resources, basic point security cover for these high value installations is not adequate, especially in the context of maritime terrorism. This also shows a gross mismatch between maritime development and maritime security.

Though not directly related to coastal security, the deep sea bed resources in mid-Indian Ocean can become an object of maritime development and hence of security. India had invested heavily in the exploration of deep sea bed resources. Consequently India was awarded the status of Pioneer Investor (Qasim, 2001, pp. 93-9), in 1987. India has been allotted an area of 75,000 sq km of deep sea bed in South-West Indian Ocean. While India has developed the technology of mining the deep sea bed nodules and extraction of metals from them, their mining is not economically viable at the moment.

Table 5

India: Offshore Oil and Gas Production

Oil (mn. tons)	1970-71	1990-91	2004-05	2010-11
Total	6.8	30.4	34.0	37.96
Offshore	Nil	19.0	22.4	Na
Gas (bcm)	**1970-71**	**1990-91**	**2004-05**	**2010-11**
Total	na	18.0	31.8	57.51
Offshore	Nil	14.1	22.9	Na

Sources: Economic Survey, 1988-89, Table 5.72,
Economic Survey, 1994-95, Table 5.35,
Economic Survey, 2006-07, Table 5.81/82 p. 144,
Economic Survey, 2010-11, pp. 266-7, and TERI, Energy Data
Document of Year 2004/2005, New Delhi, p. 80.

Ignoring appropriate Sea Governance

Though Indian decision makers took cognizance of these issues of maritime development, they failed to evolve an appropriate administrative and constitutional framework to get the maximum advantage of the new opportunities since 1970s in the field of the state's extended jurisdiction in the adjacent sea space. As will be analysed in details in Chapter IV, presidential proclamations in 1956 and 1967 and constitutional amendments in 1963 and 1976 paved the way for passing the Maritime Zones of India Act of 1976. It delimited various maritime zones of India and the degree of India's sovereign jurisdiction in each of them. These steps were not reflected in the creation of a comparable administrative framework that would ensure good governance in the newly acquired sea space.

Instead of evolving an appropriate mechanism to deal with the newly acquired sea space, decision makers continued to retain the then existing administrative structure of the fifties that was tailored to meet the requirements of a country with only three n. mile territorial waters as the adjacent sea space. The Constitution of 1951 and the related administrative infrastructure reflected that mindset. Concentration of powers dealing with maritime affairs under the Central Government and sidelining the role of the coastal states probably had seemed logical at that time but it has not proved viable with the passage of time. It was unfortunate that decision makers failed to understand the need for evolving a mechanism that would have responded positively to new opportunities and related challenges, as also mechanism for integrating coastal states more intimately in the development as also security of the larger sea space adjacent to the Indian coast.

How was sea governance managed? Often, matters allegedly related to maritime field were attached to ministries or departments in the Centre that dealt with seemingly related affairs on land. No wonder they were neglected. Under the Constitution, regulating marine fishery beyond territorial waters is entrusted to the Central Government. Fish (marine) is food. Ministry of Agriculture which also deals with fishery on land deals with that also. It is often forgotten that infrastructure for marine fishery is totally different and the EEZ covers a large sea space that is two-thirds the size of India's land mass. Since ships sail on the surface of the sea, Ministry of Surface Transport was asked to look after it. While shipping is under the Centre, all of its infrastructure is located in the coastal states. Management of ports was divided under the Central Government, state governments and UTs, with the result that development of non-major ports had been stunted and so also that of coastal shipping. Customs (Marine) formed a part of the larger department. Though the importance of the marine wing of the Customs was recognised in the sixties and the seventies, it was neglected subsequently and the Coast Guard was also entrusted with that role. Thus, two separate agencies of separate ministries were entrusted with the same role. While the Coast Guard continued to expand, Customs (Marine), that would have played a significant role not only in preventing smuggling but also in enhancing maritime security, was downgraded. As noted, maritime security was retained under the Ministry of Defence. Other departments of the Centre, leave aside the coastal states, were sidelined in that context.

On land, these departments dealing with food, transport, security (Home Ministry and Defence Ministry) are autonomous in their function. They guard their autonomy zealously. Such an arrangement is not viable in sea space. Management of shipping, port facilities, fishery, Marine Customs, offshore installations and their security cannot be seen in isolation. An effective sea space management needs a greater degree of coordination, both at the level of policy making and implementation than is required on land. Thus, a new maritime approach is essential, to address the question of sea space governance and related questions of maritime security in the coastal waters.

The most significant failure in sea space governance was the non-recognition of the positive role that coastal states could play not only in maritime development but also in the security of the adjacent sea space. The Constitution puts the responsibility of maritime development at the level of the Central Government with very limited role left for the state government. That is true of security as well. Even though territorial waters limit was extended from three n. miles in 1951 to six n. miles in 1956 and 12 n. miles in 1967, coastal states of India were not encouraged to develop the capability to extend maritime enforcement capability in their respective adjacent sea space. It was only after 2004 that coastal states were grudgingly granted that 'concession' by the Ministry of Home Affairs. Even then, under the present scenario, the role of the Marine Police is seen as that of the beat constable along the sea shore. By contrast, enforcement capability of the Navy and the Coast Guard was rapidly expanded.

While the enforcement capability of maritime enforcement agencies at the level of the Central Government needs to be strengthened, it is also important to underline two interrelated factors. The one is the need to integrate coastal states more effectively in the governance/management of adjacent sea space. The other is the need to look at the sea space as an integral unit that deserves an integrated approach rather than the present policy of seeing it as autonomous extensions of various ministries and departments of the Central Government. If nothing else, some form of formal coordination of all stakeholders for evaluating related issues, making necessary recommendations and to monitor follow up action, can become the first step towards a more appropriate framework of sea space management and sea governance. To be really effective, maritime (coastal) security can only be a part of that broader framework of sea governance.

Maritime Frontiers and Coastal Security

Another major point that needs to be underlined while analysing coastal security is that unlike land territory which has a well defined border that delimits the state's total sovereignty on land, the adjacent sea space comprises of frontiers over which the coastal state enjoys varying degree of sovereign jurisdiction. This concept of sea frontiers is necessary to evolve effective mechanisms for sea governance and, as noted above, coastal security can only be an intrinsic part of total sea governance. Unfortunately that awareness is still lacking.

Annual Report, 2007-2008, of the Ministry of Home Affairs, noted, "A coastal security system has been formulated for strengthening infrastructure, for patrolling and surveillance of the country's *coastal areas, particularly shallow areas close to the coast,* to check and counter illegal *cross border* activities and criminal activities, *using coast or sea.* If nothing else, it underlines the lack of maritime awareness among India's decision makers and their reluctance to outgrow their traditional continental mindset.

This mindset is reflected especially at the level of the thinking in the Central Government. Maritime security was not dealt with, till recently, by the Ministry of Home Affairs. As per the Government of India (Allocation of Business) Rules, 1961, Ministry of Home Affairs comprised of two main departments; Department of Internal Security, dealing with police, law and order, and rehabilitation, and Department of States dealing with Centre-State relations and Union Territories. There were several functional divisions. Border Management Division is a newly created division among 25 such divisions. It was created in 2004 only after the Kargil crisis and on the recommendation of the Group of Ministries on Internal Security. During the initial period, it focussed on 'land' borders. Even in 2002, Ministry of Home Affairs was not concerned with 'maritime' affairs since that task was entrusted to the Ministry of Defence with some inputs from the Ministry of External Affairs. Ministry of Home Affairs was concerned at best with cross-border infiltration in the marshy area of the Kutch along the Indo-Pak border and river border along India-Bangladesh border. Consequently, the Border Security Force (BSF) was equipped with a few small patrol boats in the Kutch sector. Concept of floating border outposts was introduced for effective surveillance of the river border. *Annual Report, 2002-2003*, of the Ministry of Home Affairs does not mention either maritime frontier or maritime terrorism.

Perception of the Ministry of Home Affairs *vis-à-vis* criminal activities of Non-State Actors (NSA) and terrorists began to shift gradually after 2004. The Group of Ministers, following the Kargil conflict, in the Report on Reforms of National Security System, advocated a comprehensive revamping of intelligence apparatus as also management of border and internal security. As a result, a new Border Management Division was created. The initial thrust continued to focus on land border. However, by 2004, it came to be realised that the coastal belt too needed to be considered as India's 'border' in the context of containing trans-border terrorism. That new perception, among other things, resulted in the recognition that coastal states too have a role as reflected in the recommendation for the creation of the Marine Police in the coastal states with the help of the Ministry of Home Affairs. Ministry of Defence too began to consider steps that might strengthen the infrastructure of the Navy and the Coast Guard in the context of the new role of containing threats to homeland security from hostile elements using adjacent sea space to attack and destabilise India.

The traditional perception of the Ministry of Home Affairs of looking at maritime 'frontier' of coastal states in the context of 'border' was reflected in its approach to the role suggested by it for the Marine Police; that of a beat constable along the shore, or more appropriately the coast line and its immediate water space like internal waters and estuaries. The low priority role for the enforcement agencies of the coastal states was also reflected in the attitude of the Ministry of Defence. Defence Minister A.K. Antony announced a plan for a three-tier system to protect the coastal area against terrorism. The Navy was tasked to secure 'maritime border', whatever it might mean. The Coast Guard was to patrol waters beyond 12 n. miles (territorial waters). The Coastal Police of the state was to patrol the 'shores' (*The Hindu*, November 28, 2008).

This approach to coastal security is not only conceptually wrong but also inadequate to deal with challenges posed by NSA and terrorists to India's homeland *via* the adjacent sea space. The present approach, as illustrated in the *Annual Report, 2007-2008*, of the Ministry of Home Affairs, is based upon two main variables. The one revolves around the mistaken notion that the responsibility of national security is, by and large, entrusted to the Central Government under the Constitution. Consequently the Central Government is obliging the government of the coastal states by allowing it to share it with the Union Government.

Maritime Frontier

It is often forgotten that the coast is secure when the adjacent water space is also secure. Land border or frontier is well defined *vis-à-vis* another state. By contrast, maritime security frontier is not so specifically defined. Theoretically, it stretches from the immediate hinterland to the farthest point in the adjacent water space, depending upon the nature of threat and the enforcement capability of the coastal state. The state signs maritime boundary agreements with adjacent states, largely on the basis of median line, primarily to define limits of their territorial waters, exclusive economic zone and continental-shelf. While India has signed these agreements with Myanmar, Thailand, Indonesia, Sri Lanka and the Maldives, it has still to sign such agreements with Bangladesh and Pakistan. It needs to be underlined that these maritime boundary agreements that delimit their respective maritime zones for purposes of economic exploitation, in no way reflect maritime frontier in the context of homeland security because these waters also overlap the high seas where navigation is governed by different sets of international law and terms of UNCLOS-III.

Maritime frontiers differ in concept from land frontier. Limits of state's jurisdiction are defined by its boundary on land. A state, if it so wishes, may designate a part of its own land territory inside its boundary, as its frontier. British India had designated certain areas as North-East Frontier and North-West Frontier. India and Pakistan inherited those frontiers at the time of their independence.

Unlike land frontier, maritime frontier extends beyond the state's coast into adjoining sea space. For a long time, that was restricted to a narrow three n. mile belt of territorial waters. Beyond that was the high sea, an area that was under the control of no state. Freedom of the high seas was zealously guarded by major maritime powers.

After World War II, that concept was gradually eroded, primarily due to economic reasons. Extending jurisdiction of the coastal state on 'land' submerged under water but adjacent to its shore, or sub-soil resources beyond its territorial sea limits on the continental-self, became important so as to authorise an agency to exploit those resources in an area that was, till then, beyond the sovereign jurisdiction of any state. President Harry Truman of USA took that step in 1945 when he authorised exploration of off-shore oil and gas resources in the Gulf of Mexico, adjacent to the coast of USA but beyond its three n. mile territorial sea limit. Potential of discovery of oil and gas in other off-shore waters adjacent to the coast led to the legitimisation of the concept of a new economic maritime frontier, continental-shelf, in the Geneva Conference, in 1958.

Since sea space beyond three n. miles was considered to be the high sea and thus free for exploitation by all, fishing fleets from far away states could legally fish in these waters that were adjacent to that of the coastal coast. That was objected to and certain states threatened to extend their national fishing zone upto 200 n. miles from the coast. After a great deal of debate, UNCLOS-III of 1982 legitimised the coastal states' exclusive right to exploit living and also non-living resources in the adjacent waters, upto the maximum limit of 200 n. miles from the coast.

Thus, 1970s witnessed a spurt in defining several new maritime frontiers like the EEZ, the continental-shelf and the contiguous zone. As noted, the EEZ and the continental-shelf defined the outer limit of the coastal state's jurisdiction for the exploitation of living and non-living resources in their adjacent waters. They were not security frontiers in the real sense, though coastal state had the power to ensure that these resources were not exploited by others without its consent. In the case of contiguous zone, the coastal state was given criminal jurisdiction in matters of economic offences, like the customs violation and other related issues, upto a maximum limit of 12 n. miles beyond the territorial waters. All these three maritime zones fall within the broad term of the high seas and thus foreign vessels enjoy freedom of navigation in these zones.

None of the three newly created maritime frontiers under UNCLOS-III dealt with threat to national security arising out of terrorist-related activities, though the world had started facing that new challenge. UNCLOS-III, despite the fact that it was widely discussed over a long period, had no provision that could authorise the state to extend its criminal jurisdiction beyond its territorial waters in matters of terrorist-related threat to its homeland security.

Evolution of India's Maritime Frontiers

Like several other states, India had also demarcated these maritime frontiers over the years through presidential proclamations, constitutional amendments and acts of the Parliament. These steps were taken even before the signing of UNCLOS-III in 1982. Details of these steps will be discussed in Chapter IV

Before one seeks to define India's maritime security frontiers *per se*, it is essential to identify its various other maritime frontiers like the outer limits of territorial waters, contiguous zone, EEZ, continental-shelf etc. These are recognised maritime frontiers under UNCLOS-III as also under national law. Maritime security frontiers can then be delimited within these recognised multiple maritime frontiers. These maritime security frontiers will include frontiers of economic security like the Customs waters covering the sea space of the contiguous zone, the EEZ for fishery resources and the sea space around the off-shore installations on the continental-shelf, for their safety and protection. Enactments like the Customs Act 1962, Maritime Zones of India (MZI) Act 1976, the Coast Guard Act 1978, MZI (Marine Fisheries Regulation) Act 1981 etc. provide the legal framework for enforcement of related laws in the context of crimes, mostly economic in nature, so as to ensure economic security in these different maritime zones.

Maritime security frontiers will need to be defined separately in the context of anti-state activities, particularly those related to acts of terrorism. Government of India has defined Non-State Actors (NSA) and terrorists separately in the WMD Act, 2005. Section 4, subsection iii g of that act defines NSA as a person or entity not acting under the lawful authority of any country. Section 4, subsection iii m says that terrorists shall have the meaning as assigned to this expression in the Unlawful Activities (Prevention) Act, 1967.

Another factor that needs to be underlined is that India's maritime frontiers have evolved over the years. These are still in the process of evolution. Indian Constitution, which remains the primary document, dealing with limits of India's sovereign jurisdiction, does not specifically mention maritime frontiers. It seems that the makers of the Indian Constitution were overwhelmed with what is known as the continental mind set. Article 1 (3) of Part I of the Indian Constitution that deals with "The Union and Its Territories", defines that the territory of India shall comprise of

(a) The territories of the States

(b) The Union Territories

(c) Such other territories as may be acquired.

That article even ignored mentioning territorial waters which were recognised world over as an extension of state sovereignty over its adjacent waters. Even the Indian Penal Code, in Chapter II, Section 18, says, "India means territory of India" (as defined in Article 1 (3) of the Indian Constitution).

It will be incorrect to think that Indian law makers were not aware of the term territorial waters because that term dealing with water adjacent to the coast and which fall within Indian jurisdiction had been used earlier in the Territorial Waters Jurisdiction Act, 1878. Unlike the three n. mile limit of the territorial waters, that act defined 'territorial waters' in a more liberal manner. That act deals with offences committed on the sea *within a certain distance of the coast*. It said that rightful jurisdiction extends and has always extended over the *open sea adjacent to the coast* of the Majesty's dominions "to such a *distance as is necessary for the defence and security of such dominions*" (Manohar and Chitaley, *vol. 43*, 1988, pp. 597-99).

Though the omission in Article 1 (3) of the Indian Constitution was glaring, framers of the Constitution did induct the concept of territorial waters in two separate contexts in the Constitution. Item 57 in the Union List (List I) of the Seventh Schedule lists fishing and fisheries *beyond territorial waters* as subject under the Union Government. Also, Article 297 said that all lands, minerals and other things of value underlying the ocean "within the territorial waters of India" shall vest in the Union and be held for the purposes of the Union. It seems that the purpose of these two articles was less to define India's maritime frontiers and more to assert the right of the Union Government over their resources *vis-à-vis* the coastal states of India.

Chandrasekhar Rao, commenting upon the subject, had argued that Article 1 is not a complete code on the territory of India. Indian Constitution had made provision for two categories of territory of India; land territory and maritime territory and made separate provisions for both. He also said that Article 297 deals with both; *interim* and *dominium*, and deals with properties, contracts, rights, liabilities, obligations and suit (Rao, 1983, pp. 26-7).

India's maritime frontiers began to expand over the years under presidential proclamations, constitutional amendments and acts of Parliament. Presidential proclamation of March 22, 1956, expanded India's territorial waters limit to six n. miles. By another presidential proclamation on December 3, 1956 it created a contiguous zone that extended six n. miles beyond the limits of its territorial waters, to check growing smuggling. Thus, India had created its second maritime zone, the contiguous zone, as early as 1956. Presidential proclamation of September 3, 1967 extended the limit of the territorial waters to 12 n. miles (FAO, 1987, vol. I, IND 1-12).

Under the 15th constitutional amendment of October 5, 1963, Government of India introduced the concept of continental-shelf so as to enable India to explore and exploit its oil and gas resources in that zone. Under that amendment, Article 297 of the Indian Constitution read as follows: "All lands, minerals, and other things of value underlying the ocean within the territorial waters *or the continental-shelf of India* shall vest in the Union…" (Chitaley and Rao, *vol. IV,* 1970-71, p. 781). That amendment did not define the outer limit of the continental-shelf though the concept of continental-shelf had already been accepted at the Geneva Conference on the Law of the Sea in 1958. That amendment served two purposes. It reaffirmed the right of the Central Government over sub-soil resources of the submerged area under the sea beyond the coastline and, secondly, it prepared the legal framework for starting exploring and exploiting resources especially off-shore oil and gas in the Bombay High.

Article 297 was again amended on May 27, 1976 to further expand India's maritime frontier, by providing for an exclusive economic zone that also coincided with the outer limit of the continental-shelf. The amended article read as follows: "All lands, minerals, and other things of value underlying the ocean within the territorial waters or the continental-shelf or the exclusive economic zone of India shall rest in the Union…" (The Constitution of India, 1977, pp. 355-56). The amendment added, "All other resources of the exclusive economic zone of India shall vest in the Union and be held for the purposes of the Union. The limits of the territorial waters, continental-shelf, the exclusive economic zone and *other maritime zones* of India may be specified from time to time by *any law* made by the Parliament. Thus, the 40th Amendment to the Constitution, that dealt with Article 297, has enough scope even now to create or designate maritime security zones in the context of threats posed by NSA and terrorists. As will be analysed in subsequent pages, part of the MZI Act of 1976 that deals with contiguous zone already has that provision.

The 40th Amendment to Article 297 paved the way for the promulgation of Maritime Zones of India (MZI) Act of 1976 under which India codified in one act its various maritime zones. The Territorial Waters, Continental Shelf, Exclusive Economic Zone and Other Maritime Zones Act, 1976 (No. 80 of 1976) commonly known as the MZI Act, 1976, was passed by the Parliament on May 28, 1976. It received the assent of the President on August 25, 1976. (Text in the *Gazette of India, Extraordinary*, Part II Section I, No. 121 of August 26, 1976, New Delhi, pp. 1067-1075). MZI Act, 1976, defined and delimited the following maritime zones of India: territorial waters (12 n. mile), contiguous zone (24 n. miles), and EEZ and Continental-Shelf (200 n. miles). It also spelled out the nature of India's jurisdiction as also its enforcement rights, duties and obligation in each of these maritime zones. MZI Act of 1976 will be analysed in details in Chapter IV.

Economic dimensions of new Maritime Frontiers

India's maritime frontiers, as defined under MZI Act, 1976, were formulated and approved as binding act of the Parliament long before UNCLOS-III was approved in 1982. It is also important to note that while India had signed UNCLOS-III in 1982 it ratified it only in 1995 after thirteen years. It also needs to be underlined, especially for those who swear by UNCLOS-III, that Indian Parliament has so far not passed acts that would provide legal validity in Indian courts, to all the provisions of UNCLOS-III. By contrast, Indian Parliament has passed SUA Act, 2002 to facilitate implementation of the SUA Convention of 1988, and the WMD Act, 2005 to facilitate implementation of Security Council Resolution 1540 (2004) as also WMD Convention of 2005. Thus, as far as India is concerned, it is not UNCLOS-III but MZI Act, 1976, SUA Act of 2002 etc. that carry binding legal obligations.

Under MZI Act, 1976, India has asserted sovereign rights over the territorial waters, right to intercept and inspect vessels in the context of economic offences in its contiguous zone, right to enforce its legislation in the context of fishery in the EEZ, exclusive right to exploit its sub-soil resources in the continental-shelf and to provide for 'safety and protection' of off-shore installations.

In 1947, when the limit of the territorial waters was three n. miles India had sovereign right over an area of 36,076 sq km in its adjacent water space. After 1956, when its limit was extended to six n. miles, the area of sovereignty expanded to 72, 153 sq km. In 1967, when the limit was further extended to 12 n. miles, the area covered by its territorial waters expanded to 144,307.2 sq km. Under section 5 of MZI Act 1976, outer limit of India's contiguous zone is 24 n. miles. Though India does not exercise sovereign rights over 12 n. miles of water space that extends beyond the outer limit of its territorial waters, yet it has jurisdiction over those waters in the context of its security as well. As will be analysed in chapter IV, the outer limit of the contiguous zone, which is also called India's Customs waters, constitutes India's security frontier *vis-à-vis* economic offenders as also terrorists.

Outer limit of sea space in the context of EEZ extends upto a maximum limit of 200 n. miles from the coast. This vast sea space covers an area of about 2,013,410 sq km which is almost two-thirds of India's land mass. Since it extends India's jurisdiction over living resources in that entire sea space, it also constitutes a new economic frontier though India's jurisdiction is limited only to the living resources therein.

Continental-shelf zone extends at present upto the outer limit of the EEZ. Its outer limit might be extended further under Article 76 of UNCLOS-III provided India is able to convince its extended continental-shelf boundary to the UN Commission on the Limits of the Continental-Shelf (CLCS) (Vohra, 2005, pp. 10-11). National Centre for Antarctic and Ocean Research (NCAOR), under the Department of Ocean Development, had initiated a Rs. 45 crore project to survey and establish the outer limit of India's Legal Continental-Shelf (LCS). Under that project, data upto a distance of 350 n. miles from the baseline was to be collected, analysed and documented. Data so acquired was to be analysed by the National Geophysical Research Institute, Hyderabad and the Institute of Oceanography, Goa. The report, to be submitted before 2009, was to form the basis of India's claims to the LCS that was to be presented before the International Commission of the Limits of the Continental-Shelf (*JIOS*, 2002, pp. 338-39). It is estimated that the new continental-shelf boundary, if accepted by CLCS, will cover an ocean space that is almost equal to that of India's land mass. Thus, India's new maritime frontier (outer limit of the new continental-shelf) will extend further away from the coast than as envisaged under the MZI Act, 1976. That act will need to be suitably amended. Though India has jurisdiction over the sub-soil resources of the entire zone it also enjoys special rights in the context of safety and protection around the off-shore installations as also the right to determine and specify sea lanes that would facilitate passage of vessels in those sectors under section 6, sub-section 5 of MZI Act, 1976.

Undefined Maritime Security Frontiers

Though UNCLOS-III had paved the way for a new concept of maritime frontiers for coastal states, these were only limited to exploitation of economic resources in the sea space adjacent to the state. India's MZI Act of 1976 had also defined those frontiers. By and large, they reflected the ethos of Geneva Convention of 1958 and the ongoing debate on UNCLOS-III that was in progress and whose broad outlines had been defined. India's MZI Act, 1976, dovetailed with the provisions of UNCLOS-III that was approved only in 1982, except in two cases. Both of them deal with matters of maritime security even in times of peace and clash with the ethos of absolute freedom of navigation for state actors in times of peace.

Section 4(2) of MZI Act of 1976 stipulates that foreign warships, including submarines and other underwater vehicles, may enter or pass through the territorial waters *after giving prior notice to the Central Government*. It does not deny freedom of navigation but only requires prior notification and to that extent does not, in spirit, contradict clauses dealing with innocent passage through the territorial waters of a state. Thus, outer limits of the territorial waters, over which India has sovereign jurisdiction, can be considered as the immediate maritime security frontier for India.

The second point deals with Section 5, subsection 4 (a) of MZI Act 1976 under which the Central Government is empowered to take measures, as it may consider fit, in India's contiguous zone, to ensure the security of India. Section 5, sub-section (5a) empowers the state to extend its enactments to this zone in matters relating to *security* of India. Some critics of this provision have treated it as violating the spirit of UNCLOS-III. They have inadvertently equated 'security' with 'defence'. Surely those who had framed that act knew the difference between 'defence' and 'security'.

While the theme will be discussed in greater details in Chapter IV, it is important to note that Indian law makers had in 1976 itself, through enactment, created yet one more maritime security frontier – outer limit of the contiguous zone. It is a pity that having created it, every one forgot it and treated that frontier only as the outer limit of its customs waters or frontier of its economic security and not for suppression of acts of terrorism.

UNCLOS-III, though a mile-stone in codifying the law of the sea, totally ignored the question of maritime security, thereby leaving that question to be decided by provisions under traditional international law, UN resolutions/conventions and state practices. In the context of threat of security posed by NSA, it dealt only with the question of piracy which was again defined under the narrow framework as had evolved over the centuries. Pirates were considered as enemies of mankind. Coastal states alone were empowered to take action against them in their respective territorial waters. That reasserted the concept of state sovereignty in the territorial waters. But, beyond that limit, on the high seas, maritime enforcement agencies of all states were authorised to take action against pirates and their acts of piracy. UNCLOS-III, however, does not treat criminal activities of other NSA in that light. Rather, it protects the concept of freedom of navigation and state sovereignty (flag of the ship) rather than address the question of maritime threats posed by terrorists. In all fairness, it should be realised that when UNCLOS-III was being debated, the threat from terrorist using sea space was not fully appreciated.

Threats posed by NSA and terrorists to homeland security became serious since the eighties. In the initial period they were equated with acts of piracy. As will be analysed in Chapter III, attempts were made to meet the new threat by enlarging the definition of piracy. But maritime terrorism was recognised as a specific threat by the West especially after the incident of *Achile Laura*. The IMO sought to find ways and means to meet that threat under the SUA Convention of 1988. But enforcement action under that convention was also constrained by norms of UNCLOS-III to state action in its territorial waters, *vis-à-vis* such criminal activities. Also, no preventive or preemptive measures were prescribed under SUA Convention. It dealt more with arrest and trial of persons involved in these acts.

The world began to take the question of maritime terrorism more seriously after it was viewed from the prism of the events of 9/11. Since UNCLOS-III had not provided for state action against terrorists and the NSA that supported their activities, concerned states began to initiate steps like Proliferation Security Initiative (PSI), Regional Maritime Security Initiative (RMSI), Container and Port Security, SUA Protocol etc. They also passed resolutions in the UN that could provide some legitimacy for their action in that context. Yet, these steps did not provide for the mechanism whereby a coastal state could legally define its maritime zones, related to different type of threat that could be anticipated and hence preempted beyond its territorial sea. The result was that major maritime powers usurped the right to 'defend' their maritime interest *vis-à-vis* NSA and terrorists even in far away places under state practices like RMSI, PSI, or anti-hijacking/piracy operations like those undertaken off the coast of Horn of Africa and in the Gulf of Aden.

Neutralising maritime threats posed by Non-State Actors and terrorists

Two facets of maritime security need to be clearly identified so that appropriate strategy can be enunciated to neutralise those threats. In the case of threat to maritime security that arises from state actors, there are enough provisions in international law and state practice to deal with that threat in a legitimate manner. But there is now a new and more dangerous threat that is posed by NSA and terrorists. While one can declare war on a state, how does one declare war on NSA/terrorists? If not, how can we legitimise the state's action against NSA/terrorists? The solution has been addressed by some, under the term 'war on terror' *i.e.* terror itself has been given the status of a state actor.

In the absence of any recognised naval strategy to neutralise the challenges posed by NSA and terrorists in sea space beyond the territorial waters, states that are militarily capable have sought to base their action by applying the logic of the old triad of sea denial, sea control and force projection. In the case of state actors, maritime strategy, based upon sea denial and sea control have two distinct roles in terms of weapon systems and tactics. But, in the case of NSA and terrorists, the two tend to overlap in the field of information and also enforcement action. Such a combination demands a mix of long range reconnaissance system for identification of the suspect vessel or persons, their possible target/destination and possible approach routes. Such a strategy suits isolated maritime states like Australia. Australia, in its Defence White paper, 2000, had formulated that strategy. According to that White Paper, "the key to defending Australia is to control the air and sea approaches to our continent" (Schofield, 2003, p. 42). Obviously, such a strategy and the Australian demand, that all those who approach the Australian coast must intimate the details to the government, does not accord with the concept of freedom of navigation, enshrined in UNCLOS-III. Earlier, President John F. Kennedy of USA had invoked the Rio Pact of 1947 under which a 300 n. mile maritime defence zone was established around the American continents. He had invoked it to legitimise naval quarantine imposed against USSR during Cuban missile crisis of 1962 (Mehta, 2007, p. 4). That was, however, in the context of state actors.

Others have also started expanding their maritime security frontiers beyond their territorial waters. China has projected its Customs as an instrument of that policy. It has equipped its Customs Department in South China Sea with large *Qui-M class,* 100-metre long, specially designed patrol crafts. They have a ramp at the stern that is capable of handling two high speed interceptor crafts. About 20-24 such patrol crafts were to be built (*Strategic Digest,* 2001, p. 1703). In January 2002, Israeli Navy seized a vessel flying the flag of Tonga in the Red Sea about 300 miles from the Israeli coast. That vessel was allegedly carrying 50 tonnes of armament for Palestinians which was reportedly loaded at the port of Bandar Abbas.

While these operations were nearer to the coastal waters of the concerned state, there is also the tendency to project force across the high seas over long distances to sanitise a sea space *vis-à-vis* threats posed by NSA/terrorists. Often such steps are taken by a group of concerned states either under a certain common policy like PSI or in a designated area like the northern half of Western Indian Ocean. As will be discussed in details in Chapter III, these developments have acquired added legitimacy since 9/ 11.

Multi-national Task Force 151 was created in 2002 originally to provide protection to high value shipping in the Gulf of Aden region after terrorist attacks on US cruiser *USS Cole* and French tanker *MV Limbury*. It conducts maritime security operations as part of the US-led Operation, Enduring Freedom, in an area stretching from the southern edge of the Suez Canal to the Straits of Hormuz and down East African coast upto Kenya; a 2.5 mn sq. miles of sea space. Task Force 152 covers the Persian Gulf. Vessels are contributed mostly by NATO members and these task forces have close liaison with the Vth Fleet of USA (Rix 2007, pp. 36-8).

One of the tasks of these taskforces is to keep watch on 'suspect' vessels. *M.V. So San*, was spotted 600 miles off the coast of Yemen. It was intercepted by Spanish frigate in December 2002. The suspect vessel was fired upon and then boarded by Spanish troops. Explosive experts from USA also joined. The suspected cargo included 15 *Scud* ballistic missiles and related accessories. The ship was reportedly proceeding to Yemen. Since Yemen was a partner of USA in the war on terrorism, the ship was allowed to land its cargo in Yemeni port. The interception of *MV So San* had obviously violated norms of UNCLOS-III on freedom of navigation but the incident was allowed to die down.

The sudden increase in acts of piracy/hijacking of vessels in the Gulf of Aden and along the coast of the Horn of Africa has also legitimised force projection in far off seas to provide security to international navigation, *vis-à-vis* the criminal activities of hijackers/pirates. Several countries including South Korea, Russia and China have sent their warships to that region. India too has deployed its warships there. Beside rescuing some vessels from being attacked and also by arresting some Somali and Yemeni personnel on the high seas, the Indian Navy had the unique distinction of sinking a large Thai fishing boat that had been hijacked, in a mistaken belief that it was the 'mother ship' used by the hijackers/pirates.

Delimiting Maritime Security Frontiers of India

The spurt in maritime threat posed by NSA/terrorists has at best evoked only knee-jerk responses. There is as yet no accepted definition of maritime security frontier beyond territorial waters of individual states, *i.e.* in the high seas, that define the jurisdiction as also the nature of enforcement action by state actors *vis-à-vis* NSA/terrorists.

Attempt to define maritime security frontier/frontiers under the terms as laid down in UNCLOS-III will prove to be a futile exercise. Primary focus of different maritime zones, as defined under UNCLOS-III, is to promote economic exploitation of sea resources while reiterating the concept of freedom of the high seas. This does not address the newly developing maritime threats that not only threaten freedom of the high seas but also use the high seas to target the homeland *via* its adjacent sea space. While defining maritime security frontiers one will have to address several considerations like port security, security of high value installations on the coast, smuggling activities, both overseas and coastal, that are closely related to acts of terrorism, possible misuse of fishing vessels and related fish landing sites and fishery harbours, security of off-shore oil and gas installations on the continental-shelf, SLOCs, both overseas and coastal etc. These concern multiple agencies and departments in public as also private sectors. It also involves multiple enforcement agencies. In such a case, security frontiers will overlap, thereby requiring a more robust mechanism not only for information sharing but also for enforcement action so as to provide for synergy among multiple agencies involved and to avoid duplication and hence to make the best use of limited resources.

Under these circumstances, India's maritime security frontiers can be broadly delimited as follows. The first is the coastal belt along the shore and its immediate sea approaches. It will cover port/harbour, high value installations on or near the coast, fishery harbour, fish landing sites as well as beaches that can be approached from the sea, base facilities of several maritime enforcement agencies like the Navy, the Coast Guard, the Customs, Fisheries Department and the Marine Police. The maximum outer limit of this frontier will coincide with that of the territorial waters while simultaneously covering a designated zone on land along the coast line. This has the added advantage that under the present legal norms, coastal state can extend its full criminal jurisdiction upto the outer limit of the territorial waters.

The second maritime frontier can coincide with the outer limit of India's contiguous zone for two reasons. The one is that under Article 33 of

UNCLOS-III the coastal state has the right to prevent smuggling and related activities in this zone. Thus, the coastal state has the right of search and seizure of suspected foreign vessels and if necessary, to detain the vessel and the crew. The second reason is that under section 5, sub-section 4(a) and 5(a) of MZI Act, 1976, it is already designated as the security zone of India. Since this sub-section of MZI Act of 1976 is almost forgotten by decision makers, it needs to be examined if India's anti-terrorism laws have jurisdiction in that security zone *vis-à-vis* non-Indians as well. If not, they need to be suitably amended in the context of section 5 sub-section 5 (a) of MZI Act, 1976. Beside keeping an eye on smuggling and terrorism related acts, this zone will also be important in the context of SLOCs both overseas and coastal, as well as security of some of the off-shore installations in India's continental-shelf. That widens the nature of second tier of India's maritime security zone.

The third tier of security zone will cover sea space around the off-shore oil and gas installations in the continental-shelf. Though the continental-shelf at present covers the area upto the outer limit of the EEZ, yet the focus of maritime security zone will only be the specific sea space around these installations. Security of this specific zone will have two main components; basic point security of the high value installations *per se*, and security-related management of surrounding sea and air space *i.e.* area security. That will require SLOC protection, both overseas and coastal, as well as monitoring large number of fishing vessels that will be operating in or transiting through those waters. While, basic point security of the platforms will have to be handled by suitably armed and trained special teams located on or around those platforms, SLOCs can be monitored by the Navy, the Coast Guard and the Air Force. It will be necessary to involve fishery authorities and fishing communities to evolve a mechanism to share information as well as to regulate movement of Indian fishing vessels in these sensitive zones.

The fourth security zone will comprise of the EEZ. Though notionally this sea space stretches from the outer limit of the territorial waters to the outer limit of the EEZ (200 n. miles), yet a significant portion of that sea space will already be covered under other maritime zones. For practical purposes, security dimension in the remaining sea space can be divided into two parts. The one will be limited to a distance of about 100 n. miles from the coast or about 75 n. miles from the outer limit of the contiguous zone. Monitoring and protection of SLOCs, both overseas and coastal, as well as regulating fishing on those waters will be the main requirements. India's fishery laws as also mechanism for their enforcement will need to be drastically revised, keeping in view, the rapid increase in the number of fishing vessels as also their capability to stay away from the shore for a longer period and to fish further away from the coast. The draft Fishery Bill, 2009 had proposed radical changes in the context of fishery in these waters. That draft bill raised some security related questions. It is hoped that the revised draft and the final bill will take care of these security related issues.

The bill also proposed to open India's EEZ to foreign fishermen, particularly from India's immediate maritime neighbours. These vessels that will have easy and legitimate access to India's coastal waters will need to be monitored more effectively in the context of maritime security. Present arrangements are outmoded and need radical restructuring. Hence, this zone of EEZ will become increasingly vulnerable. The fishery departments, both at the level of the Central Government as also of the states and UTs, will be forced to play increasing roles in the context of maritime security. Sea space of the EEZ, will also be important in the context of monitoring overseas SLOCs that pass through these waters. Thus, securing India's maritime frontiers will also help to monitor and protect major international SLOCs.

India's fifth maritime security frontier beyond its EEZ will include the high seas, as defined under Article 86 of UNCLOS-III. This zone will extend beyond the outer limit of the fourth zone. This sea space also constitutes the part of high seas beyond the EEZ over which no coastal state can exercise any jurisdiction. The only exception is the criminal jurisdiction that all states enjoy in the case of piracy under UNCLOS-III (Articles 100-107).

Till recently, anti-piracy measures were confined to seizure of the vessel, arrest of the culprits and their trial under the law of the land. Also, anti-piracy measures were based mostly on international cooperation in information sharing and possible alert. Now, as in the case of Gulf of Aden and waters off the Horn of Africa, state actors have reacted proactively even in cases of hijacking and are deploying warships and maritime reconnaissance aircrafts to preempt acts of piracy and hijacking. Force projection on high seas in the context of war on terror and in the context of checking proliferation of weapons of mass destruction (WMD) has been accepted as an accepted part of state practice. Thus, previous notions of freedom of navigation on the high seas is undergoing a fundamental change.

Though traditional international law and clauses of UNCLOS-III do put certain constraints on state action *vis-à-vis* threats posed by NSA and terrorists *via* the adjacent sea space, efforts are afoot to evolve state practices that are complemented by resolutions and conventions of UN Security Council and IMO that are giving shape to a new *de facto* international law that seeks to strengthen the state's action in meeting the new challenge. Together they not only help legitimise state action in apprehending and punishing the criminals but also to preempt their designs by taking preventive actions, even in waters that under UNCLOS-III, fall under the broad category of the high seas. It is, therefore, time that concerned authorities in India define their respective maritime security frontiers and spell out necessary enforcement actions so as to legalise the action taken by various enforcement agencies in these zones, in forestalling anti-national activities of these criminal elements.

2 | MARITIME DIMENSIONS OF TERRORISM

While discussing maritime terrorism two interrelated factors need to be underlined. The one is that maritime terrorism needs to be seen as an intrinsic part of the broad spectrum of terrorism except that what maritime terrorists seek to do is approach the designated target *via* the adjacent sea space. While it is possible that terrorists may use the sea for transfer of men and material at any one point along the coast to another point in the same country, it is more likely that they would use the maritime route to reach the target from their base in another country. Thus, maritime terrorism *ipso facto* acquires a transnational equation.

The second factor that needs to be noted is that terrorists, including maritime terrorists, now-a-days operate within a global network framework. Hence, efforts to combat maritime terrorism also require a global networking system. This is especially true in the field of information sharing as also in efforts that are afoot to legitimise state actions on 'war or terror', specially on the high seas. Over the past decade, many steps have been taken by state actors as also under the auspices of the UN Security Council and the IMO that are providing a degree of legitimacies to actions of state actors, to face the new challenges in the sea space of their security concern.

Non-State Actors and terrorists: defining the terms

Through the two terms Non-State Actors (NSA) and terrorists are used interchangeably, these are defined separately under WMD Act, 2005 of India. The Weapons of Mass Destruction and Their Delivery Systems (Prohibition of Unlawful Activities) Act, 2005, also known as the WMD Act, 2005, under section 4 defines them separately. Under section 4, sub-section iii (g) of that act, a non-state actor is a person or entity not acting under the lawful activities of any country. Section 4, subsection iii (m), while defining the term 'terrorist', said that it would have the meaning as assigned to that expression in the Unlawful Activities (Prevention) Act (UAPA), 1967. Thus, as per these two definitions, while the terrorist is essentially a criminal, NSA need not necessarily be so, except when the actions are so defined under various laws. For example, while NSA has the right to import goods that are legally permitted by the government of the day, smuggling them will make that a criminal act.

Though acts have defined NSA and terrorists separately, yet their activities sometimes tend to coalesce. In such cases, activities of NSA fall within the purview of acts dealing with terrorism. A smuggler, whose 'normal' activities consist of smuggling consumer goods and who would be persecuted under the Customs Act, could become liable for arrest, trial and punishment under UAPA, if his activities can be proved to be linked to acts of terrorism. It was alleged that fishermen of Tamil Nadu had used their fishing crafts to transfer material, including what could be used in combat, to the LTTE of Sri Lanka and to smuggle persons belonging to the LTTE, illegally, across the Palk Straits. The RDX that was off-loaded on the coast of Maharashtra by boats belonging to local fishermen was used during the Bombay blasts of 1993. Sometimes, trading vessels of NSA are also used for acts related to terrorism. Hence, though NSA and terrorists are, in the eyes of law, related to two different sets of criminal activities, their activities like smuggling, will need to be monitored more closely to see that NSA and terrorists do not form a nexus. This widens the scope of homeland security.

Unlawful activities of various NSA and terrorists need to be analysed under three main heads. The first comprises of activities that do not specifically target peace, security and stability of the state. They include illegal fishing, smuggling of consumer usables, acts of pollution etc. Activities of the second group would include armed robbery on board vessels near the coast and piracy on the high seas. Activities of the third group aim at undermining peace, stability, socio-economic harmony and thus the very foundation of the state system. They have no hesitation in targeting even the unarmed civilians. Their activities include illicit trade in arms, ammunition and explosives, that may include WMD-related material, smuggling of terrorists, transfer of funds, attacks on value targets like off-shore installations as also on the shore, including civilian targets as seen during the terrorist attacks on Mumbai in November 2008. The objective is to spread terror among the public at large and thereby to undermine public confidence in the state.

Evolution of modern terrorism

Terrorism is use of violence, outside the accepted framework, especially by NSA, to intimidate the adversary, so as to achieve the desired objectives, be they socio-economic, political or even revenge. One can trace it back in India, to mythology. Ashwathama, son of Guru Dronacharya, killed the sons of the Pandavas soon after the great battle of Kurukshetra, while they were sleeping, to avenge the death of his father and other dear ones who allegedly were killed by treachery. He was tracked and punished with eternal banishment. Reportedly, he is still believed to be alive. If so, he would be the founder of the terrorist movement.

During the medieval period, the assassins (or *hashasheen*) were the most dreaded groups. Their zone of operation covered the space between Iran and the Mediterranean Sea. They would launch suicidal attacks against high state officials, including heads of the state. The Sheikh, who had created that organisation, the Bin Laden of those days, had his hideout in a castle named Eagle's Nest. It was built on top of a high mountain peak. The Mongols attacked and destroyed it. The assassins have resurfaced now in the guise of suicide bombers.

Terrorism is a newly constituted term. They were known as nationalists, rebels, insurgents and even anarchists. They were motivated by factors like anti-colonialism and anti-imperialism or even by radical Leftist ideology. Bader Meinhoff of Germany, Red Brigade of Italy and Red Flag of Japan were examples of such 'terrorist' groups who not only hijacked aircrafts and attacked airports but also held high-level personnel as hostages. Some radical groups among the Palestinians also followed that tactic. Attack on the Israeli team at the Munich Olympics in 1982 and the hijacking of four airliners in Jordan in 1970 as well as that of Italian cruise liner *Achille Laura* were main highlights of their activities. Such activities were also undertaken by other terrorists groups like the Khalistanis and Islamic groups sponsored by Pakistan.

Organisations fighting for the cause of the Palestinians, against *Apartheid* in South Africa and for the rights of Tamil minority in Sri Lanka began to be dubbed as terrorists after the mid-seventies. Nelson Mandela, who became the President of South Africa after the first real democratic election in 1994, was designated as a terrorist. Interestingly, it took 14 years for the US Congress to pass a law in May 2008 that removed his name from America's list of terrorists. The Chairman of the PLO, Yasser Arafat, who was recognised by the Government of India as the President of the State of Palestine after 1988, was also dubbed as a terrorist and denied the *visa* to address the UN General Assembly session in New York, in 1988. A special session was held in Geneva so that he could address the UN General Assembly.

Thus, terrorism, as we understand today, is a post-1970 phenomenon. Though the debate as to whether violence associated with the national liberation movement constituted terrorism or not delayed the UN passing resolutions that sharply defined acts of terrorism, several conventions were passed against hijacking of aircrafts, hostage taking etc. Radical Islam had not emerged as a motive force behind such acts till the late seventies though radical Islamic movements had been gaining ground in states like Egypt, Sudan, Saudi Arabia, Iran and even Pakistan. The capture of the Holy Mosque in Mecca in 1978 by an indigeneous radical Islamic group can be said to have heralded in that new movement. Assassination of President Sadat during an Army Parade in 1981, after he had signed a peace treaty with Israel in 1979, was probably the next major terrorist attack motivated by groups that advocated radical interpretation of Islam. The Islamic Revolution in Iran, General Zia's policy of "Islamization" of Pakistan as well as the support offered to the so-called 'Mujahedeen' in Afghanistan not only by the Arab-Islamic world but also by the West, helped the radical Islamic groups to develop the Afghanistan-Pakistan axis as a safe, large and suitable strategic base for their future operations. The rest is an open book.

Events of 9/11 had a great impact upon India's world view on terrorism. The world also began to alter its perception on challenges faced by India in that field. As per the *Annual Report* of the Ministry of Home Affairs (MHA), it was realised that India's fight against forces of terrorism had to be globalised (MHA, *A R., 2001-2002*, p. 6). Ministry of Defence (MoD) was more forthright in underlining not only the transnational roots of terrorism but also the impact of radical Islam in that context. *Annual Report* of the Ministry of Defence (MoD) of *2001-2002* stated that India had been a victim of terrorism for many decades much before the West experienced its deadly reality in September 2001. The terrorist menace in Jammu and Kashmir has its roots in Pakistan and is supported financially and militarily by a section in the government and inhabitants of that country. It continued, "Terrorists organisations have long arms and global reach. The world, therefore, has to fight a united battle by pooling resources in order to remove the scourge from the face of the earth (MoD, *A R., 2002-2003*, pp. 9-10). Its *Annual Report, 2004-2005*, highlighted the role of fundamentalism and extremism (MoD, *A R., 2004-2005*, p. 7). The rise of Islamic fundamentalism as well as the increasing incidents of terrorism and political violence, with its attendant repercussion on the security of India, was further underlined in its *Annual Report* next year (MoD, *A R., 2005-2006*, p. 8).

It will not be wrong to say that terrorism, like any other movement, needs a strong motive force that would sustain it against heavy odds. That base could be radical left ideology like the Naxal movement which believes that power flows through the barrel of a gun. It could be the belief that they have no option but to resort to violence to attain their objective. The LTTE was a prisoner of that mindset. Religion could also become a motivating factor for terrorism especially when the participants are offered reward in 'afterlife'. It appears that now religion has largely replaced ideology as the motivating factor for violence thereby posing a serious challenge to secular values of modern society. No one knows how long this contest between religious radicalism and secular-liberal values will continue and what long term damage it will do to peace, security and stability not only of regional but even global order.

In many cases, use of violence is rationalised as a means to attain a given objective. However, it often degrades as an end in itself and the original objective is forgotten. In such a case it can end only after a complete victory of one and total annihilation of the other. Sri Lanka is an apt illustration. But can one repeat a Sri Lanka worldwide? India's experience in Kashmir and the North-East since past six decades and America's policy in Afghanistan and Iraq tell a different story. Thus, we will have to live with terrorism for a long time to come. Hence, we need to evolve policies that would be suitable for a long-term confrontation with an enemy that can strike anytime, anywhere while using any tool.

Terrorism and India

It is important to look at the question of terrorism from two separate but interrelated perspectives: Indian and international. India has suffered due to direct acts of terrorism on at least four separate counts; Pakistan-inspired and supported low intensity conflict as a part of its continuing confrontation, insurgency fuelled by feelings of ethno-political separatism, fallout of insurgency in Sri Lanka and the Naxal movement.

It is unfortunate that Pakistan could never evolve a national mindset that was independent of the so-called Hindu-Muslim divide that had led to the partition of British India in 1947. Consequently, hostility towards India almost became the rationale for its survival as a nation. The fact that several Muslim invaders had been able to defeat Indian rulers, including Muslim rulers, in the past, had given an eronous perception that Pakistan, as a Muslim state, could also easily defeat India (a Hindu state). That pretention of military prowess was dealt a blow in 1971 if not in 1965. Pakistani ruling elite adopted a new three pronged policy. The first was to acquire nuclear bomb to pose what was presumed to be an ultimate deterrence to India's superior conventional war-fighting capability. The second was to raise the level of state-sponsored low intensity conflict to bleed India. The third was to accelerate the process of 'Islamization' so as to strengthen Pakistan's Islamic base. *Nizam-e-Mustafa* policy of General Zia was one such example. This three-pronged approach has been pursued by Pakistan's ruling elite since the days of Zulfikar Ali Bhutto onwards.

Thus, India has been a prey to state-sponsored terrorism for decades. It will continue to face it in the future as well. Over the decades, that bilateral confrontation has spilled over at regional level when bases in Nepal and Bangladesh and in some of the Gulf states began to be used in these terrorist-related activities. The Mumbai blast of 1993 and terrorists attack on Mumbai in November 2008 were part of the maritime dimension of that ongoing confrontation.

Pakistani authorities in their strategy to weaken India have tried to use domestic insurgency movements in India. India had inherited the North-East Frontier as a part of its share in British India. The British had done little to integrate the people of that region, who were divided into various ethnic groups and sub-groups, into the main stream of India's socio-economic and political ethos. Instead, the region was almost deliberately kept isolated and backward. That feeling of alienation fed insurgency after India's independence. Destabilised Myanmar helped the insurgents in obtaining arms and also refuge when pursued by Indian forces. Insurgency in the North-East needs a separate study. However, it is being contained and hopefully the area will be integrated within the mainstream of India.

Naxal movement is a post-1962 phenomenon when the radical group from the Communist movement in India broke off and launched what can be termed as an armed struggle to attain the political objectives. It spread over the decades to other areas in India that had a poor record of 'governance' combined with strong nexus between political power and muscle power. Radical Naxal ideology, that power flows through the barrel of the gun, began to draw local recruits. Though the movement challenges the political system, it does not challenge India as a nation state. Hence, it differs radically from insurgency in some parts of the North-East or the one fuelled by so-called radical Islamic movement that has roots beyond India. Reportedly, Pakistanis are wooing the Naxalites also.

Nearer home, the case of Tamil militancy in Sri Lanka illustrates how the Tamil movement, primarily based upon real or perceived political and economic discrimination of Tamil minority at the hands of Sinhala majority, could gradually evolve from a protest movement to a militant movement, insurgency and armed struggle and finally as a 'terrorist' movement. Sense of ethno-religious as also politico-economic discrimination began to grow among the Tamil population in Sri Lanka after Buddhism-linked Sinhala language, identity and hence nationalism, was deliberately projected as a part of political strategy by some Sinhala politicians and some of their foreign supporters. According to K. Venkataraman, a person named Col. Olcott had turned up in Colombo and was responsible for the revival of Buddhism and the Sinhala cause (Venkataraman, 2006, p. 224). It is possible that the move was initiated to counter the policy of Sri Lanka's government under the leadership of Sri Bandarnaike who was not only promoting the policy of non-alignment but was also developing close relations with China, as reflected in the barter trade in rice, rubber and tea. He was assassinated by a Buddhist monk.

Increasing frustration among Sri Lankan Tamils gradually began to take more radical forms. Several groups emerged to lead the cause. Of them, the Liberation Tigers of Tamil Eelam (LTTE), under Prabhakaran, emerged as the most radical as also the most intransigent. Tamil movement in Sri Lanka received support in the initial stages in India, both in Tamil Nadu as also at the level of the Central Government. Over the years, opposition turned into insurgency and after the ethnic riots of 1983 into an armed secessionist movement. The word 'terrorist' was not used even when the Indian Peace Keeping Force (IPKF) confronted the LTTE in 1987. There was still the hope of a political settlement. IPKF was deinducted under growing 'domestic' opposition in India as also on the request of President Premadasa who had arranged a truce with LTTE. After that, Indian policy was by and large defensive. It sought to deny safe haven to LTTE in India as also essential supplies to it.

The LTTE came under greater pressure in India following the assassination of Rajiv Gandhi who, as the Prime Minister, had not only signed the India-Sri Lanka Accord of 1987 but had also sanctioned the use of IPKF against the LTTE. LTTE gradually began to be branded as a terrorist organisation. The *Annual Report* of the Ministry of Defence, *2001-2002* noted, "LTTE's efforts to operate from India and their growing nexus with Indian militant organisation, who also prefer ideologies rooted in violence, continue to cause serious concern…Assassination of Rajiv Gandhi and the 'suspected' role of the LTTE highlighted the dangers of *terrorism* in the context of the security environment in the region" (MoD, *A R., 2001-2002*, p. 6). Annual Report of 2002-2003 was more specific, "LTTE remains a *proscribed terrorist organisation* in India and its leader, a proclaimed offender under the law (MoD, *A R., 2002-03* p. 6). Interestingly, while the Annual Reports of the Ministry of External Affairs had named the LTTE as a terrorist organisation, it was declared not as a *terrorist* but only as an *unlawful association* under UAPA, 1967 (*The?? Hindu*, May 6, 2005). Prabhakaran was declared a proclaimed offender in the trial of assassination of Rajiv Gandhi. That charge was dropped after his death was confirmed, as per Indian legal practice (Subramani, *The Hindu*, October 26, 2010).

Though the LTTE was criticised by several states, it was not treated as a terrorist organisation in many states. The Nordic countries and Japan tried to broker peace between LTTE and the Government of Sri Lanka. That process virtually collapsed by 2007. Since 2008, the Armed Forces of Sri Lanka, with the active and passive support of many states, were able to mount heavy and sustained military pressure upon the LTTE and finally succeeded in militarily defeating it and in occupying the "heart land" of the LTTE. But it will be wrong to presume that it will be an end to Tamil militancy. It will operate clandestinely from places all over Sri Lanka and abroad. It may even seek to activise and strengthen its links with ideological and ethnic supporters in India. Thus, Tamil militancy/terrorism is likely to continue to be a potential threat unless a political settlement is achieved that is acceptable to the radical groups of Tamils as a viable alternative to their basic demand of Tamil Elam in Sri Lanka.

India and International Terrorism

Beside these acts related to terrorism that directly target India, India is also affected by the fallout of terrorism at the global level. As noted earlier, the international community was already threatened by isolated acts of terrorism and had passed several conventions to meet the new challenge. But terrorism was designated as the most serious challenge to international peace and security only after the West and its regional allies in West Asia like Israel, Egypt and Saudi Arabia became the prime targets of groups, inspired by radical interpretation of Islamic theological formulations by certain Islamic scholars like Ibn Tamiyya, during the medieval period and Mohammad bin Abdul Wahab of Arabian Peninsula, Mawlana Maududi of Indian sub-continent and Hasan al-Banna and Syed Kutb of Egypt in the contemporary era.

While attempts were made to suppress their views they began to acquire increasing legitimacy even among the educated. These views were even promoted since the end of the seventies to serve narrow domestic political ends of some ruling elites in states like Saudi Arabia and Pakistan as also by USA against USSR. Those who had let loose the genie soon found that they could not put it back in the bottle. Also, those who were seeking to promote USA as the sole super power after the breakup of USSR, designated terrorism as the new global challenge. 'War on terror' became the new basis for USA's world leadership agenda. Unfortunately, this war on terror had resulted in the confrontation with radical Islam and almost proved the hypothesis of clash of civilizations. This confrontation between one-time allies began to take a serious turn after US-led troops increased their military presence in the Gulf after the Kuwaiti Crisis of 1990-91 and its aftermath. India has been affected by the fallout of this war on terror especially when it seemed to be siding with USA in this new cold war at the global level. Those Islamic groups, like the *Taliban* and *Al-Qaida* that were not against India early have now begun to target India as an enemy of their pan-Islamic coalition.

Though USA and its diplomatic missions had been targeted even earlier, as in 1998, war on terrorism acquired greater political and legal acceptance even in UN after the events of 9/11. Terrorism, in any form, is now accepted as a crime against humanity. Security Council passed several resolutions against it and indirectly legitimised US-led coalition's military offensive in Afghanistan in 2001 and its immediate adjacent frontier. After the end of the Cold War, that was explained in ideological terms as a contest between democracy and free market economy *vs* socialism and centralised economy, the new cold war is projected as a contest between democracy and modern values *vs*. radical Islam and medieval values as propounded by its ideologues. Thus, the new cold war has also acquired its own ideological overtones.

Maritime Terrorism

Maritime terrorism, an offshoot of terrorism *per se*, is conceptually different from other maritime crimes since it aims at using violence, unrestrained by political, economic, social or even humanitarian constraints so as to achieve the goals as determined by the specific group or the umbrella organisation or by the state who use them to plan and execute such acts at national and/ or international level. Traditional international law or UNCLOS-III that deal with maritime affairs have no provision for terrorism though insurgency and belligerency were reorganised and provided for in the past. UNCLOS-III does not provide for actions *vis-à-vis* maritime terrorism, though other maritime crimes by non-state actors like acts of piracy, slavery and illicit traffic in narcotic drugs or psychotropic substances are recognised and states are asked to cooperate in suppressing them.

Criminal acts linked to maritime affairs were formally recognised in the Convention for the Suppression of Unlawful Acts against the Safety of Maritime Navigation (the SUA Convention) of 1988. It was in response to the hijacking of the cruise liner, *Achile Laura*, on October 8, 1985, by a group belonging to one of the radical Palestinian movements. Since a US citizen was killed in that incident, USA wanted the case to be tried under the crime of piracy. While some supported the US stand, others opposed it (Halberstam, 1988, 269-70). Under traditional international law, as also under UNCLOS-III, act of piracy needs two ships and has to have private gains as its objective. Both these facts were absent in the case of *Achile Laura* which was hijacked by 'terrorists' who had boarded the vessel as passengers, and who had political objectives.

The event had occurred when the VIth Committee of the General Assembly of the UN was discussing the question of international terrorism. It passed a resolution requesting the International Maritime Organisation (IMO) to study and recommend appropriate measures to combat such threats. The IMO conference discussed the question and adopted the SUA Convention by consensus in its meeting in Rome in March 1988. An associated Protocol dealing with fixed platforms on the continental-shelf was also adopted at that time. 'Terrorism' was a politically sensitive term those days. Hence, to achieve consensus, its use was avoided. Rather, criminal acts, that otherwise would have been classified as acts of terrorism, were listed in Articles 3(1) of the SUA Convention. The question will be discussed in details in Chapter III that deals with maritime terrorism and international responses.

The term 'maritime terrorism' began acquiring greater legitimacy after 2000, when the West began to be targeted on the sea. Though terrorists had targeted state actors like India, Sri Lanka and the Philippines *via* the adjacent sea space even prior to that, such acts were not taken seriously by the international community. The term, 'maritime terrorism' was employed only after the West itself began to be so targeted by radical Islamic groups after military interventions in the Persian Gulf region. The attack on *USS Cole* (DDG-67), an American guided missile destroyer, on October 11, 2000, while it was being refuelled at Aden port, could be said to mark the beginning of maritime terrorism for the West.

A small boat, loaded with about 500 lb of high explosives and manned by a two-member team, was detonated close to the side of the American warship. That tore a hole of 40 by 40 feet in the hull. The blast also killed 17 sailors while 39 were wounded. Serious damage was caused to the warship. According to Peter Lehr, a similar attack was planned earlier in January 2000 against *USS The Sullivans*. It failed because the suicide attack boat was probably overloaded and had capsized due to high waves in the open sea. *USS Cole* was repaired at the cost of $250 mn while the total cost of the attacking boat was estimated at about $50,000 (Lehr, 2008, pp. 180-81).

A similar attack followed in October 2002 when the French tanker, *M.V. Limburg* was targeted at the Yemeni oil port of Mina al-Dabah near the town of Mukallah. The tanker was already carrying 400,000 tonnes of oil from the Iranian oil terminal at Kharg and was to load an additional 1.5 mn tonnes of oil at the Yemeni port before sailing to its destination in Malaysia. It was attacked by a small boat which impacted on the port side of the tanker. The tanker burst into flames after violent explosion. The fire was brought under control within hours. Several crew members were hurt. About 90,000 barrels of oil (about 12,000 tonnes) were spilled. The double hull of the tanker saved it from greater damage (Lehr, 2008, pp. 181-82). A Yemeni group called the Islamic Army of Aden-Abyane, that figures in the American list of terrorist organisations, claimed responsibility for the attack. It sought to justify the attack on the ground that the tanker was going to supply fuel to the American Vth Fleet for an attack against 'our Iraqi brothers'. It was also said that the real target was an American frigate that was close to the tanker (Naravane, 2002). The French had become the target of attack especially after their involvement in US-led attack on the *Taliban* and *Al-Qaida* in Afghanistan after 9/11. A car bomb had also killed eleven French naval engineers in Karachi on May 6, 2002. Probably, they were involved in the construction of French *Agosta-class* submarines that were being built for the Pakistan Navy.

Oil terminals in Iraq also came under attack. A small boat filled with explosives launched the attack in the early hours of the morning of April 24, 2004 on Basrah oil terminal. The target was the VLCC tanker *Takasuza*. The suicide boat was fired upon by security personnel. Though two attackers on the boat were killed in action, the tanker could escape the intended blast only because the 700 lb explosive charge had failed to explode. Another attack was also launched, almost at that very time at *Khor al-Amaya* oil terminal in South Iraq, across the Kuwaiti border. A slow moving *dhow* was employed. When the search and seizure team reached the *dhow*, the *dhow* exploded, reportedly killing two and injuring nine personnel of the US Coast Guard that were employed in that sector (Lehr, 2008, pp. 182-84).

Al-Qaida was projected as the main motive force behind the new threat of maritime terrorism. According to Barrett Bingley, *Al-Nashiri*, allegedly the head of *Al-Qaida's* naval operations who was captured in November 2002, had prepared a 180-page dossier that listed maritime targets of opportunity. It also gave details of the vulnerable places in the ship, as also use of limpet mines, how to turn LNG tanker into a floating bomb, etc. (Bingley, 2004, pp. 357-358). It is also reported that *Al-Qaida* owned a fleet of sea-going vessels that operate under various flags of convenience and are capable of being used in terrorist-related operations. (Arabinda and Withana, 2008, pp. 216-17).

Overblowing the issue

Experts on maritime terrorism seem to have let their imagination run wild and have anticipated all sorts of scenarios where terrorists would use the sea space as also vessels, installations etc. as means as well as targets of their criminal activities. US Secretary of Defence, William Cohen, as per the Report of the Quadrennial US Defence Review, May 1997, had warned that a paradox of the new strategic environment was that American military superiority actually increased the threat of nuclear, biological and chemical attack against USA by creating incentives for adversaries to challenge the US asymmetrically (Forbes and Rumley, 2008, p. 51).

Containers became a subject of special interest both in the context of smuggling of terrorists as also for delivery of WMD and terrorism-related material (Sakhuja, 2002, p. 3). US-led Container Security Initiative (CSI) was one such response. Some experts have cautioned against over blowing such threats and advocate the need for a more realistic appraisal of the threat perception.

Undoubtedly, Islamic militants had targeted *USS Cole* and French tanker *Limberg* in 2000 and 2002 respectively. But, no such major attack has taken place since then. No tanker or CNG carrier has been captured by the terrorists and taken to a port to be exploded there. Undoubtedly, one oil tanker carrying oil from Saudi Arabia was hijacked in North-Western Indian Ocean and taken to the coast of Somalia for ransom. But no such hijacked tanker would be allowed even to approach the port or the coast of any other state. It would either be recaptured or sunk in mid-ocean. No WMD-related material in quantity that can be a cause for serious concern has been found on board hundreds of ships intercepted under PSI. Those that were found were dual-use material destined for state actors (so-called states of proliferation concern).

The fear of attack on oil tanker also needs to be assessed more rationally. The long-drawn Iraq-Iran War (1980-88), that had serious impact on oil-related infra-structures as also tankers in the confined space of the Persian Gulf, presents an example of how the impact of so-called tanker war and attack on oil terminals did not seriously hamper either the production or the export of oil from that region even when the combatants were state actors armed with modern weapons. During those years 543 vessels were struck. Of them, 80 vessels were sunk (Roy, 2002, p. 405). During the war, Iran's oil terminal on the Kharg Island was repeatedly attacked by Iraqi Air Force but with little real effect on its functioning. According to Peter Lehr, attacks by sea borne improvised explosive devices (IED) are hardly likely to have more than nuisance value if proper security measures are taken (Lehr, 2008, pp. 182-83).

Martin Murphy, while evaluating the threat of maritime terrorism, noted that a lack of necessary skill and practical difficulties facing terrorists while attempting to operate in the present-day maritime system, may render many of the nightmare scenarios, feared by government and port authorities, as unlikely. According to him, ports are large and hard to destroy though explosion would cause death and destruction. While oil tankers or CNG carriers are supposed to be exploded near the port, how do the terrorists, even if they are able to hijack them and bring them near the port, get them to explode on command? Crude oil is difficult to ignite. Hundreds of large ships and tankers were hit in the Gulf during the so-called tanker war, yet, few of them exploded. Even the oil spills have been contained. Between 834,000 to 1,500,000 tonnes of crude oil was spilled in the northern half of the Persian Gulf during the fag end of the Kuwaiti war with no military or strategic effect, though it caused environmental damage. Tanker spills are much smaller (Murphy, 2006, pp. 20-1).

Benjamin Friedman also questions the induced fear psychosis of terrorism. According to him, people overestimate risks that they can picture and ignore those they cannot. America's Council on Foreign Relation Report of 2003 mentioned that emergency responders were drastically underfunded and dangerously unprepared. It had recommended spending $25 bn per year. The post-9/11 fear psychosis was partly responsible for it. It had generated a feeling that terrorists can strike any place any time with any weapon. Countering that exaggerated threat became the guiding principle of anti-terrorist thinking. Government's warnings and 24-hour news network enhanced that feeling of insecurity and of danger. USA squanders billions of dollars annually protecting the state and locations that face no significant threat of terrorism. Federal spending in that context grew from $616 mn in 2001 to $ 3.4 bn in 2005. According to Benjamin Friedman, Homeland Security spending would approach $ 50 bn in 2006. It did not include missile defence. That spending was roughly equal to China's defence spending (Friedman, 2005, pp. 22-4).

The real issue while formulating an effective policy to counter threats, even those posed by terrorists, is to differentiate between threat *per se* and general vulnerability. Often, ill-defined vulnerability rather than a well-defined and 'practical' threat has been made the basis of counter-terrorism policy and related initiatives. USA and Canada have responded to such a maximum threat perception. According to Benjamin Friedman, US Federal Port Security Program had distributed about $ 600 million to hundreds of ports in USA. The US Coast Guard budget had grown to $ 6.3 bn per year since September 11, 2001 (Friedman, 2006, p. 24).

Canada was equally keen to seal off its maritime approaches. It was reportedly building an underwater tripwire system that would warn of potential terrorists approaching by ships in ports or in shallow waters – above and below the water's surface. The system was designed to use acoustic and electro-magnetic sensors networked with satellite and other communication links. According to Ross Graham, Director-General of Defence Research and Development, Canada (DRDC) Atlantic, the system, dubbed as Rapid Deployable System (RDS), can also be deployed to monitor the choke points overseas. It is effective upto a depth of 500 metres. A working model was being prepared at the cost of US $ 5.6 mn and was expected to be ready for field trial by 2005. Only then, was the government to decide if it was worth funding a full-scale model. Related to it was the plan to spend Canadian $ 50 mn to install a High Frequency Surface Waves Radar System, capable of tracking even far off surface targets. For an effective check, it was to be coordinated with the role of maritime patrol aircrafts. The purpose was to keep track of suspicious vessels approaching North America (*Defence News*, February 16, 2004).

Maritime Terrorism: Indian context

While what decision makers do need to do is take note of wider global scenario, it is equally important to evaluate realistically, threats in India's homeland security that can be posed by NSA and terrorists *via* the adjacent sea space, for the simple reason that India's maritime environment and threat perception differs widely *vis-a-vis* those of the West.

Though smuggling by sea was a common phenomenon in India, the first time when linkages between sea-borne smuggling and terrorism was highlighted, was in 1993, when large quantities of high explosives like the RDX, that was used in those blasts, were landed on the coast of Maharashtra and brought to Mumbai by persons allegedly linked to the Daud Ibrahim group. Post-blast response was, at best, knew jerk. The usual patrols by the Indian Navy and the Coast Guard was given a new designation — *Operation Swan*. Attempt was also made towards patrolling the 'sensitive' coast of Maharashtra by a joint team comprising of the Navy, the Coast Guard, the Customs and the Maharashtra police. Reportedly, trawlers were hired for that purpose. Such as exercise, without an appropriate strategy, could not have yielded results. Despite these efforts, smuggling continued as usual. Terrorists, however, did not think it fit to use sea space for their activities in these waters till November 26, 2008 when they reached Mumbai by using a hijacked trawler from Gujarat.

Before the Mumbai blast of 1993, Tamil Nadu's sea space had been regularly used as a supply route for Tamil militancy in Sri Lanka. No special efforts were made except for the so-called *Operation Tasha* and *Operation Nakabandi* after the deinduction of IPKF from Sri Lanka. India was not the primary target of LTTE's terrorist activities though LTTE drew support from it sympathisers in Tamil Nadu. One wonders if special steps were initiated to better monitor that region even after the assassination of Rajiv Gandhi. Indians did not take steps to sanitise the adjoining sea space for two main reasons. The one was linked to domestic political reasons since many Tamil Nadu political parties were actively supporting Tamil militancy in Sri Lanka. The other reason was the presence of thousands of trawlers and other fishing vessels in that area. They even intruded into Sri Lanka's territorial waters for fishing and were consequently apprehended by Sri Lanka's Navy. Many of these fishermen were allegedly involved in smuggling activities also. So-called 'plight' of Indian fishermen and the issue of Katchchativu had acquired political focus rather than the terrorist threat to homeland security *via* the adjacent sea space.

Some moves were initiated after the Group of Ministers 'discovered' that India has a maritime border which also needed to be secured. Moves were initiated. Plans were drawn and funds were ear-marked for a five-year period. As will be analysed in Chapter VI, they were most inadequate. The events of November 26, 2008 (26/11), when terrorists landed on the coast of Mumbai proper to attack several value targets, highlighted the level of unpreparedness in combating maritime terrorism. The so-called 'public anger' led to rolling of some political heads but with no practical results in the context of strengthening homeland security. The Navy and the Coast Guard got more funding to improve their capability by acquiring more vessels and aircrafts and to establish more bases. 26/11 was, however, important because it forced decision makers to take a new look at the entire question of maritime security.

Contrary to 1993, when maritime terrorism had not been made an issue, media focus on events of 26/11 had pushed the question of maritime terrorism as a major issue though it was seen in the limited context of coastal security. It remains to be seen if governments, both at the Centre and in coastal states, really revamp the entire machinery of sea governance and related maritime security or hope that the public memory, short as it is, can be ignored till another incident shocks the nation and causes more heads to role. Terrorists would love that publicity as an added bonus for their criminal activities.

Now that maritime terrorism, or threat to homeland security *via* adjacent sea space, has been accepted as a real long term threat, it will be important to underline the possible nature of the threats so that the broad spectrum of threat and hence an appropriate framework to meet it can be more logically evaluated without being conditioned by the formulas propounded by Western strategists and their spokesmen in the South, including India. The zones of threat as also nature of threat can include threat to offshore oil and gas platforms on the continental-shelf, major SLOCs, both overseas and domestic, smuggling of men and material related to acts of terrorism, attack on high value targets in the harbour like oil and CNG tankers, cruise liners, dockyards, bases operated by the Navy and the Coast Guard, as also targets on the coast like refineries, nuclear installations, hubs of communication and of tourist interest etc. In maritime terrorism, access to these targets are *via* the adjacent sea space that can extend from coastal waters to the high seas. As seen in Chapter I, this sea space constitutes India's maritime frontier. That entire maritime frontier and not only the coastal waters needs to be monitored and if possible sanitised in the context of neutralising the challenges posed by maritime terrorism.

Maritime Terrorism: domestic, regional and international linkages

Terrorism, supported from across the land border and maritime terrorism are two different concepts. While terrorists crossing the land border can be confronted along a border or LoC that is well demarcated, terrorists approaching the coast or targeting value objects in adjacent sea space have a vast sea space to operate from. This sea space can extend beyond a country's territorial waters into the high seas where the coastal states have limited jurisdiction. This provides a more conducive environment for the terrorists to operate. Hence, meeting the threat posed by maritime terrorism needs maritime cooperation at bilateral, regional as also at international levels. The nature of cooperation can include information sharing and cooperation in a mutually agreed framework for patrolling of maritime borders for curbing criminal activities that target other states as well. Such cooperation is essential to forestall efforts by militants in one coastal state for targeting foreign vessels in the adjacent waters like attacks on *USS Cole* and *MV Limburg* or tankers in Iraqi oil terminals. Vast sea space of the high seas which is normally left unguarded and in which even criminals can operate with relative freedom under the concept of freedom of the high seas, reiterated under UNCLOS-III, is used to transport men and material from a 'safe' place across the sea to the 'targeted' area in another country.

LTTE had been using that grey area to supply material to its cadre in Sri Lanka from overseas sources. Reportedly, Indian militants in the North-East were also able to acquire arms and ammunition from abroad, mostly from sources in South-East Asia *via* the Malacca Strait and the Andaman Sea. The attack on Mumbai in November 2008 and the transfer of RDX for Bombay blast of 1993 are other examples of the linkage between terrorists operating at regional and international level.

Since there are limits to a state's capacity to fully sanitise, on its own, waters adjacent to its coast, homeland security will also depend upon the degree and type of cooperation that the concerned coastal state is able to obtain from its regional/maritime neighbours and from the international community.

Role of maritime neighbours becomes a critical factor in enhancing homeland security. Their roles can be divided into three broad categories; positive, neutral and negative. Positive role is played when these neighbours or even international actors are willing to cooperate in a bilateral or multilateral framework to combat the common threat. Neutral neighbours can be divided into two categories. Those that are neutral for reasons of domestic political compulsions. Bangladesh at least till recently could have been placed in that category. Other states are neutral because they are themselves unable to control their waters and coast. Somalia can be illustrated as an example of what can be termed as a failed state that is unable to exercise effective jurisdiction over its adjacent waters. The third category is that of a state which, because of political and military adversary relationship, will not only not cooperate but is likely to allow terrorists to use its territory to launch their operation against the maritime neighbour. Events of 26/11 have once again underlined that attitude.

Pakistan has always been a hostile neighbour and the passage of time seems to have further fuelled the fire of vengeance if not hatred *vis-à-vis* India in certain sections in that country. While these elements continue to use the land border for infiltration of terrorists, events of 26/11 have demonstrated their willingness to use the sea space also as a medium to promote terrorist activities against India. The statement of the arrested terrorist, Ajmal Kasab, mentioned the links of *Lashkar-e-Taiba* and elements in Pakistani Navy in facilitating the attack on Mumbai. David Coleman Headley also collaborated the role of Pakistan's Navy in this terror attack (*The Times of India*, July 20, 2010). Reportedly, elements in Pakistan are also trying to infiltrate the Maldives so as to use it as a base for their operations against India.

North Arabian Sea region has been and will remain crucial in the context of India's homeland security. That is also the area where bilateral and multilateral cooperation between India and regional powers is minimum. India has, of late, succeeded in opening dialogue on this question with some regional powers like Oman, UAE and Djibouti. Since most of the regional powers, except Iran, are very much part of the US-led coalition, anti-terrorist maritime cooperation between India and the countries of the Arabian Sea region will also depend upon the nod from USA. This will mean introducing India as a regional partner in maritime security, a place that is now reserved, under the broad framework of American strategy, for Pakistan since Operation Enduring Freedom of 2001, if not earlier, and its links with the Central Command (CENTCOM) whose zone of operation covered Pakistan.

Cooperation with Iran will also depend upon two inter-related perceptions on both sides; how will USA look at it? There has been muted criticism even of India-Iran naval visits in certain American circles. The perception of Gulf Cooperation Council (GCC) members will also need to be noted in that context. The Islamic Republic of Iran, a *Shia* dominated state, is seen as expanding its zone of influence in Iraq, Syria and Lebanon. Thus, a newly emerging *Shia* axis is seen as a challenge to *Sunni* dominated West Asia. Secondly, though the present political setup in Iran is not a perfect example of a liberal democratic state, it offers a model of an Islamic Republic that can offer an alternative on one hand to the system of monarchies in the Gulf as also to the ultra-conservative and extremist model of Islamic state as propounded by *Al-Qaida, the Taliban* and similar radical (*Sunni*) Islamic groups.

While India has close political and economic relations with several of the littoral states of this region yet, except for Oman, it has still to develop relations that would actively help India meet the challenge of maritime terrorism. No wonder, northern half of the Arabian Sea has become the prime focus of India's strategy to meet the new challenge of maritime terrorism.

Sri Lanka and the Maldives in Central Indian Ocean region are of prime concern as far as India's homeland security is concerned. As discussed, Sri Lanka is relevant from the point of Tamil-Sinhala divide in Sri Lanka as also because of the fallout of that divide in India, especially in the neighbouring state of Tamil Nadu. The ethnic linkage and the emotional outburst of so-called popular support in Tamil Nadu for the Tamil cause in Sri Lanka was already a matter of domestic concern in India. It was seen in the outbursts of pro-LTTE leaders like Vaiko (G. Gopalaswamy), leader of the Marumalarchi Dravida Munnetra Kazhagam, who had even warned of a blood bath in Tamil Nadu if the slightest harm befell V. Prabhakaran. (*The Hindu* April 9, 2009). This warning was taken seriously at that time because the LTTE's hard core group was trapped and was using local Tamil civilians as shields. Vaiko had said that Tamils of India would take up arms. He also warned that India would not remain one country if Sri Lankan President Rajapaksha did not stop the war and if India did not urge him to stop the war. Rajapaksha refused to do that on the pleas that it would give LTTE time to regroup. Before things could take an ugly turn in India, Sri Lanka's forces were able to defeat LTTE's armed wing without any serious fallout in Tamil Nadu. That, however, does not mean the end to emotional attachment in Tamil Nadu towards Tamils of Sri Lanka. It remains dormant and can be exploited again if Sri Lanka's government is unable to resolve the question in the near future.

India's homeland security is also closely related to peace and stability in the Maldives. The long north-south chain of Islands of the Maldives, which are also in close proximity to the chain of islands of the Lakshadweep, poses peculiar problems of maritime security of a long chain of small islands inhabited by a population that is being targeted by radical Islamic groups. Reportedly, Pakistan is seeking to woo some citizen from the Maldives as a part of the *jehadi* network against India. Such a move will also destabilise peace and security of the island republic. Reportedly, like the previous regime, the present regimes in the Maldives are also aware of this threat. Thus, there is common concern and hence ground for bilateral cooperation in strengthening homeland security of India as also of the Maldives.

There is no doubt that India has built bridges of bilateral and multilateral cooperation with its maritime neighbours in Central Indian Ocean region. This level of cooperation has reached a higher level of bilateral understanding and has led to fruitful cooperation among their respective enforcement agencies. This is also true in the case of Mauritius and the Seychelles.

The Andaman Sea and the Malacca Straits are important in the context of India's maritime security. In that context, the Andaman-Nicobar group of islands have attracted attention. Vice-Admiral Vinod Pasricha, the then Chief of Eastern Naval Command, Visakhapatnam, had expressed his concern as early as December 1999 at the growing anti-nationalist activities in and around these groups of islands. He was referring to instances of infiltration by foreigners in these waters and in the islands. He said that 150 cases of such infiltration were apprehended in November 1999 alone (*The Hindu*, December 12, 1999).

The issue had become a matter of prime concern for the Tri Services Andaman-Nicobar Command. An amphibious exercise was witnessed by India's Defence Minister, A.K. Anthony, which, among other things, included a mock amphibious exercise code named Blazing Khukri. As a part of that exercise, an island held by 150 heavily armed groups allegedly belonging to Andaman Liberation Front was secured by Indian forces. (*Hindustan Times*,

March 25, 2007). One hopes that the imaginary Andaman Liberation Front does not become a reality in future.

Malacca Straits – Andaman Sea route is also important in the context of transfer of arms to the terrorist groups in India also. Thai Navy had intercepted a 16-metre boat after a chase from the Thai port of Ranong. Even though large amounts of arms and ammunition were dumped into the sea during the chase, patrol boats of the Thai Navy captured about two tonnes of various types of weapons. They included two rocket-propelled grenade launchers, two recoil-less guns, M-79 granade launchers, 20 assault rifles and about 10,000 rounds of ammunition. Four persons, reportedly belonging to Manipur Revolutionary People's Front, were apprehended. Six crew members were from the Arakan region of Myanmar. The boat was reportedly, heading towards Cox's Bazar (*Jane's Defence Weekly*, March 26, 1997, p. 11).

The *Hindustan Times*, September 12, 1998, quoting Indian intelligence sources, had reported that several shipments of arms were sent from Ranong in Thailand to Cox's Bazar in Bangladesh. They were mainly destined for the insurgents in the North-East (Lehr, 2008, p. 189). That arms transfer continued. Two persons from Bangladesh, who were accused in the case of big arms haul in Chittagong in 2004, said that those arms were meant for the United Liberation Front of Asom (ULFA). They also said that important political leaders as also officials of the intelligence agencies of Bangladesh were directly involved (Habib, *The Hindu*, 2009).

Though important, India's cooperation in the context of meeting new maritime challenges cannot be limited to its regional neighbours alone but also needs to be extended to others at the international level. India, which was isolated at international level during the Cold War era, succeeded since the nineties in integrating itself as an important partner in the evolving maritime order. Its first significant gesture was the offer to escort high value US ships between Singapore and the Andaman Sea, *via* the Malacca Straits, in 2001-2002 in support of *Operation Enduring Freedom* against *Al-Qaida* and the *Taliban* in Afghanistan. Indian Navy as also Indian Coast Guard have developed close contacts with their counterparts in USA, France, Japan, South Korea, Vietnam etc. India has been conducting joint exercises with navies of these states. They include, among other things, steps necessary to prevent non-proliferation of WMD as also other counter-terrorism measures. India is also an active partner in Japan-sponsored ReCAAP that focusses on meeting challenges of piracy in South-East Asia.

India cannot force its security parameters upon others, be they regional powers or international actors. But it can discuss appropriate measures with them and seek cooperation at various levels that dovetail with the policies of other parties. It must, however, be underlined that efforts made by India to strengthen its own homeland security will also protect the interests of others, both regional and international actors. As noted in Chapter I, India's maritime security frontier extends deep into what is termed as the high seas. That vast sea space also covers vital SLOCs between the Arabian Sea and its natural extension to the Bay of Bengal *via* Central Indian Ocean. Thus, a robust homeland security framework will also directly contribute to India fulfilling its international obligations in the context of protection of major SLOCs in its vicinity. But, India needs to define its priorities. Protection of international SLOCs is the logical result of India's own homeland security policy and not an end in itself.

Maritime Terrorism International Legal Norms & State Practices

3

International Law and Maritime Terrorism

Traditionally, public international law dealt with legal dimensions of interstate relations only. Apart from exceptions like piracy and slavery, it did not deal with relations between state and non-state actors (NSA) who indulged in acts of armed conflict. Even when it did so, it sought to offer the NSA the status of a *de facto* state actor so that it could be accommodated as a combatant within the then existing legal framework. Under such cases, terms like armed resistance, rebellion, insurgency, belligerency etc. were defined more sharply and rights and obligations of concerned NSA were delimited in that context.

Crimes like piracy on the high seas, were even then considered as crime against humanity. Pirates were the only NSA that were never given the status of combatant. According to Charles G. Fenwick, a noted scholar of international law, "being *hostes humani generic*, they were outside the role of international law" (Fenwick, 1965, pp. 504-05).

Traditional international law had also sought to differentiate between lawful and unlawful combatants. While state actors were *ipso facto* treated as lawful combatants, there were provisions for giving a *de facto* status of lawful combatants to certain categories of belligerents or insurgents. This question assumes importance when one seeks to differentiate between acts of insurgency or belligerency and acts of terrorism. That issue had dominated political and legal debate for decades, both in the United Nations and even outside it, when a large number of states of the South had argued against treating insurgents or freedom fighters as terrorists.

In Latin America, during the nineteenth century, several political groups rose against the then ruling state authorities. In that context, it was held that where a *de facto* political organisation had been setup, giving promise of being able to maintain itself and conducting military and naval operations *in accordance with the laws of war* and where, on the other hand, the present state was exercising the belligerent rights of visit and search and of blockade, the situation must be recognised as one of public war. In such a case, Fenwick argued that the effect of the *recognition by third states of belligerent rights* on the part of insurgents was to confer upon them a *de facto* international character in respect of rights and duties of legal warfare (Fenwick, 1965, pp. 165-66)

Some experts of international law have sought to make a distinction between acts of maritime violence by insurgents on the high seas and piracy. According to Fenwick, the general practice was not to regard the capture as piratical if limited to the property of the state against which the insurgents were in revolt. But, he insisted that recognition of the insurgents as belligerents was essential (Fenwich, 1965, p. 506). D.P. O'Connell also concedes those points. But, he adds that where the insurgents crossed the line between enforcing the blockade directed against the government they are fighting and the plundering of foreign ships or molestation on the high seas of foreign nationals, they lost the right of insurgency and became pirates (O'Connell, 1984, pp. 975-76).

L. Openheim, another noted scholar on international law, mentioned that the law of nations did not treat civil war as illegal and created for other states, the right and the duty to grant recognition of belligerency, under certain conditions. Among other things, they included the existence of a civil war, accompanied by a state of general hostilities, occupation and a measure of orderly administration of a substantial part of national territory by the insurgents, observance of the rules of warfare on the part of the insurgent forces acting under responsible authority, practical necessity for third states to define their attitude towards the civil war etc. He argued that in the absence of those conditions, recognition of belligerency constituted illicit interference in the affairs of the state affected by civil disorder, an international wrong analoguous to the premature recognition of a state or a government (Oppenheim, 1972, p. 249).

Belligerency, insurgency or even civil war is recognised under international law, and a state can define its policy in that context. Terrorism had no such well defined and accepted status in international law till recently. But, of late, terrorism is acquiring a legal status. This is especially true after great powers declared so-called war on terror. Thus, a state can now declare a group as a terrorist organisation, if it seeks to target it under its policy of 'war on terror'. The *Taliban* were not a terrorist group till the US-led coalition decided to target it. LTTE was not considered as a terrorist organisation by USA till 1997. It was so labelled only after it reportedly got linked to groups like that of Abu Sayyaf in the Philippines that were also targeted by USA under war on terror (Gunaratne, 2001, p. 16). In 2008, FBI of USA asked those who were donating funds to charities related to Tamils in Sri Lanka to stop and alleged it to be a front organisation of *Al-Qaida* by saying that LTTE had inspired terrorist network world wide including *al-Qaida* in Iraq (*The Times of India*, January 12, 2008).

Maritime Security and Constraints of UNCLOS-III

Though UNCLOS-III was a major step in updating international law dealing with sea space yet certain articles and their traditional interpretation have posed serious constraints in the way of maritime states, taking measures to protect their homeland from possible threats posed by NSA and terrorists, using their adjacent sea space to launch their criminal operations. UNCLOS-III was drafted keeping in view inter-state relations, primarily for exploitation of living and non-living resources of the sea by coastal/island states. It also aimed at reinforcing traditional concepts like freedom of the high seas in the light of economic rights given to these states. Some of these provisions directly and indirectly provide legal grey areas that can be exploited by criminal elements. These provisions deal with freedom of navigation on the high seas, right of innocent passage, hot pursuit, rights of flag states, right/penally on visit and seizure of vessels on the high seas etc. It will be important to analyse these provisions to find ways and means to enable the coastal states to legitimise their enforcement action in these waters that extend from the coast to the high seas that includes the territorial waters, the contiguous zone, the EEZ and the continental-shelf.

Freedom of navigation in adjacent waters:

These waters comprise of sea space that extends from inland waters to the territorial waters, the contiguous zone, the EEZ and the continental-shelf. It seems that UNCLOS-III, while trying to balance freedom of navigation and state sovereignty and maritime security, gave preference to freedom of navigation over state sovereignty and maritime security. While writers like Natalino Ronzitti claim that the state enjoys full sovereignty in its internal waters (Ronzitti, 1990, p. 5), Article 8(2) of UNCLOS-III seeks to put limits on state sovereignty even in its internal waters, in the context of freedom of navigation. As per Article 8(2), "Where the establishment of a straight baseline in accordance with the methods set forth in article 7 of UNCLOS-III has the effect of enclosing as internal waters areas which had not previously been considered as such, a right of innocent passage as provided in this Convention shall exist in those waters". Such a clause will cause confusion for enforcement agencies like the Marine Police that are going to be primarily responsible for maritime security of coastal waters, including internal waters.

These constraints are also in place in the territorial waters over which the state is supposed to exercise complete sovereignty. Analysis of Articles 17-25 of UNCLOS-III, that deal with right of innocent passage, criminal jurisdiction over foreign flag vessels as also rights and duties of the coastal state, will make the point clear. While UNCLOS-III was framed to rationalise interstate maritime relations in times of peace, some of these provisions can be misused by NSA and terrorists to pose a threat to maritime security of a state.

Under article 17, ships of all states, whether coastal or land-locked, enjoy the right of innocent passage through the territorial sea. Under article 18(2), the passage has to be continuous and expeditious except under exceptional circumstances like distress or SAR operation. Article 19 deals with the details of innocent passage. While article 19(1) says that the passage is innocent so long as it is not prejudicial to the peace, good order or security of the coastal state, sub-clause 2 of the same article seeks to define what does not constitute 'innocent passage'. Contents of article 19(2) can be discussed under three different heads; those that primarily address state actors, those that address NSA, and those that are common to both.

Sub-sections of article 19(2) that primarily address state actors are as follows:

- ➢ any exercise or practice with weapons of any kind (b)
- ➢ launching, landing or taking on board of any aircrafts (e),
- ➢ launching, landing or taking on board any military device (f) and
- ➢ carrying out of research or survey activities (j).

The following sub-sections of article 19(2) primarily address activities of NSA. They are:

- ➢ loading and unloading of any commodity, currency or person contrary to the customs, fiscal, immigration or sanitary laws and regulations of the coastal state (g)
- ➢ any act of wilful and serious pollution contrary to this Convention (h)
- ➢ any fishing activities (i), and
- ➢ any act aimed at interfering with any systems of communication or any other facilities or installation of the coastal state (k).

Following sub-clauses of article 19(2) address state actors as also NSA and terrorists:

- ➢ any threat or use of force against the sovereignty, territorial integrity or political independence of the coastal state, or in any other manner in violation of the principles of international law embodied in the Charter of the United Nations (a),
- ➢ any act aimed at collecting information to the prejudice of the *defence or security* of the coastal state (c)
- ➢ any act of propaganda aimed at affecting the *defence or security* of the coastal state (d); and
- ➢ any other activity not having a direct bearing on passage.

A point worth noting in sub-paras c and d are the use of two different words '*defence or security*' of the coastal state. Thus, UNCLOS-III does differentiate between the *defence* of a state *vis-à-vis* another state or group of states, and *security* of the state that can be threatened by criminal activities of NSA and terrorists operating from vessels, flying the flag of another state, but operating in the territorial waters of the targeted state. This distinction between defence and security also helps to analyse other articles of UNCLOS-III in the context of 'defence' against state actors and 'security' *vis-à-vis* NSA and terrorists. Since the main thrust of this monograph is on threats to homeland security, posed by NSA and terrorists *via* the adjacent sea space, the element of 'security' as listed in UNCLOS-III will need to be focussed upon rather than interstate relations in times of peace.

UNCLOS-III limits the powers of the coastal state in the context of criminal jurisdiction in the territorial sea over foreign flag vessels passing through those waters. Under article 27 (c) the coastal state cannot arrest a person or conduct investigation in connection with any crime committed on board the ship during its passage through the territorial waters, except in the following cases:

➤ if consequences of the crime extend to the coastal state (a)

➤ if the crime is of a kind to disturb the peace of the country or the good order of the territorial sea (b), and

➤ if such measures are necessary for the suppression of illicit traffic in narcotic drugs or psychotropic substance (d)

All these provision can authorise actions against NSA and terrorists. The coastal state is also bound to take action if its assistance has been requested by the master of the ship or by a diplomatic agent or consular officer of the flag state.

Article 27 (5) restricts the rights of a coastal state in matters of criminal jurisdiction over foreign flag vessels, exercising right of innocent passage, over crime committed upon the ship before it had entered its territorial waters, except for crimes related to EEZ of the coastal state or to pollution on the high seas. Natoliano Ronzitti explains it by saying that the vessel arriving from the high seas is not immediately threatening the coastal state but is traversing the territorial sea in lateral passage. In that case, the vessel cannot be considered to have committed a breach of innocent passage "even if it aims at waging terrorist activities in a third country". Article 19 (2) of UNCLOS-III applies only when the activities are prejudicial to the coastal states and are committed in its territorial waters. One, however, wonders if Article 27 (5) does not put obstacles in the implementation of SUA Convention, 1988 and WMD Convention, 2005 or UN Security Council Resolution 1540 (2004) on non-proliferation of WMD.

Contiguous zone that extends to a maximum of 12 n. miles beyond the outer limit of the territorial sea limit of a coastal state formally constitutes, under Article 86 of UNCLOS-III, part of the high seas, as far as freedom of navigation is concerned. However, under Article 33 (1a), the coastal state has been given the right to exercise the control necessary to prevent infringement of its customs, fiscal, immigration or sanitary laws and regulations 'within its territory or territorial sea'. This sub-section introduces a degree of confusion as to whether a coastal state's criminal jurisdiction, even in matters of customs etc, extends upto the outer limit of its contiguous zone and, if so, does it cover foreign flag vessels as well.

While a coastal state's full sovereignty does not extend to the 12 n. mile zone beyond the territorial waters in the contiguous zone yet it has been given the right to exercise its jurisdiction in a limited manner as defined in Article 33 (1a). Thus, an attempt has been made to differentiate between *sovereignty* and *jurisdiction*. This provision needs to be read along with Articles 19 (2g) and 21(1h) also that deal with similar subjects in the territorial sea. Hence, one can argue that the coastal state reserves the right to visit foreign vessels in its contiguous zone in case of suspected violation of Article 33(1a) as also Articles 19 (2g) and 21(1h). In such cases, Article 33 (1a) also empowers the coastal state with the right to enforce its criminal jurisdiction on the contiguous zone in cases of criminal activities of the NSA and terrorists if they come under the purview of that article. In fact, section 5 of India's MZI Act 1976 does extend the state's right of enforcement in its contiguous zone in the context of matters related to national security. It needs to be underlined in this context that UNCLOS-III in article 19 (2c) and 19 (2d) has also made the distinction between two words; defence and security, in the context of innocent passage in territorial sea of a coastal state.

Articles 55 and 56 of UNCLOS-III deal with EEZ (and continental-shelf) of the coastal state. Article 55 seeks to find an equitable balance between the right of the coastal state in exploitation of living and non-living resources of that sea space by saying that the purpose was to establish specific legal regime under which the rights and jurisdiction of the coastal state and the rights and freedom of other states are governed under relevant provisions of the Convention. According to Article 56 (1a), the coastal state has the sovereign rights (not sovereignty) for the purposes of exploring and exploiting, conserving and managing natural resources, both living and non-living, of the waters superjacent to the seabed and of the seabed and its sub-soil for the economic exploration and exploitation. As will be noted, UNCLOS-III also sought to maintain, to the extent possible, right of freedom of navigation in this sea space of the EEZ that falls under high seas under Article 86 and 87 of UNCLOS-III.

Article 73 defines the rights of the coastal state in terms of exploitation of living resources in the EEZ that under Article 57 extends to a maximum limit of 200 n. miles from the baseline along the coast. In its EEZ, the coastal state, in the exercise of its sovereign rights to explore, exploit, conserve and manage the living resources of the EEZ, can take such measures including boarding, inspection, arrest and judicial proceedings, as may be necessary, to ensure compliance with the laws and regulations adopted by it in conformity with the Convention. Thus, the state, under its own laws, can exercise criminal jurisdiction over foreign fishing vessels that are found violating those laws and fishing illegally in the EEZ. However, since EEZ is also to be treated as the part of the high seas, foreign fishing vessels can exercise freedom of navigation in the entire EEZ, if they are not indulging in illegal fishing there. Since fishing vessels are normally the preferred mode of operation of NSA and terrorists, the coastal state is helpless in preventing them from operating in its EEZ, at least beyond the outer limit of its contiguous zone, in support of NSA and terrorists. Thus, UNCLOS-III puts constraints on a state's efforts to check activities of NSA and terrorists even in its adjacent waters, under the concept of freedom of navigation on the high seas.

UNCLOS-III provides for exploitation of sub-soil resources in the continental-shelf of the coastal state under Articles 56 (1a) and 60 (1), as also Articles 77 and 81. Article 60 (1b) provides for the construction of installations related to exploitation of sea bed resources. Yet, under Article 60(7), these structures may not be established, where infringement may be caused, for the use of 'recognised' sea lanes essential to international navigation. Also, according to Article 78 (2), the exercise of the rights of the coastal state over the continental-shelf must not infringe or result in any unjustifiable interference with navigation and other rights and freedoms of other states as provided for in this Convention.

UNCLOS-III only takes cognizance of the question of 'safety' (not security) of the off-shore installations in the continental-shelf. It must be recognised that the framers of UNCLOS-III at that time had only 'accidents' in mind and not acts of terrorism. But one can also argue whether a safety zone of 500 metres is enough to avert accident especially as oil tankers are growing in size and need more sea space to manoeuvre. As per Article 60(4), the state may, where necessary, establish reasonable safety zones around such artificial installations which would ensure the safety of navigation as also of the installations. However, under Article 60 (5), it limits that zone to a maximum of 500 metres around them. This distance can be covered by a vessel doing even 10 knots in about two minutes. Such a provision will only facilitate a terrorist attack since that vessel can operate unchecked on the adjacent high seas upto a range of 500 meters under Article 60 (5) of UNCLOS-III. That short time is insufficient even to anticipate the intention of that vessel.

Freedom of the high seas

Freedom of the high seas is based upon two interrelated concepts; *Mare Liberum* and *Domino Maris*. Hugo Grotius had propounded the concept of *Mare Liberum* (freedom of the sea) to refute Portuguese claims, based upon the Papal Bull, of their sovereignty over the waters of the Indian Ocean. Hugo Grotius provided the Dutch, who also wanted to enter the maritime trade in the Indian Ocean region, a legal basis to refute the Portuguese claims to sovereignty over the seas. It must also be underlined that the Dutch warships lent their weight to buttress the legal doctrine. It is often forgotten that laws are made by those who also have the power to enforce them. Those with power can even refuse to abide by them. USA has as yet not ratified UNCLOS-III and hence is not legally bound by its constraints. USA Navy, in *The Commander's Handbook on the Law of Naval Operations*, had even coined the term 'international waters' to describe collectively the high seas, the EEZ and the contiguous zone (Bateman, 2007, pp. 27-56).

The other concept, *Domino Maris*, was propounded by Cormelius Bynkeshock in around 1702. He had argued for the extension of the coastal state's sovereignty over the adjacent waters and in that context, he promoted the 'cannon-shot' doctrine. He argued that the coastal state be allowed to exercise its sovereignty upto the outer limit of the gun shot fired from the coast. Three nautical miles distance (one sea-league) from the coast was accepted as the limit of state sovereignty over the waters adjacent to its coast. Beyond that was the 'high seas', sea space over which no state could claim sovereign rights and hence was free for all. The concept of three n. mile territorial waters limit and the high seas beyond it remained in operation till the end of World War II.

In the post-war period, technology was available to exploit sub-soil resources in the continental-shelf further away from the coast. There was also the growing demand for oil and gas. Some states in Latin America wanted to reserve the sea space of upto 200 n. miles from their coast for their exclusive fishing. There was also the demand for expanding the outer limit of the territorial sea to 12 n. miles. These new demands were finally met under provisions of UNCLOS-III.

While UNCLOS-III provides the coastal state the right of enforcing its domestic laws in respect of economic exploitation of living and non-living resources in the larger sea space of EEZ, which includes the continental-shelf area as well, it also simultaneously lays down, under Articles 58 and 86, that the sea space beyond the territorial waters was the high seas. Though UNCLOS-III does mention that provisions of Article 86, dealing with high seas, applies to the sea not included in the EEZ, the territorial sea and the internal waters of a state, yet the same article also adds that it does not entail the abridgement of freedom enjoyed by all states in the EEZ in accordance with Article 58 (1); i.e. freedom of the high seas. Thus, under Article 86, read along with Article 58 (1), the entire sea space beyond the territorial waters limit of coastal states constitutes the 'high seas'. This sea space includes the contiguous zone also. Any ship flying the flag of a state has the absolute right to sail upto the 12 n. mile distance from the coast. Thus, the basic premise of freedom of navigation on the high seas puts serious constraints on evolving an effective policy to deny that sea space to NSA and terrorists whose vessels can also enjoy unrestrained freedom of operation in waters adjacent to the coasts of all states.

The concept of freedom of navigation on the high seas is also an extension of state sovereignty in that sea space. The flag of the vessel signifies the nationality of that vessel and is the symbol of sovereignty of that state. As noted, this concept of sovereignty of the flag state is extended even in the territorial waters of another state under Article 27 (1) of UNCLOS-III. Under that article, criminal jurisdiction of the coastal state does not extend on board a foreign flag vessel passing through its territorial waters except under some specific conditions as stated before.

On the high seas, freedom of navigation can be denied only under three circumstances. All states can take action on the high seas against a ship engaging in the transport of slaves (Article 99), indulging in acts of piracy (Articles 100-105), and in illicit traffic in drugs (Article 108). But the state's responsibility under Article 108 is seriously restricted. Under Article 108 (1), all states are asked only to cooperate in the suppression of this illicit traffic. But, it stops short of suggesting enforcement measures on its own as is done in the case of piracy. This grey area in the interpretation of Article 108 can hinder state action on the high seas in the suppression of trade in narcotics which is often related to illicit trade in arms and explosives as also terrorism.

Under Article 87, freedom of the high seas is to be enjoyed only by the state actors. The flag of the vessel denotes the nationality of the vessel and misuse of a flag is prohibited. Under Article 92 (2), "a ship which sails under the flag of two or more states, using them according to convenience, may not claim any of the nationalities and may be assimilated to a ship without nationality". Any state then has a right to intercept such a ship on the high seas for appropriate action. Thus, though UNCLOS-III is not implicit on the subject, a ship not legally entitled to fly the flag of a state can be intercepted on the high seas by authorised vessels of any state actor under principle of universality. A Warship of any state has the right, under Article 110 (d) to intercept and check, i.e. exercise the right of visit, any ship on the high seas that is suspected of being without a nationality. These provisions can be applied, under UNCLOS-III, to intercept hijacked vessels that are operated by the criminal elements in the sea space of the Horn of Africa, the Gulf of Aden and other parts of Indian Ocean even without any proof of their having indulged in piracy or hijacking.

Under UNCLOS-III, enforcement of state's criminal jurisdiction on the high seas can be undertaken only by a warship or any other government vessel so empowered. Under Article 110, such vessels have the right to board a ship on the high seas that is suspected to be engaged in salve trade, piracy or is without legally accepted nationality, for the purpose of verifying papers. It has the right to affect seizure under Article 107, if circumstances so demand. In that case, the ship, along with the crew can be taken to the port for suitable legal action under the law of the land. However, UNCLOS-III has also provisions for liability for wrongful boarding and seizure under Article 106, 110(3) and 111(8). That often acts as an inhibiting factor and favours NSA and terrorists who use ships carrying the flag of convenience to operate in the sea space beyond 12 n. miles limit of the state's territorial waters, to carry out their activities.

The coastal state also enjoys the right of hot pursuit on the high seas. The pursuit has to commence from the zone where the relevant state law was violated, be it the territorial sea, the contiguous zone or the EEZ/continental-shelf. Under article 111 (3), it must be continuous till the ship that is being pursued is intercepted or 'escapes' into the territorial waters of another state. That provision respects the sovereignty of other coastal states. No foreign vessel can exercise criminal jurisdiction over another vessel in another state's territorial waters.

But that provision need not be made an excuse for discontinuing the hot pursuit in another state's territorial waters since UNCLOS-III also allows for right of innocent passage even to a warship. Hence, the state that is exercising the right of hot pursuit on the high seas can still maintain the pursuit and inform the appropriate enforcement authorities of the concerned coastal state so that they can themselves intercept and seize the vessel and take suitable action under their own law or repatriate the culprits. Such an understanding among regional states on a bilateral or multilateral level, in the case of criminal activities of NSA and terrorists, will plug a major gap in the context of regional cooperation to ensure peace and security in adjoining sea spaces in the region, without violating the norms of UNCLOS-III.

The right of hot pursuit, to be an effective instrument of state policy in meeting the new threat to homeland security *via* its sea space, implies that the coastal state not only has a credible mechanism for detecting the violation of state laws and regulations in these different maritime zones, but also has an integrated command and control system as also the capability to pursue and intercept the culprit, by using surface vessels and/or aircrafts at its disposal. Thus, capability for effective hot pursuit becomes an intrinsic part of the total package of homeland security. Many states of the South lack that capability and culprits are able to escape without being apprehended. Bilateral or regional cooperation can help to overcome that constraint. Very often, such a cooperation is seen as eroding the state sovereignty in its territorial sea. But, such a cooperation will only help to buttress state capability and hence strengthen the basis of state sovereignty.

The most important but often neglected article of UNCLOS-III in the context of threats posed by NSA and terrorists and which underlines the very sanctity of the concept of freedom of navigation on the high seas, is Article 88. As per that article, freedom of the high seas shall be reserved for peaceful purposes. There are provisions under traditional international law that regulate freedom of navigation during state of war between states. Those provisions are not applicable to NSA and terrorists. Hence, it can be argued that principle of universality that governs state action on the high seas, like suppression of crimes like slavery, piracy etc. should also be applicable for enforcement of Article 88, especially now that the UN agencies have passed resolutions and conventions against terrorism-related crimes as also proliferation of WMD. Article 88 of UNCLOS-III, in this context, should also be read along with Article 2 (5) and 51 of the UN

Charter that give the Member State not only the right of individual and collective self-defence but also confer upon states, the obligation to support UN action.

UNCLOS-III: Acts of piracy and other crimes

The only issue in which UNCLOS-III gives a free hand to the international community to take unilateral action on the high seas is in the context of piracy but even in that case, it underlines all the preconditions that were applied to it when the territorial sea limit was only 3 n. miles from the coast and the rest of the ocean space was the high seas.

Since ancient times, piracy had been considered a crime against humanity and every state had the right to suppress it not only in its own waters but also on the high seas. Piracy was suppressed by the end of the eighteenth century. But the issue remained alive under traditional international law. The Harvard Research on International Law Group did produce a draft convention on piracy in 1932. But, it remained on paper only (Joyner, 1984, p. 213) though the draft became the basis for debate on the subject after World War II. After the formation of the UN, International Law Commission, in its report to the General Assembly in 1955, offered its own suggestions. That report became the basis of the provisions on piracy under the Convention on the High Seas or the Geneva Convention of 1958. That convention dealt with the question of piracy under the age-old formale. Article 15 described it as an illegal act of violence committed for *private* ends on the *high* seas and directed against *another* ship. The Geneva Convention also applied the principle of universal jurisdiction to entrust the right to seize pirates and the pirate ships to warships of all states on the high seas, under provisions of Articles 14, 19 and 21.

The question of piracy has been dealt with, at length in UNCLOS-III. It has almost reproduced the related provisions under the Geneva Convention. Zou Keyuan has discussed the question in detail (Keyuan, 2005, pp. 117-34). Under the principle of universal jurisdiction, Article 100 of UNCLOS-III authorises all state actors to take action to suppress acts of piracy on the high seas. Article 101 reiterates the traditional concept that defined acts of piracy under Geneva Convention of 1958. While Article 105 authorises seizure of a private vessel, Article 106 warns of the liabilities if the seizure was wrongful. While Article 110 (1a) authorises seizure of the ship on grounds of piracy, Article 110 (3) warns of the possible liability. While Articles 106 and 110 (3) are designed to prevent arbitrary action on the part of state actors, they also simultaneously inhibit the officer commanding the state's enforcement vessel under Article 107, from risking his 'neck' in any official enquiry on the matter. Will his plea of 'good faith and intention' save him from being made into a scape goat in the game of international law or UNCLOS-III, these constraints of UNCLOS-III inhibit state action against piracy, now being linked to hijacking of ship, in the Horn of Africa, Gulf of Aden and waters of north-western part of the Indian Ocean. As will be analysed subsequently, anti-piracy operations have acquired a new thrust and international cooperation, largely because of inadequacies of UNCLOS-III provisions.

There is no provision for terrorism in UNCLOS-III. Some attempt was made to equate piracy with maritime terrorism so that principle of universal jurisdiction could be applied. According to Natalino Ronzitti, if terrorism is equated with piracy, nobody would question the legality of intervention since states are allowed to seize pirate vessels even though no act of piracy has been committed. (Ronzitti, 1990, p. 10). Leading scholars like I.L. Oppenheim had earlier offered their definition of piracy that could also be stretched to include acts of maritime terrorism. According to him, piracy must be defined as every *unauthorised act of* violence against persons or goods committed on the open sea. That definition avoided terms like private gain and high seas, while stressing upon unauthorised use of violence on 'open sea' (Oppenheim, 1955, pp. 608-09). The SUA Convention, 1988, reflects that view.

Under UNCLOS-III, piracy is related only to crimes committed for private gains. 'Private' ends can be interpreted as opposed to 'public' i.e. state-actor ends as objectives or end of terrorists' activities. In that case, economic gratification may be absent. Hatred and vengeance, in the context of 'wrong' done, can sometimes be more powerful 'private' ends than economic ends *per se*. UNCLOS-III also deals with activities of NSA under two other crimes; transport of slaves (Article 99) and illicit traffic in narcotic drugs or psychotropic substances (Article 108). Though UNCLOS-III applies the principle of universal jurisdiction in both cases, there are some limitations. Under Article 99, every state shall take effective measures to prevent and punish the transport of slaves, in ships authorised to fly its flag and to prevent the unlawful use of its flag for that purpose. This article makes prevention of slavery (an out-moded concept now) the responsibility of the flag state only. No other state has been so authorised under that article. That, however, contrasts with Article 110 (1b), under which a warship of another state is authorised to visit a ship if there is reasonable ground for suspecting that the ship is engaged in the slave trade. UNCLOS-III is silent on the follow up action. This is one of the examples of several grey areas in UNCLOS-III.

Article 108 deals with illicit traffic in narcotic drugs or psychotropic substances. While 108 (1) asks all states to cooperate in its suppression, none of these states are given the power of follow up action. Under article 108 (2), the responsibility lies primarily with the flag state. According to that article, "Any State, which has reasonable ground for believing that a *ship flying its flag* is engaged in illicit traffic in narcotic drugs or psychotropic substances, *may request the cooperation of other states* to suppress such traffic". It does not specify the mode of that cooperation. Interestingly, while Article 110 (1), that deals with the right of visit in connection with piracy and slave traffic, does not mention traffic in illicit drugs as a ground for the visit.

Bypassing constraints of UNCLOS-III, pre 9/11

As noted, UNCLOS-III, the alleged basis of law of the seas today, has virtually no provisions that are specific to deal with modern challenges to meet threats to maritime security posed by terrorists. Since amendments to UNCLOS-III or framing a new UNCLOS-IV would have taken decades to be debated on and approved, the international community has taken steps through United Nations and its agencies, like the International Maritime Organisation (IMO), Security Council and General Assembly as well as through individual and multilateral state practices, to gain legitimacy for their actions in that context. Thus, a new customary international law is being evolved that also needs to be taken note of, in the context of meeting challenges posed by NSA and terrorists.

Role of IMO

The IMO has played an important role in suggesting new steps in meeting the challenges of piracy and terrorism. The IMO, an organisation under UN that deals with maritime affairs, was the most appropriate organisation to deal with issues like piracy and other acts of maritime violence that were not covered or were inadequately covered under UNCLOS-III. Among these steps, resolution widening the scope of piracy, the SUA Convention of 1988 and related SUA Protocol of 2005, need special mention.

As noted, international action to suppress acts of violence against vessels under piracy is constrained under the terms of the UNCLOS-III, on several grounds. Under UNCLOS-III, such acts must be committed for private ends, at least two vessels should be involved and the crime must be committed on the high seas. Rear Admiral O.P. Sharma had suggested that Article 101 of UNCLOS-III be amended so that requirement of a second ship be deleted. He had also advocated that the phrase 'for private ends' be substituted by 'without due authority' (Sharma, 2000, 160-61).

Till World War II, the territorial sea limit was only three n. miles. Beyond that was the high seas. That limit has now been extended to 12 n. miles. Also, a large sea space falls under the sovereignty of island states under the concept of archipelagic state (UNCLOS-III, Article 46-54). Consequently, the space of the high seas has shrunk. Many of these acts of 'violence against shipping are being committed when the vessels are within the limits of the territorial sea of a given state. Under UNCLOS-III, these acts do not qualify as international criminal acts but are to be treated only as criminal acts under the law of the coastal state. Not only has the coastal state got the sole responsibility of preventing those crimes but the coastal state alone has the right of hot pursuit in such a case. No one wants to dilute the clauses of UNCLOS-III lest it be seen as an effort to erode the sovereignty of the state over its territorial waters. Often, inability of several coastal states to monitor their adjacent waters, offers 'safe haven' to NSA for their criminal acts.

Attempts were made to bypass the legal constraints under UNCLOS-III by using the good offices of International Maritime Organisation (IMO). By 1980s, incidents of attack on ships in waters in South-East Asia and along West African coast had increased greatly. Sweden drew attention of the Maritime Safety Committee (MSC) of the IMO to this growing challenge. The MSC prepared a draft which was adopted as Resolution A 545 (13) by the IMO Assembly, in 1991. That resolution bypassed the legal constraints on the use of the term 'piracy' under UNCLOS-III, by clubbing it with armed robbery. It urged member states to take all steps to "prevent and suppress acts of piracy and armed robbery from the ships in or adjacent to their waters". Though the constraint of high seas was not removed, the coastal state was asked to shoulder the responsibility for acts of crime in its territorial waters. It also broadened the concept of piracy by including armed robbery. Thus, it respected the concept of state sovereignty in territorial waters and kept itself well within the limits of UNCLOS-III while seeking to widen the scope of piracy.

Unlike IMO, which is a UN agency and hence bound by its laws, the International Maritime Bureau (IMB) of International Chamber of Commerce (ICC) could define an act of piracy without those legal constraints. It must also be underlined that the definition of IMB has no sanction under international law. It defined piracy as an act of boarding any vessel with the intent to commit theft or any other crime and with the intent or capability of using force in furtherance of that act. This definition does away with the requirement of two ships as also high seas, as required under terms of UNCLOS-III (Paleri, 2004, pp. 136 and 328). Under this definition, even minor thefts onboard ships at anchor in the harbour, could be listed as acts of piracy. Jayant Abhyankar, Deputy Director of ICC, IMB, commented that while IMB's definition of piracy may be contrary to that in UNCLOS-III, that distinction was irrelevant in the eyes of the victim (Abhyankar, 2000, p. 141).

It needs to be underlined that the right, under UNCLOS-III, of a coastal state to exercise criminal jurisdiction for violation of the rights provided to it under various categories as listed above, is possible only when the state has an appropriate legal regime that provides for it as also an adequate enforcement capability to pursue its objectives. In the absence of these two interrelated factors, the state may claim prerogatives without really enjoying them. That also indirectly undermines good governance in adjacent sea space and, therefore, poses threat to maritime security for other users of that sea space.

Also, only a state that has such a capability can take steps not only to neutralise threats to its homeland but also contribute to regional and international maritime security from threats posed by NSA and terrorists. It also needs to be noted that major international SLOCs, in what is termed as the high seas under Article 86 of UNCLOS-III, often traverse the contiguous zone and the EEZ of the coastal states. Hence, capability to monitor and enforce laws in these zones also enables the state to contribute effectively towards maintaining peace and order even on the high seas near its adjacent waters; and thus contribute to the maritime security at regional and even global level.

The SUA Convention, 1988

In the post-World War II period, terrorism had become a value loaded term. Use of violence in anti-colonial and anti-imperial conflicts, as also by Palestinians against Israel and its supporters etc were politically defended in the South. Hence, even while several conventions against hijacking of aircrafts, hostages taking etc were signed, use of the term 'terrorism' was avoided for the sake of achieving political consensus. The question of maritime terrorism was also handled in a similar fashion.

Since UNCLOS-III had not dealt with the issue of maritime terrorism that question was taken up by International Maritime Organisation (IMO). It was founded in 1959 and till 1982, was known as Intergovernmental Maritime Consultative Organisation (IMCO). The IMO was entrusted with the task of providing a framework *vis-à-vis* maritime terrorism, after the Italian cruise liner, *Achille Laura,* was hijacked in October 1985, by a group of Palestinians belonging to Abu Nidal group. An American tourist on board the ship had died in that context. That action could not be defined as an act of piracy under international law or under UNCLOS-III.

The *Achille Laura* incident had occurred when the VIth Committee of the General Assembly of the UN was debating the question of international terrorism. On the suggestion of Italy, Austria and Egypt, the General Assembly, in its Resolution 40/61 of December 9, 1985 (paragraph 13), entrusted the matter to the IMO. Italy took the lead in preparing the draft which was debated extensively. The IMO Conference, held in Rome in March 1988, adopted the convention by consensus. The Convention on the

Suppression of Unlawful Acts Against the Safety of Maritime Navigation, 1988, or in short, the SUA Convention, 1988, was opened for signature on March 10, 1988. The IMO Conference had also approved of a protocol, dealing with security-related issues of fixed platform on the continental-shelf. The Convention entered into force on March 1, 1992. Initially, the rate of ratification was slow. Only 52 members had signed it till the end of December 2000. Events of 9/11 speeded up the process and about 142 states ratified it by the end of December 2006. The SUA Convention (and associated protocol) of 1988 was ratified by India also. While India has not enacted laws in the context of UNCLOS-III, not even on piracy, it took serious note of SUA Convention of 1988. Indian Parliament passed the Suppression of Unlawful Acts Against Safety of Maritime Navigation and Fixed Platform on Continental Shelf. Rajya Sabha passed that bill in November 21, 2002 while the Lok Sabha did so on December 10, 2002. Thus, India's own SUA Act, 2002 is a major Indian document in the context of state practice *vis-à-vis* acts of maritime terrorism. That document will be analysed in depth, in Chapter IV.

For political reasons, the title of SUA Convention of 1988, avoided the use of the term 'terrorism', though the focus was made clear in the preamble itself. It recalled Resolution 40/61 of December 1985 of the UN General Assembly, that had unequivocally condemned as criminal, all acts, methods and practices of terrorism wherever and by whomsoever committed, including those which jeopardised friendly relations among states and their security. Article 3 of the SUA Convention 1988, makes it clear that it targets acts of terrorism without specifically using the term 'terrorism'. Thus, acts were defined without using the term 'maritime terrorism'.

As per Article 3 (1), a person commits an offence if that person unlawfully and intentionally:

(a) Seizes or exercises control over a ship by force or threat thereof or any other form of intimidation,

(b) performs an act of violence against a person on board a ship if that act is likely to endanger the safe navigation of that ship,

(c) destroys a ship or causes damage to a ship or to its cargo,

(d) places or causes to be placed on a ship, by any means whatsoever, a device or substance which is likely to destroy that ship or cause damage to that ship or its cargo,

(e) destroys or seriously damages maritime navigational facilities or seriously interferes with their operation,

(f) communicates information which he knows to be false, thereby endangering safe navigation of the ship, and

(g) injures or kills any person in connection with the commission or the attempted commission of any of the offences set forth in sub-paragraphs (a) to (f).

Under Article 3 (2), any person who commits such acts as listed in Article 3 (1) or attempts to commit them or abets the commissioning of such acts or threatens others to do that, is also held accountable.

Though SUA Convention of 1988 does not use the term 'piracy' or hijacking of ships on high seas, so as not to clash with the very restrictive provisions of UNCLOS-III on that subject, most of the offences listed in Article 3 (1), especially 3 (1) (a), (b), (c), and (g), can be directly related to acts of piracy or hijacking even on the high seas in the northern part of Western Indian Ocean. Under Article 3 (2), persons indulging in those acts can be held accountable for those acts. They can be apprehended by the naval vessels and tried even under SUA Convention of 1988, especially by those states like India that have ratified that Convention and have passed domestic laws to enforce it, even if no act on piracy has been passed.

Robert Bechman tried to link piracy, armed robbery and maritime terrorism with SUA Convention. He was referring to the delay by states in not ratifying that convention. He tried to illustrate it by giving the example of seizure and trial, in India, of *MV Alondra Rainbow*, a Japanese vessel that was pirated in South-East Asia. According to him, "If India had been a party to the 1988 SUA Convention, *i.e.* had ratified it at the time of the incident, the pirates would have been charged under one of the offences setout under the Convention. Also, if Indonesia had been a State Party to the same Convention, it would have been under a legal obligation to cooperate with India, in connection with the criminal proceedings against the pirates under that Convention" (Bechman, 2006, p. 36).

There is a grey area in the interpretation of modern international law dealing with maritime security that needs to be further examined in the light of modern requirements. If these offences can be related to acts of piracy, then under the principle of universality, it is no longer the sole responsibility of the coastal state's jurisdiction. Under Article 111 of UNCLOS-III, such a ship or person involved in the criminal acts listed under Article 3 (1) of SUA Convention of 1988 can even be apprehended on the high sea by the warship of any other state. Experts have, however, tended to analyse SUA Convention of 1988 as being only state centric and not falling under the norms of universalism. Even subsequent attempt to enlarge its scope as under SUA Protocol, 2005, could not overcome the narrow constraints of UNCLOS-III. Major shortcoming of the SUA Convention, 1988, is that the responsibility for its implementation is entrusted to the coastal state that has ratified it. As seen, not all states have ratified it and enacted appropriate domestic laws so as to give effect to it. Under Article 5 of the SUA Convention, states were expected to make the offences, listed under Article 3, punishable by appropriate penalties. SUA Convention also deals with extradition and/or trial of persons who have been apprehended for violating the terms of the Convention.

IMO also approved, along with the SUA Convention of 1988, the Rome Protocol for the Suppression of Unlawful Acts Against the Safety of Fixed Platforms Located on the Continental-Shelf, 1988. Only those states that had ratified the SUA Convention could be a party to that Protocol. Under Article 2(1) of that Protocol, any person commits an offence if that person unlawfully and intentionally:

(a) seizes or exercises control over a fixed platform by force or threat thereof or any other form of intimidation;

(b) performs an act of violence against a person on-board a fixed platform;

(c) destroys a fixed platform or causes damage to it which is likely to endanger its safety,

(d) places or causes to be placed on a fixed platform, by any means whatsoever, a device or substance which is likely to destroy that fixed platform or likely to endanger its safety, or

(e) injures or kills any person in connection with the commission or attempted commission of any of the offences listed above.

Under Article 2 (2), those who were accessory to the crime were also held responsible.

SUA Convention, 1988 and the associated Rome Protocol on Fixed Platform on the Continental-Shelf, despite their limitations, deserve to be taken seriously in the context of the state's strategy, to meet challenges posed by NSA and terrorists to maritime dimensions of homeland security. Offences listed in Article 3 of the SUA Convention and Article 2 of the associated Rome Protocol on the platform on the continental-shelf are the offences that are likely to be committed by NSA and terrorists, also against the state. Thus, they give international legitimacy to the state's own legal initiatives in meeting those challenges. Though the Convention and the Protocol are by and large state-centric in enforcement, yet they do offer a mechanism for mutual cooperation among the signatories to meet the new threat. For example, exchange of information to facilitate trial or smooth process of extradition is easier in these cases. Lastly, the states that have ratified these documents are entrusted with the task of framing new and suitable domestic laws to facilitate their enforcement. India had to enact its SUA Act, 2002, in that context.

Impact of 9/11

Though maritime terrorism is a relatively recent phenomenon, terrorism has been seen as a threat at least since 1970s if not earlier. In 1970s, terrorists targeted aircrafts, airports and internationally protected persons like diplomats. The Palestinian attack on Israeli athletes during the Munich Olympics in 1982, was seen as a manifestation of terrorism that targeted innocent persons. The matter related to terrorism was raised in the General Assembly since 1972 but there could be no consensus on defining acts of terrorism. Those were the days when struggle against colonialism and racism (apartheid) as also Palestinian movement were drawing political and diplomatic support from several states. Consequently, the international community passed several conventions dealing with acts related to terrorism but without naming them specifically so. Some of these conventions were Convention of Seizure of Aircrafts and on Safety of Civil Aviation of January 26, and October 14, 1971, Crimes Against Persons of International Significance on February 2, 1971, against Internationally Protected Persons including Diplomatic Agents on February 20, 1977, against Taking of Hostages on December 4, 1979 etc. It was only in 1985 when the General Assembly could arrive at some consensus on the question of terrorism that a compromise Resolution 40/61 of December 9, 1985 was passed by the General Assembly. The resolution also called upon Member States to remove causes that gave rise to such acts of terrorism.

By 1999, UN Security Council began to deal with the question of terrorism. That coincided with the end of the Cold War and the new threat posed by radical Islamic groups especially under the tutelage of *Al-Qaida* and the *Taliban*. These resolutions were passed under Chapter VII and hence were mandatory in nature. Resolution 1269 of October 19, 1999 was the first of the series. Events of 9/11, (Sept. 11, 2001) led the Security Council to pass, on September 12, 2001, the Resolution 1368 (2001). It was a sweeping resolution. Its preamble said that terrorist acts caused threats to international peace and security. It expressed determination to combat them 'by all means', by implication, even by use of force by states. It also recognised the inherent right to individual and collective self-defence in accordance with article 51 of the UN Charter. Thus, the resolution, for the first time, recognised the right of military self-defence as applicable against terrorist acts perpetrated by non-state actors also. This resolution was not specific to events of 9/11 but was recognised as legitimising the state's right to use force against terrorists under the UN Charter; a major milestone in the legal context of antiterrorist operation. Other resolutions of the Security Council on terrorism included Resolution 1373 (2001) of September 28, 2001. It prescribed that states should take certain specific action against terrorism. A Counter-Terrorism Committee was constituted to follow the actions taken. Resolution 1377 (2001) supplemented it (*Singh*, 2006, pp. 145-48).

None of these resolutions touched upon maritime terrorism specifically, though they do help to legitimise action against acts of terrorism on land, air and sea, especially where there is no specific provision under UNCLOS-III. As will be discussed subsequently, the Security Council passed Resolution 1540 (2004) and UN Convention on WMD (2005), that, in some ways strengthened the state's action in the context of confronting the threat of maritime terrorism. In the meanwhile, other steps were initiated, both within the framework of UN as also outside it, that have introduced new features of state practice in the context of the state's action against maritime terrorism.

Though UN did pass resolutions in the context of terrorism *per* se, none of them had directly addressed the issue of maritime terrorism. However, some concerned agencies like the IMO, as also state actors, began taking concrete steps to meet the new challenges and to give a degree of legitimacy to state action in their fight against this new threat. Thus, new chapters began to be added, especially after 9/11, which helped to expand the scope of law of the sea that was fossilised at 1882. IMO and Security Council took the lead in these matters.

It was presumed that ships and port/harbour facilities could become the target of terrorist activities. The new International Ship and Port Facilities (ISPS) Code aimed at evolving a common code that could be applied to state actors, ship operators, and port/harbour authorities. Each state was obliged to certify that ships that flew their flags and enjoyed related facilities under their jurisdiction were code-compliant. USA had taken the initiative in that direction and had activised the IMO towards establishing new international standards for improving security practices on vessels and in ports (Flynn, 2006, p. 9).

The 22nd Session of the IMO, held in November 2001, soon after the events of 9/11, unanimously agreed on the need to evolve new measures to cope with the emerging threat of maritime terrorism. A special group of IMO met in February 2002, to consider a US proposal in that context (Bowbrick, 2003, p. 228).

Following a conference in IMO Headquarters in London, during December 9-13, 2003, IMO introduced a more comprehensive security regime for international shipping and to strengthen maritime security. Consequently, the Conference of the Contracting Governments to the International Convention for the Safety of Life at Sea, 1974 (SOLAS Convention, 1974), adopted several amendments to that Convention, as also recommended the new ISPS Code. Changes recommended were to be affected by January 1, 2004 and were to be in force by July 4, 2004. While some of the recommendations were mandatory, others were in the nature of guidelines. India was a party to the SOLAS Convention of 1974 and had also participated in the deliberations leading to the signing of the new ISPS Code. The Ministry of Shipping is the nodal agency in India for implementing the ISPS Code. The Indian Registrar of Shipping has been designated as the authority responsible for implementing the provisions of the ISPS Code (For details, see Paleri, 2004, pp. 170-72, Sakhuja, 2002, pp. 395-96 and Vasan, 2006, pp. 152-54).

Some of the new security-related regulations include the Ship Identification Number (SIN) and the carriage of Continuous Synopsis Record (CSR). Both help in the monitoring of the movement of the vessel. Other regulations deal with ship-port interface and deal with facilities serving the type of ships mentioned in the ISPS code. They include passenger ships, cargo vessels of 300 GRT and above, and mobile off-shore drilling units. Ports and ships are required to be audited and certified for the level of their preparedness, under the code. Reportedly, India has extended the provision of ISPS code to its ships operating in coastal waters also.

Resolutions of the Security Council & UN Charter

Security Council passed several resolutions on terrorism since 9/11. Terrorism is not treated as a crime against humanity though Security Council Resolution 1368 of September 12, 2001 and Resolution 1373 of September 28, 2001 maintained that terrorism threatened international peace and security. Resolution 1373 made it obligatory for all states to prevent and suppress it in their territories (including territorial sea), through all 'lawful' means. It needs to be noted that this resolution does not cover enforcement on the high seas i.e. sea space beyond 12 n. miles of territorial waters.

Resolutions of the Security Council need to be read in the context of Article 2 (5) and article 51 of the UN Charter. Under article 2 (5), all

Members of the UN are obliged to give the UN every assistance in any action that it takes in accordance with the present Charter and to refrain from giving assistance to any state against whom UN is taking preventive or enforcement action. The framers of the UN Charter had taken only state actors into consideration and not non-state actors while framing the Charter primarily for the reason that it addresses actions of state actors only and not of non-state actors, except in the context of human rights.

Article 51 legitimises the state's action under the right of individual and collective self-defence. Though article 51 does not specify terrorism or terrorists as adversary, it does not prohibit it either. The article says, "Nothing in the present Charter shall impair the inherent right of individual and collective self-defence if an *armed* attack occurs against a Member of the United Nations until the Security Council has taken measures necessary to maintain international peace and security". The action has to be reported to the Security Council for it to take suitable action so as to maintain or restore international peace and security. Actions of a state involving use or threat of use of force against NSA and terrorists can, thus, be legitimised under Article 51 of the UN Charter. This can empower the concerned state to take appropriate action, including use of force *vis-à-vis* crimes listed under Article 3 of the SUA Convention, 1988 as also resolutions of the Security Council and various conventions that deal with terrorism, including maritime terrorism.

Though the UN Security Council has not passed a resolution that focusses upon maritime terrorism *per* se, Resolution 1540 (2004) that authorises state action against proliferation of WMD and its delivery system has clauses that can partly legitimise the state's action against WMD-related terrorism on the high seas also. Like other resolutions, Resolution 1540 (2004) was a part of the total package of initiatives led by USA in strengthening the regime of non-proliferation of WMD at the global level. Hence, it has to be analysed in the context of Proliferation Security Initiative (PSI) and its Statement of Interdiction Principles of 2003. While PSI sought to skirt the grey areas in UNCLOS-III dealing with freedom of navigation while defining the terms of interdiction of vessels even on the high seas, Security Council Resolution 1540 offered such actions, a limited legitimacy. (Text of Resolution 1540 (2004) in Singh, 2006, pp. 155-61).

Like PSI, Resolution 1540 also seeks to combine two issues; non-proliferation of WMD at global level and post-9/11 emphasis upon international efforts to curb WMD terrorism. Like PSI, it also seeks to target, on grounds of non-proliferation, the state that had not signed the NPT and/or those who were considered rogue states by US-led coalition. During the debate on Resolution 1540, the delegate from Malaysia, who was representing the NAM, argued that the draft resolution had ignored the basic question of general and complete nuclear disarmament. The delegate from Pakistan defended Pakistan's status as nuclear-weapon state and argued that the proposed resolution should be applied only to NSA and terrorists and not to state actors. The Indian delegate too made similar reservations. Despite these reservations, US-led resolution, while targeting NSA/terrorists as well as so-called 'states of proliferation concern' (Iran and North Korea at that time), also left the door open that could enable the Security Council to target those nuclear-weapon powers that had not signed the NPT.

Resolution 1540 (2004), in its preamble, reaffirmed its support for the multilateral treaties "whose aim is to eliminate or prevent the proliferation of nuclear, chemical or biological weapons and the importance of all state(s) that are parties to these treaties to implement them fully in order to promote international stability". The Preamble also targets NSA and terrorists, especially those identified in the list established and maintained under Security Council Resolution 1267 (1999) and Resolution 1373 (2001). It also asked states to coordinate their efforts at national, sub-regional, regional and international level, in that context. This aspect of international cooperation was reiterated in Article 3 (c) and Article 7. It also urged states to take steps in accordance with their national legal authorities to counter this threat. Government of India passed its WMD Act (2005) partly in response to Resolution 1540. Details will be discussed in Chapter IV.

WMD Convention, 2005

As noted, non-proliferation of WMD and related delivery systems had become an intrinsic part of war on terror. Several states were not fully satisfied with provisions under various resolutions, conventions and protocols of international organisations like the UN and IMO. These states felt that they did not provide them with enough enforcement powers to take individual or collective action to counter possible WMD–related threats, that could be posed not only by NSA and terrorists but also by some so-called 'rogue states'. Iraq had been projected as a possible source of threat in that context and the full-scale war to destroy the *Baathi* regime there, was launched in 2003 on the ground that Iraq was on the path to producing WMD. As is known, US administration was proved wrong on that count. But, interestingly, USA launched the new Proliferation Security Initiative (PSI) in May 2003, soon after the Iraqi war was formally terminated unilaterally by President Bush of USA.

PSI was one facet of five interrelated moves that were made between 2002-2005. They were the PSI (2003), Security Council Resolution 1540 (2004), UN Convention for the Suppression of Acts of Nuclear Terrorism (2005), Petersburg Initiative (2005) and SUA Protocol (2005). Unlike Security Council Resolution 1540 (2004) that was adopted so as to offer some legitimacy to US-led initiative on PSI, the General Assembly had been debating the question of nuclear terrorism for years. General Assembly's Resolution of 2005 was the final outcome of General Assembly's Resolution 51/210 of December 1996 under which an *ad hoc* committee had been constituted to discuss modalities for an international convention for the suppression of acts of nuclear terrorism. Thus, it was not a response to PSI. Also, the debate had spread over years and had reflected the views of the states of the South, especially in the context of respect for state sovereignty as also provisions of UNCLOS-III. Also, unlike Security Council Resolution 1540, it is restricted to acts of NSA and terrorists only and does not target so-called rogue states.

The General Assembly passed the resolution on that subject on April 13, 2005. The resolution was subsequently termed as International Convention for Suppression of Acts of Nuclear Terrorism, 2005 or the WMD Convention (2005). It was opened for signature at the UN Head Quarters, New York, on September 14, 2005, so as to coincide with the 60th Anniversary Summit of the UN. (For text of the Convention see Singh, 2006, pp. 169-93). India signed it in July 2006. Till the end of September 2008, India and Russia were the only two nuclear-weapon states that had signed it. No other nuclear weapon power, even those who had been promoting PSI and Security

Council Resolution 1540, had signed it. Probably one reason could be that it had not targeted the so-called rogue states.

This Convention, under Article 1, restricts itself to nuclear threats posed by NSA and terrorists. It also defines in detail, terms like 'radio active material', 'nuclear material', 'nuclear facility', 'nuclear device' etc. Article 2 defines acts that constitute offences under this convention. Among other things, they include possessing radio-active material and device, *with the intent to cause death, bodily injury, damage to property and environment and to damage nuclear facility.* Under Article 5, each state party to the convention shall adopt measures to establish as crime, under its national law, offences listed under Article 2 of the Convention and to prescribe appropriate penalties that take into account the grave nature of these offences.

Article 9 recommends that each state party should take measures to establish jurisdiction over the offences set forth in Article 2. Under Article 9 (1b), the state has jurisdiction if the offence is committed on board a vessel flying the flag of that state. Articles 11 and 13 deal with extradition procedures. Article 15 is very specific on extradition. It cannot be refused on the ground of being a political offence.

The Convention emphasised sovereign equality and territorial integrity of states and non-intervention in domestic affairs of other states (Article 21). Article 22 mentions, "Nothing in this Convention entitles a State Party to undertake in the territory that includes territorial waters of another State Party, the exercise of jurisdiction and performance of functions which are exclusively reserved for the authorities of that other State Party under its national law. Though the UN Convention on nuclear terrorism formally came into force in 2006, India's WMD Act of 2005 is modelled more on it rather than on the recommendations of Security Council Resolution 1540.

SUA Protocol, 2005

Provisions of SUA Convention, 1988 and associated Protocol on off-shore platforms were found by some states to be inadequate under their post-9/11 threat perception and hence needed to be updated. Working out a new Convention would have proved to be time consuming and might have faced serious opposition from some quarters. Hence, under the diplomatic pressure of USA, IMO's Legal Committee in its 83rd session decided to 'review' the SUA Convention of 1988. IMO's General Assembly passed Resolution A-924(22) titled Review of Measures and Procedures to Prevent Acts of Terrorism which Threaten the Security of Passengers and Crew and the Safety of Ships (Paleri, 2007, p. 263). In April 2002, IMO's Legal Committee agreed to establish a Correspondence Group, led by USA, with the short-term aim of developing a working paper on the scope of possible amendments for consideration at its 85th session in October 2003, as also a long term aim to draft the amendments and make a memorandum to the IMO Assembly to convene an international diplomatic conference in order to consider and adopt amendments to the SUA Convention of 1988. All states and interested international organisations were invited to participate in the working of the group. IMO's Secretary-General, Efthimios E. Mitrapoulos, said on October 17, 2005 that the Protocol aimed to fill the legal vacuum (For details about SUA Protocol 2005, see *Beckman*, 2006, pp. 36-49).

The US delegation, as representing the lead country for the Correspondence Group, prepared and introduced draft amendments to SUA Convention of 1988. Some of these amendments not only enlarged the scope of offences but also sought to legitimise boarding and seizure of ships on the high seas in the context of likely violation of these offences. Some of these proposed amendments faced serious opposition. It needs to be underlined that the IMO was not the appropriate body to discuss issues related to non-proliferation of WMD. There were other more competent bodies like the International Atomic Energy Agency. Consequently, the Legal Committee worked on a revised draft protocol and completed its work by the time the 85th session was to be held in April 2005.

IMO's Diplomatic Conference on the Revision of the SUA Convention was held to adopt amendments to the SUA Convention of 1988 as also associated protocol on offshore platform. The SUA Protocol of 2005 was formally adopted in London on October 14, 2005. It was opened for signature on February 14, 2006 and formally entered into force 90 days after the twelfth country had signed it without reservation. Only those states could sign the SUA Protocol of 2005, that had already ratified the SUA Convention of 1988. Article 1-16 of the SUA Convention of 1988, as amended under the 2005 Protocol and its annexure, constitute the new Convention for Suppression of Unlawful Acts Against the Safety of Maritime Navigation, 2005, or the SUA Protocol, 2005, as it is commonly known. It needs to be noted that the use of the term 'terrorism' has been avoided.

Main amendments to the previous SUA Convention of 1988, as incorporated in SUA Protocol, 2005, largely relate to preventing proliferation of WMD-related material, including the delivery system, and also creating conditions that could help in boarding of and seizures of such vessels on the high seas. Some of these points had led to serious debate as also to reservations by some countries, including India, that had signed SUA Convention, 1988. India's objections to SUA Protocol, 2005, was based on the fear that it might be targeted as a non-NPT signing nuclear weapon power with an advanced missile delivery system. Those fears are no longer valid now that the international community has recognised India as a legitimate nuclear-weapon power. Also, some of the provisions of SUA Protocol, 2005, can help legitimise India's action *vis-à-vis* terrorists even on the high seas. Hence, it is time that Indian policy makers undertake a review of their policy not only *vis-à-vis* SUA Protocol of 2005 but also PSI, 2003.

Seven new offences were added to the offences as listed in Article 3 of SUA Convention of 1988. These included acts of terrorism like using a ship as a weapon or as a means of carrying out terrorist attacks. Already, explosive-laden boats were being employed to target other ships. So-called security experts were also busy building scenarios of how large ships like a tanker or a CNG carrier could be hijacked and employed by terrorists to cause serious damage to the port and the coastal environment besides posing threat to life and property.

Other set of offences deal with non-proliferation of WMD and related delivery systems. Security experts were busy speculating how terrorists could employ WMD-related material against their intended targets. The Protocol sought to include transport of WMD-related material by sea, as an offence. It must be noted that this issue was also being debated by the UN General Assembly. It was also the basis of state-level initiatives like Proliferation Security Initiative (PSI) and associated Security Council

Resolution 1540 of 2004. Debate in the General Assembly had led to WMD-related Convention of 2005.

Amended Article 3 also makes it an offence for any person who had committed any offence under the SUA Convention of 1988 to transport by sea, the SUA Protocol of 2005 or any form of act associated with terrorism-related convention of UN. This offence goes beyond the scope of the original SUA Convention of 1988 which had focussed on offences that threatened the safety of maritime navigation only. SUA Protocol of 2005 lists UN Conventions dealing with acts of terrorism and allows for the inclusion of such conventions that may be adopted in the future as well.

USA, in its original draft, had sought to include in Article 8, provisions for boarding and even of seizure of a suspect vessel on the high seas. A ship sailing on the high seas enjoys sovereign immunity of the flag state under Article 92 of UNCLOS-III. It can be intercepted only by stretching Article 94(6). Under that Article, a state that has clear ground to believe that proper jurisdiction and control, with respect to a ship, have not been exercised can only report the facts to the flag state. Upon receiving such a report, the flag state shall investigate the matter and, if appropriate, take any action necessary to remedy the situation. To bypass the concept of sovereignty of the flag state over the vessel, US draft had included the clause of 'tacit understanding' that would have enabled the enforcement agency of any state to take action even on the high seas if there was no response to its request within four hours.

This proposed amendment also faced strong opposition. Consequently the draft amendment had to be dropped. Thus, under Article 8 of the SUA Protocol of 2005, boarding of a foreign vessel is not possible without the express consent of the flag state. USA, however, succeeded in bypassing that by including in the Protocol, provision that allow State Parties to the Protocol to declare in advance, their authorisation for boarding of their flag ships under certain conditions. Since these are non-binding provisions, there was no objection. Lest acts of terrorism be qualified as political offence by some states, Article 11 bis? of SUA Protocol, 2005, made it expressly clear that extradition may not be refused on the ground that it was a political offence.

It will not be far from the truth to say that SUA Protocol of 2005 had become a part of the wider global effort led by USA against proliferation of WMD and related maritime terrorism. As Robert Beckman puts it, "It should be noted that the 2005 SUA Protocol is consistent with the US-led Proliferation Security Initiative (PSI) and is complementary to it". He argued that the Protocol, under Article 8, provides that State Parties could conclude agreements or arrangements between themselves to facilitate law enforcement operations that would be carried out under boarding provisions. Joining the PSI would arguably be one such arrangement. He added, "Articles 8 bis and 13 of the 2005 Protocol specifically provides that State Parties are encouraged to develop standard operating procedures (SOPs) for joint operations and to consult with other states with a view to harmonising SOPs" (Beckman, 2006, p. 46).

It is important to note in this context that even those states including India that are neither parties to PSI nor have ratified SUA Protocol 2005 are making SOP as a part of their agenda in bilateral and multilateral naval exercises with US Navy and are, therefore, complying with the political agenda of PSI as also SUA Protocol 2005 without the concerned states formally joining the PSI or signing SUA Protocol, 2005. Indian Navy is, thus, contributing, through joint naval exercises, what the Government of India is formally unwilling to accept, probably for domestic political reasons.

Actions outside internationally sanctioned institutions

Some states that were unhappy with politico-legal constraints under internationally sanctioned institutions, like the UN, sought to bypass them and began taking initiatives outside these institutions and hoped to partly legitimise them through resolutions passed by the Security Council, the General Assembly, the IMO etc. Such initiatives included the Proliferation Security Initiative (PSI) of 2003, Petersburg Initiative of 2006. Container Security Initiative (CSI), Regional Maritime Security Initiative (RMSI), Regional Co-operation Agreement in Asia Against Piracy (ReCAAP) etc.

The Proliferational Security Initiative (PSI)

The PSI is linked to US Naval Security Strategy of September 2002 and the related policy of preventing attacks on USA as also to establish and maintain an international coalition to fight so-called war on terror (*Military Balance, 2003-2004*, p. 12). The Bush administration had given top priority to National Strategy to Combat Weapons of Mass Destruction. As noted, destruction of WMD had been a major argument to justify war on Iraq in 2003. According to Michael Byers, John Balton, the then Under-Secretary for Arms Control and International Security, was charged with 'fixing the legal problem' (Byers, 2003, pp. 14-5).

President Bush formally announced the Proliferation Security Initiative in Krakow, Poland, on May 31, 2003, coinciding with the end of the conventional war in Iraq. Though USA's allegations against the *Baathi* regime in Iraq had subsequently proved to be untrue, USA continued to make counter-proliferation of WMD the main plank in its strategy of war on terror. USA was able to obtain support of several interested partners. Formal accord, as reflected in the Statement of Interdiction Principles, was arrived at in Paris during the third meeting of eleven core members in September 3-4, 2003. Subsequently, USA was able to cajole many other states to join the PSI. Till December 2008, 93 participants had endorsed PSI. But only 20 among them constitute the Operational Experts Group which meets regularly to coordinate PSI-related activities. They include USA, its European allies, Japan, Australia and Russia.

The Statement of Interdiction Principles constitutes the core of the PSI. (For full text see *Singh*, 2006, pp. 149-53). According to Article 1, not only NSA but also state actors are subject to interdiction. The term used is 'states and non-state actors of *proliferation concern*'. That Article also said that these states and NSA of proliferation concern 'generally refers to those countries or entities that the PSI participants involved establish should be subjected to interdiction activities'. Thus, a group outside the UN took upon itself the task to designate states/NSA as proliferators of WMD, and PSI was created to target them. An international system parallel to established international organisations was sought to be established to target a few entities as desired by these states. To say the least, it was a very arbitrary proposition.

The Statement of Interdiction Principles also included clauses that were designed to answer the concerns of states of possible violation of freedom of navigation in PSI-related action. Article 4 dealt with those measures and introduced the concept of 'prior consent' of those that wish to join the PSI. The flag states had to be given prior consent to allow ships flying their flags to be searched and if need be, seized by enforcement agencies of others who are part of PSI even on the high seas. (Article 4 b, c and d). Under Article 4 (a), these states also agreed that vessels flying their flag will not transport WMD-related material. USA has succeeded in obtaining 'prior consent' of several states who offer their flags to ships owned by nationals of other states (flag of convenience). These states include Liberia, Panama, the Marshall Islands, Croatia, Cyprus, Belize etc. (Song, 2007, p. 106).

While PSI participants might give their consent, UNCLOS-III, under Article 23 does not prohibit carriage of WMD material by ships on the high seas or even the passage of nuclear powered ships. It, however, provides guidelines if these vessels wish to exercise their right of innocent passage even through the territorial waters. In such a case, Article 23 of UNCLOS-III insists that they should "carry documents and observe special precautionary measures established for such ships by international agreements". It is well known that not only do vessels carry WMD-related material but several great powers operate nuclear powered ships which often carry nuclear warheads. India not only had operated an ex-Soviet nuclear-powered submarine (*INS Chakra*) for three years in the past but is also actively pursuing a policy to acquire such submarines of its own which would be armed with missiles, carrying nuclear warhead.

PSI can be faulted on other grounds as well. Those who had proposed PSI, had failed to provide guidelines about what constitutes 'proliferation' that is a threat to security. Also, the term 'WMD' and the delivery system are so open-ended that any activity, even for peaceful purposes, especially of state actors so targeted, is to be unilaterally decided by those who judge them to be 'proliferators'. They are not accountable to any other international organisation.

It is well understood that PSI was being driven by USA. Thus, only those states that are targets of US policy like Iran and North Korea would have been the focus of activities under PSI while states like Pakistan and

China will be left out for political considerations, despite their proven records as culprit in this context. The threat of WMD proliferation/insecurity *via* Pakistan is much greater now because of the close nexus between so-called *jehadi* terrorism and some highly placed official agencies in Pakistan and radical Islamic elements in the armed forces. Pakistan also has ties with similar agencies in some other Islamic states as well.

The PSI has no clear policy on non-proliferation of ballistic and cruise missiles. The Missile Technology Control Regime (MTCR), also a product of non-UN initiative, had at least defined the guidelines for missiles that could be used for carrying nuclear warhead upto a certain distance. Thus, it fixed a maximum range of 300 km and a warhead of 500 kg as the limit for transfer of missiles from one country to another. PSI has neither fixed such a guideline nor has endorsed the norms of the MTCR.

PSI also lacks political legitimacy since it was not the end product of a discussion/consensus at internationally recognised institutions but was an initiative approved by a select few states. Those who have not accepted it are not bound by it. And, even USA cannot afford to implement it fully. Will a Chinese ship, carrying parts of the *Babur* cruise missile to Pakistan, be intercepted by warships of US-led coalition?

Petersburg Initiative, 2006

The meeting between President George Bush and Vladimir Putin in July 2006 in St. Petersburg, led to yet another initiative to counter the threat of nuclear terrorism. Unlike the PSI, Security Council Resolution 1540 (2004) or the SUA Protocol of 2005, the new initiative targets only threat of nuclear terrorism from NSA/terrorists and not from the so-called rogue states. This group is also a coalition of the willing but unlike the PSI, it is joined by states like China, Pakistan and India that had not joined the PSI and who had raised reservations on Resolution 1540 (2004). India took almost two years to sign it. Saudi Arabia and UAE are other important members.

This new global initiative had already held three meetings in Morocco, Turkey and Kazakhstan before the Madrid meeting that was held in June 2008. This meeting was to be attended by officials from European Union, the International Atomic Energy Agency as well as representatives of related industries. The focus was to monitor the availability of nuclear materials, building of weapons, target and attack scenarios. It seems that the primary focus of the new initiative has shifted from the so-called 'rogue states' like North Korea and Iran to possible leakage from Pakistan's I.Q.Khan-led nuclear network to NSA and terrorists, especially those believing in radical Islam and the so-called *jehadi* groups that were becoming more and more vocal in Pakistan-Afghanistan frontier.

India's focus on non-proliferation of WMD was not as much on state actors as NSA and terrorists, as is clear from its WMD Act of 2005. Hence, though rather late, India's membership of the new group is in keeping with the Indian policy. India has thus not only fulfilled its mandatory obligation under Chapter VII of UN Charter by enacting WMD Act, 2005, as required by Resolution 1540 (2004), as also by ratifying UN Convention on WMD-related terrorism of 2005, but it has now joined the Petersburg Initiative that was co-sponsored by USA and Russia and supported by China as also several other states and the IAEA. This brings India closer to the US-led PSI, which is also supported by Russia but not by China. It remains to be seen if this initiative will be operationally useful in confronting nuclear terrorism of NSA and terrorists or will be yet another futile exercise by state actors in their confrontation with NSA and terrorists.

Container Security Initiative (CSI)

The enhanced post-9/11 threat perception, especially in USA, envisaged multiple scenarios under which terrorists could target USA and its allies *via* the sea. Experts, seeking to prevent the misuse of containers by terrorists, proposed the Container Security Initiative (CSI). This step was taken along with the new ISPS Code. The fear that containers could be used to target the homeland led to the newly created US Customs and Border Protection Agency (CBP). It was established within the Department of Homeland Security. It demanded that the ocean carriers must electronically fill cargo manifest outlining the content of US-bound containers, 24 hours in advance of their being loaded overseas. These manifests were then to be analysed against the intelligence database at CBP's National Targeting Centre to determine if the container might pose a risk. If so, it was likely to be inspected overseas itself before it could be loaded on a US-bound ship under the CSI.

It was feared that containers could be used by terrorists to smuggle not only WMD-related material, particularly material for what is termed as a 'dirty bomb', in which depleted uranium or such other radio-active material in bulk can be scattered widely through use of explosive devices, but also terrorists themselves. That led several states to accept the procedure as laid down under the CSI. Many states in Europe and in the Pacific coast are a party to CSI. As of November 2005, there were 41 port agreements in place where the host country permitted the US Customs inspector to operate within its jurisdiction and agreed to pre-loading inspection of any targeted container.

Though laudable as a means to defeat the activities of NSA/terrorists, CSI is not easy to implement at the global level. Reportedly, in 2006 itself, about 220 million containers were shipped around the world. The sheer volume makes it almost impossible to screen all of them. Screening technology includes use of X-rays, Gamma rays and neutron scanning devices. X-rays and Gamma rays have limitations like lower penetration of steel, difficulty in identifying cargo without definite shape etc. Drugs and explosives can be packed in a variety of ways and home-made or improvised explosives like a mixture of ammonium nitrate and fuel-oil bomb can be packed even in plastic oil drums.

Very few developing countries can afford the cost or the expertise to operate the technology related to CSI. Countries that feel threatened seek to apply the CSI among themselves and concentrate upon equipping selected ports where the facilities can be installed. Countries can also enter into bilateral agreement under which they agree to allow experts from their countries to be stationed at each other's ports to monitor containers that are being destined for the ports of these countries. India and USA have such a bilateral agreement. In India, Nhava Sheva Port at Navi Mumbai is equipped for CSI. India is also investing in R & D in this area. The Electronic Corporation of India Limited (ECIC), in collaboration with OSI System Inc., was to manufacture a scanning and security system for ports and airports for inspection of cargo (Lale, 2006, p. 182).

Related to the ethos of CSI is another initiative called the Customs-Trade Partnership Against Terrorism (C-TPAT). Under it, importers and transportation companies agree voluntarily to conduct self-assessment of their company operations and supply chains and then put in security measures to address any security-related vulnerability that is detected. At the multi-lateral level, US customs authorities have worked with Brussels-based World Customs Organisation on establishing a new framework to improve trade security for all countries (Flynn, 2006, p. 7).

Regional Maritime Security Initiative (RMSI)

Since the concept of state sovereignty in territorial waters and that of freedom of the high seas have been seen as major constraints in efforts to neutralise threats posed by NSA and terrorists, efforts have been made to evolve consensus among major maritime powers and associated regional powers to evolve a mechanism that will help in monitoring the sea space in a more organised and cooperative environment. RMSI aims at that.

RMSI aims at monitoring sea traffic in areas of special concern, primarily by warships and maritime reconnaissance aircrafts of members of US-led coalition with or without active participation of regional states. Like PSI and CSI, RMSI also reflected the initiative taken by USA in this regard. The Chief of Naval Operation's guidelines for 2005 had listed, among other things, establishing 'expanded military intercept operations as a *core* Navy responsibility (Holmes and Winner, 2004, p. 128). RMSI also represented the strategy of sea control in the context of threat of WMD from rogue states as also NSA and terrorists.

This strategy raises several issues of maritime law during the state of 'non-war'. Can a state or a group of states operate in the sea space near other coastal states in far off regions and designate that area as a region of their security concern? How different is RMSI from the earlier strategy of maritime force projection in far off regions? USA and its allies have been pursuing that strategy for decades in the Indian Ocean, especially around the Persian Gulf, at least since mid-sixties. Today, Combined Task Force CTF-151 and CTC-152 under US-led coalition as also taskforce sent by European Union operate in north-western Indian Ocean. Except for Pakistan, which is represented in CTF-152, no other regional power is part of these so-called regional maritime security initiatives.

Is RMSI a part of continuation of that strategy of force projection at a wider level or is a new facet of maritime strategy related to containing threats of maritime terrorism posed by NSA and terrorists as well as of non-proliferation of WMD? It needs to be underlined that this strategy of sea control *vis-à-vis* NSA and terrorists was adopted in the post-9/11 period and especially after Operation Enduring Freedom against *Al-Qaida* and the Taliban. Initially its focus was on the northern half of the Indian Ocean and its natural extensions like the Red Sea and Bab al-Mandeb region. Subsequently, it was extended to cover East Mediterranean and South-East Asia.

Attempts have been made to legitimise RMSI by stretching the interpretation of Article 51 of the UN Charter to include 'preemptive action' of a state for self-defence as also by basing it on several resolutions/ conventions of UN and IMO. Capability to monitor and enforce such a sustained operation in far away regions is not possible by one state alone. To be really effective, it has to be a multilateral operation with inputs from at least a few regional actors.

Indian Ocean remains the region of primary concern in the context of RMSI. Reportedly, hundreds of vessels sailing in the Arabian Sea were scanned by warships of USA and its allies, since the beginning of Operation Enduring Freedom in 2001 and the subsequent thrust on non-proliferation of WMD. The noteworthy illustration of this operation was the interception of the North Korean vessel *MV So San*. It was an allegedly 'stateless' vessel at the time when it was intercepted in December 2002, in the Gulf of Aden while it was on its way to Yemen. It was intercepted about 600 miles off the coast of Yemen by the Spanish frigate *Navarra* which was a part of the international flotilla patrolling the Arabian Sea. When challenged, the master of the ship refused to identify the vessel. He also refused to stop the vessel after the frigate had fired warning shots. After that, the ship's guns blasted the mast cables to enable Spanish Special Operations troops to land on the deck by helicopter. US Navy's explosive experts also joined the Spanish members to locate the 'real' cargo on board the vessel. The team found 15 SCUD missiles, two dozen tanks, rocket fuel addition and about 100 other barrels of unidentified chemicals. Despite the high profile interception, it was decided to release the ship and its cargo as Yemen was a strategic partner in the US-led war on terrorism against *Al-Qaida*. Also, SCUD missiles did not come within the prohibited range of MTCR and hence there was no reason to stop its delivery at that time. If the interception had taken place after PSI was in operation and/or after Security Council Resolution 1540 (2004) was approved, may be USA would not have released the North Korean ship so easily.

Commodore Anthony Rix, who was in command of the Multilateral Task Force 151 between March-September 2005, in an article in *RUSI Defence Systems*, wrote that Task Force 151 was created in 2000 after terrorist attacks on *USS Cole* and *MV Limburg*. Its operational zone included an area stretching from the southern edge of the Suez Canal to the Straits of Hormuz and down to East African coast to Kenya; some 2.5 mn square miles of sea space. By contrast, operational zone of Task Force 152 was limited to the sea space around the Gulf. The objective was to deny terrorists the use of maritime environment. Now piracy or hijacking of ships and crew for ransom has emerged as the new focus of operation of Task Force 151. This task force comprises of about ten frigates and destroyers from countries that include USA, UK, France, Germany, Italy, Spain, Canada, Australia, New Zealand and Pakistan. Pakistan is probably the lone representative of the region. No GCC member is involved. Commodore Rix maintained that Task Force 151 had not taken on at that time (2005), law enforcement operations. Rather, it concentrated upon intelligence operations, preplanned operations in certain designated areas, theatre security operation activities with regional navies etc. (Rix, 2005, pp. 36-9).

Was this the model that US administration was trying to thrust upon the littoral states of the Malacca Straits also? Singapore is a partner in PSI and has shown willingness to join the US-led initiative in war on terrorism. However, other regional actors like Malaysia and Indonesia have declined to join the US-led initiatives arguing, among other things, that it violates their territorial sovereignty. They also took serious objection to the way USA was pushing them into joining RMSI. According to Rommel C. Banlaos, US model of "follow the leader" differs radically from the cooperative model of the ASEAN members. Their model relies more upon *musyawarat*, i.e. intense dialogue and consultations, to generate consensus or *mufakat* on contentious issues facing the region. The practice of *musyawaat dan mufakat* encourages ASEAN members to cooperate on various issues, through informal and incremental mechanism.

This ethos was also reflected in the ASEAN Concord II of Bali, reached on October 7, 2003, on promoting regional solidarity and cooperation. It said that the member states would exercise their rights to lead their national existence free from outside interference in their internal affairs. It also recognised the sovereign rights of the member states to pursue their individual foreign policy and defence arrangements, taking into account the strong interconnection among politics, economics, social and cultural aspects in consonance with ASEAN Vision 2020, rather than a defence pact, military alliance or a joint foreign policy (Banlaos, 2008, pp. 254-55).

Sharply in contrast to the ASEAN ethos, was the way the US sought to impose RMSI in South-East Asia. Admiral Thomas Fargo of the US Pacific Command launched the controversial concept of RMSI during his testimony before the US House of Representatives' Armed Services Committee on March 31, 2004. He said that RMSI aimed to operationalise the PSI and the Malacca Straits Initiative (MSI) to promote regional security in the midst of growing maritime security threat. The ASEAN had accepted neither the PSI nor RMSI because of strong opposition from Indonesia and Malaysia who were 'cautious' of American strategic intensions (Banlaos, 2008, p. 256).

According to Peter Lehr, some of the ASEAN members believed that it would trap them in major powers' geopolitical game. They were also apprehensive of vast power asymmetry and its long-term effect upon the role of regional powers. Probably, the lessons of the near permanent presence of US-led coalition in the Gulf and the Arabian Sea were before them. Peter Lehr also touched upon a sensitive spot when he observed that, to some extent the difference between the major power users of the Malacca Straits and the 'Muslim' littoral states are linked to ideological idiosyncrasies and prejudices. Major powers' attempt to link threats of piracy in Straits of Malacca to maritime terrorism, was a case in point. According to him, littoral states believed that it was an extension of their war on the so-called Islamic terrorism in the Middle East (Lehr, 2008, pp. 192-94).

Though India has not formally joined PSI or RMSI, its maritime strategy of offering protection to SLOCs in adjacent sea space as also its regular naval exercises with states that subscribe to PSI and RMSI, like USA, UK, France, Japan, Singapore and Russia, underline its policy of offering support to war on terror without politically or diplomatically compromising its status as a nuclear-weapon power.

Regional Cooperation Agreement on Combating Piracy and Armed Robbery Against Ships in Asia (ReCAAP)

Malacca Straits and South China Sea have been in focus since late 1980s, in the context of the growing threat of piracy and armed robbery on board the ship. Littoral states of the Malacca Straits have been under pressure from major users of the sea lane, like Japan, to enhance the security of this vital choke point. More than 100,000 vessels transit through it per year. The figure is expected to double by 2020. Besides, there are about 80,000 regional fishing vessels operating in these waters. Malacca Straits, with its innumerable islands and rugged terrain is not an easy place to monitor. Does the responsibility of maintaining a secure transit in such a long and narrow waterway fall on regional powers alone, who incidentally are not its major users? Or, do they not need support from other users also? Article 43 (a) of UNCLOS-III stipulates need for burden sharing. Under that article, user states and states bordering a strait should 'by agreement' cooperate in the establishment and maintenance of necessary navigational and safety aids or other improvements in aid of international navigation. Article 43 (b) provides for such cooperation for the prevention, reduction and control of pollution from ships in those waters.

Japan has been deeply involved in trying to evolve a mechanism for such a cooperation between regional powers and major users. Unlike the US model of RMSI, Japanese model was closer to the ASEAN model of mutual negotiations and consensus building.

The Regional Cooperation Agreement on Combating Piracy and Armed Robbery Against Ships in Asia (ReCAAP) is the first regional government-to-government agreement to promote and enhance cooperation against the menace of piracy and armed robbery in Asia. It was proposed by Japanese Prime Minister Junichiro Koizumi in October 2001. The 'region' is supposed to include 16 states; ten ASEAN Members, plus, Bangladesh, China, India, Japan, Republic of Korea and Sri Lanka. Negotiations were finalised in November 2004 in Tokyo. The Agreement was opened for signature on February 28, 2005. By June 15, 2006, twelve countries had signed it. Reportedly, Malaysia and Indonesia had stated their 'preparedness to cooperate' without formally signing the agreement with ReCAAP Information Sharing Centre.

ReCAAP comprises of three interlinked components; information sharing, capacity building and operational cooperation. ReCAAP has established an Information Sharing Centre (ISC) as the hub of its information network. It is a permanent body with a full-time staff. Singapore is the hub of ISC. It is expected that ReCAAP will help improve the response of its members at state level as well.

Almost parallel to ReCAAP, Japan has also succeeded in creating Asia Maritime Security Initiative (AMARSECTIVE-2004) in June 2004. It aims at anti-piracy cooperation among regional coast guards (Paleri, 2006, pp. 310-11, 315) India has joined that initiative as well. Coast Guards of India and Japan often hold joint exercises with anti-piracy as one of the objectives (Paleri, 2006, pp. 235-36).

Initiatives at individual state level

Besides multilateral agreements and initiatives, many states have announced their individual state-specific regulations that aim at monitoring ships far away from their coast. USA, probably the most self-terrorised state, had plans to crafts a maritime NORAD that would monitor the movements of any ship that would be found moving towards its coast. It was supposed to be comparable to the air-defence system that was established during the Cold War era on the frontier across Canada and USA *vis-à-vis* USSR. Canada, had, since January 2003, prohibited vessels from coming within 500 metres of its military ports at Halifax, Nova Scotia, and those at Esquimalt and Nanovsa Bay in British Colombia. On December 24, 2005, Australia had expressed its intention of announcing a Maritime Identification Zone, 1,000 miles from the Australian coastline. A vessel proposing to enter Australian ports was required to provide comprehensive information regarding its identity, crew, cargo, location, course, speed and intended port of arrival. One wonders if such requirements do not amount to denial of freedom of navigation on the high seas.

Apart from reinforcing the security of one's coastal zone, a state can also offer help to other states on a bilateral basis, for improving the ability of that state to protect its immediate sea space. Needless to say, these transfers of equipment are made to states whose security concerns are deemed vital for protecting regional interests of the donor state. USA has been supplying patrol crafts to states like Djibouti, Yemen and Kenya. In June 2006, it supplied four 44-feet ex-US Coast Guard patrol boats to Djibouti's Navy. It also sent a team of experts to train the locals in operating these boats. Djibouti also provided facilities when USA hosted, in August 2006, training exercise Natural Fire. US forces that included about 400 Marines conducted the exercise along with troops from Tanzania, Kenya and Uganda. In all, about 1,000 troops participated. USA also donated ten gunboats and spares etc. in August 2006 to Yemen to help it secure the coast line along the Gulf of Aden. USA also donated in October 2006, six powerful armoured speed boats to Kenya to patrol its sea coast (*Forbes and Rumley*, 2008, p. 63). India too has been offering its expertise and also patrol crafts to island states like Sri Lanka, Maldives, Mauritius and Seychelles.

Conclusion

Survey of provisions of international law, UNCLOS-III, various resolutions and conventions of UN and IMO as well as several initiatives at multilateral level and at the individual state level point to the fact that the global community is witnessing the evolution of a new international law, may be at present at *de facto* level, that seeks to design a framework that would legitimise their individual and collective efforts to meet the new challenge posed by NSA and terrorists to maritime security.

In that process, states of the developed North have taken steps to sanitise not only their adjacent sea space but also to ensure better monitoring of major SLOCs and choke points as also to legitimise enforcement measures taken by them against threats posed by terrorists in far off places also. By contrast, states of the South have either ignored that aspect or have taken only symbolic and inadequate steps in that direction. The near total absence of maritime enforcement agencies of littoral states of Arabian Peninsula, along the Horn of Africa especially of Saudi Arabia, Oman and UAE, in managing the new menace of piracy/hijacking of ships and its crew for ransom in the sensitive area of their adjacent sea space, is a pointer in that direction. Such a non-response, directly and indirectly, legitimises the naval presence of non-regional powers in that region.

Responsibility for ensuring maritime security *vis-à-vis* threats posed by NSA and terrorists in waters adjacent to the coast, rests primarily with the coastal states since these elements can operate only when they have a secure home base nearby. It is only when they are either reluctant or are incapable, due to lack of adequate resources, in performing that role that initiative for providing maritime security in that area is taken over by other concerned states. It is illogical to claim the privilege of state jurisdiction over adjoining waters without corresponding means to shoulder accompanying obligations.

This is becoming increasingly important in the context of threats posed by NSA and terrorists. It is important to underline in this context, that major users of these sea lanes, instead of criticising and even blaming coastal states of the South for inaction, should seek to offer help through proper forums so as to enable these states to overcome their handicaps and fulfil their obligations.

For long, littoral states of Indian Ocean region have been neglecting their obligation to take effective steps either individually or through multilateral regional cooperation, in protecting even their adjacent sea space and international SLOCs. Even now, many states, on one pretext or the other, refuse to share that responsibility. This has made their respective coast lines and coastal waters, a fertile ground for criminal activities of NSA and of terrorists. They need to convert the 'hostile' coast into a 'secure' coast by ensuring good governance in their respective sea space.

A hostile coast can never ensure maritime security either for the coastal state or for international community, using that sea space. Even India, despite its claims to being an emerging maritime power and a major regional power, had also, till recently, lagged behind in evolving an effective maritime mechanism for ensuring security of its own homeland. Some steps have been initiated in that direction since 2004-2005. Such a mechanism of coastal security of individual states would automatically spill over in the adjacent sea space and will help not only the coastal state but also other users of that sea space and thus help it fulfil its international obligation in meeting the new threat to maritime security. That will also help fill the gap left due to inadequacies in UNCLOS-III, as also various resolutions and conventions in meeting the new challenge.

Traditional international law, as also UN Charter and UNCLOS-III have state-centric focus. Hence, they do not provide legal means to legitimise state action against the new threat to maritime security, posed by NSA and more so by terrorists who have developed transnational linkages. Consequently, states have been forced to pursue a multi-pronged policy so as to legitimise their action in combating the new threat. That includes reinterpreting UN Charter, especially Article 51 that provides for individual and collective self-defence. After the events of 9/11, provisions of the UN Charter are being invoked by equating threats posed by terrorists with that posed by state actors. Efforts are being made to reinterpret articles of UNCLOS-III, by differentiating between defence *vis-à-vis* states and security *vis-à-vis* NSA and terrorists, so that steps initiated by state actors in various maritime sones, including the high seas, against NSA and terrorists can be differentiated from those that target state actors. States have also passed resolutions under IMO and Security Council to enlarge the scope of enforcement action beyond the prescribed limits of UNCLOS-III. States have also resorted to various initiatives outside the framework of institutions legitimised under the UN, like the PSI, CSI, RMSI, ReCAAP etc.

Thus, one has witnessed at least since 1988, the evolution of new international norms that seek to provide legitimacy for state action against maritime terrorism. Over the years, these will be accepted as *de facto* international law on the subject. Indian decision makers who are planning to evolve a legal framework for combating maritime security, need to take note of these developments and to incorporate them while reframing the legal framework and state practices to legitimise state enforcement action against NSA and terrorists.

4 | INDIA-MARITIME THREATS, LEGAL NORMS AND STATE PRACTICES

New threats and outmoded legal systems

Maritime threats to homeland security by Non-State Actors (NSA) and especially by terrorists is a recent phenomenon for India. Acts of maritime terrorism can be traced to the 1980s. Over this short period, threats have snowballed and have assumed a serious proportion. Responses have been sporadic. A comprehensive legal framework, both at the level of international norms as also domestic norms that would clearly and comprehensively lay down the legal framework has not been put in place so far.

Undoubtedly, there are several acts that can be applied in the case of maritime threat to homeland security, posed by NSA and terrorists. This chapter will seek to examine them and analyse if they are adequate as they are to meet the legal requirements and to facilitate adequate enforcement measures especially in preempting the act, or they need to be redefined and streamlined in the context of the fast changing environment of maritime insecurity.

Laws have been passed to deal with crimes committed by 'ordinary' criminals as also by NSA and by terrorists. As noted earlier, Indian decision-makers have differentiated between NSA and terrorists. India's WMD Act, 2005, defines them separately. Under Section 4, Subsection (iii) g, a Non-State Actor is a person or entity not acting under the lawful authority of any country. He need not necessarily be a terrorist. By contrast, Section 4, Subsection (iii) m defines terrorists in the context of the Unlawful Activities (Prevention) Act, 1967 (UAPA, 1967). Interestingly, SUA Act, 2002, of India does not make a distinction between NSA and terrorists but clubs them under one head, under Section 3, but does not use the word 'terrorists'. It categorises all those acts as 'unlawful'.

Normally, a state has full jurisdiction over criminal activities committed on land – its 'territory' as also on board an aircrafts or vessel under its flag. But, crimes related to maritime affairs that affect the state can also be committed beyond its immediate land border, be it in the territorial waters or on the high seas beyond it. As noted in Chapter III, UNCLOS-III does provide for state action in sea space beyond its land border, in the context of criminal activities of NSA like piracy, drug trafficking and slave trade. But it has no provisions for dealing with acts of terrorism.

How logical is it to allow maritime security of a nation to be held hostage to outmoded sets of laws and conventions, like UNCLOS-III, that offer legal framework for action, however restrictive that may be, against piracy, slavery and trafficking in prohibited drugs but not terrorism? UNCLOS-III ignores the security aspect of a state by hiding behind the argument, that concept of 'security' of a state could be abused to deny freedom of navigation.

P. Chandrashekhar Rao refuted this argument According to him, a right can be exercised properly or abused, "In fact, there is no right which may not be abused. The right itself, if it merits recognition on the basis of valid grounds, cannot be jettisoned because of the possibility that it might be abused. No one denies the need to reduce or eliminate abuses. But, what is at stake for the maritime power in this context is not so much the freedom of navigation as their global maritime interests. It can scarcely be contemplated that a state must remain passive while acts prejudicial to its security are mounted from just across its territorial sea.... It is decidedly illogical to allow self-protection against the smuggling of merchandise but to disallow self-protection against the smuggling of arms and men to rebels (Rao, 1983, pp. 333-34).

No state, in times of peace between state actors, is interested in denying freedom of navigation to other state actors. However, state actors should in turn also take cognisance of the fact that 'war on terror', unlike conventional wars, is a continuous process. The entire world community has condemned terrorism both within the UN and outside it. Member states have also been urged to cooperate in various ways in combating this menace. Thus, the state's action to 'sanitise' waters adjacent to its coast and even on the adjoining high seas, in the context of war on terror, should not be treated as efforts to undermine UNCLOS-III, especially clauses dealing with freedom of navigation.

One can even apply norms of self-defence in the context of meeting the challenge posed by maritime terrorism. As analysed in the previous Chapter, UN Charter provides for it under Article 2 (4) and 51. State action, in this context, can be defined under four heads; theatre of operation, scale of operation, level of weaponry to be employed and finally graduation of force and scale of response (O'Connell, 1984, pp. 1094-95). In the context of India, combating maritime threat to homeland by NSA and terrorists, the theatre of operation will be generally restricted to waters adjacent to the coast, though it can even extend to areas further away, as in the case of anti-piracy/hijacking patrol in the Indian Ocean area. Level of weaponry is likely to be much below that employed in conventional naval warfare among states. The graduation of force and scale of operation will also be conditioned by the threat posed by these new adversaries. Such operations by state actors in adjacent waters should not be seen as security threats to freedom of navigation of other state actors. Rather, they should be seen as means to sanitise the adjacent sea space and thus to ensure freedom of navigation for all.

NSA/Terrorism: Indian Laws, Acts and State Practices

Efforts will be made in this chapter to analyse various laws, acts and state practices that have evolved over the years, in India and which are likely to be employed, to meet the challenges to homeland security posed by NSA and terrorists *via* its adjoining sea space. These acts and laws can be divided into three parts; acts and laws that apply to criminal activities in general, those that apply to actions of NSA and those that target the terrorists. How much maritime content they have will also be worth analysing.

The Indian Penal Code

Though the Indian Penal Code (IPC) was not framed keeping terrorism or maritime crimes in mind, yet it contains sections that can be applied in the context of criminal acts that can be related to terrorism, piracy etc. (For text of IPC, see *The Indian Code, Vol. III*, 1956). Since India had no law specific to acts of piracy, those involved in the piracy of the Japanese vessel

MV Alondra Rainbow were tried in the court in Mumbai, under various sections of IPC. If India had passed the SUA Act, 2002, earlier, they could have been tried under that as well.

Various sections of IPC can be divided into two broad categories-Sections on crimes that are aimed against the state and the 'allied' powers, and those that are directed against the 'subjects'. Both these categories can be applied to criminal activities of NSA and terrorists, though the primary focus of IPC was and remains 'land' centric. The 'continental' or 'land based' mindset of the framers of IPC is reflected in Chapter II, Section 18. It states that 'India' means the territory of India (except the State of J & K). There is no mention even of territorial waters, though under MZI Act, 1976, Government of India, by notification, extended the provisions of IPC and CrPC over the entire EEZ of India (MoD, *A.R. 1981-82*, pp. 26-27). IPC, however, reflects the concept of state sovereignty. As per Chapter I, Section 4 (2), its provisions apply to any person on any ship or aircrafts registered in India *wherever it may be*. As noted, provisions of IPC are applied to offences against the State as also offences against persons. In neither case is the term 'terrorism' employed.

Sections 121 to 126 deal with offences against the State. Article 121 deals with activities related to waging war against the Government of India or attempting or abeting insurrection. Punishment ranges from death to life imprisonment and fine. Section 121 (A)a? deals with conspiring to perform these acts within India or outside India. Section 122 deals with attempt to collect men, arms, ammunition etc to wage a war against the State. Punishment ranges from 10 years to life imprisonment and fine.

Provisions of IPC are also extended to cover similar criminal activities directed against other State actors. Section 125 deals with waging war or attempting to do so against the government of *any Asiatic Power, in alliance or at peace with the Government*. Punishment can extend upto life imprisonment. Section 126 applies to whosoever commits depredation or makes preparations to commit depredation on the territory of any power in alliance or at peace with the Government. Punishment can range from seven years imprisonment to life imprisonment and fine and forfeiture of property so used. As noted, provisions of Section 125 of IPC, apply selectively – only to *Asiatic Power in Alliance with or at peace with the Government of India*, while Section 126 omits the phrase "Asiatic Powers" and widens the scope to 'any Power' in alliance with or at peace with the Government. These two sections indirectly convey the impression that similar actions against governments that are hostile to the Government of India are not offences under IPC; a concept that goes not only against the principle of universalism, but also various resolutions of the UN and conventions on terrorism.

Several sections of IPC deal with criminal offences committed against the person and property of individuals. When read along with sections of India's SUA Act, 2002, they strengthen the hands of enforcement agencies in their action against the criminal activities of NSA and terrorists committed on vessels or on off-shore platforms. Though these sections of IPC do not specifically mention the maritime facets of the criminal activities, they do overlap offences listed in Article 3 of the SUA Convention, 1988 and India's SUA Act, 2002 that incorporates provisions of SUA Convention, 1988. Section 286 of the IPC deals with explosive substances. This section also needs to be read along with amendment to the Explosive Substances Act of 1908 that was passed by the Parliament on December 4, 2002. This amendment includes the use of explosives like RDX, PETN as also remotely controlled explosive devices. That amendment raises the level of punishment upto long years of rigorous imprisonment and even death (MHA *A.R., 2001-2002*, p.19). Sections 299 to 304 of IPC deal with various aspects of homicide, Section 342 deals with wrongful confinement. Sections 349 to 352 deal with use of criminal force and assault, theft and robbery, kidnapping and abduction. Article 380 specifically deals with theft on board a vessel. It carries a punishment upto seven years of imprisonment as well as fine. Section 390 deals with robbery and dacoity.

Other acts specific to Non State Actors

Several acts have been passed that specifically target criminal activities of NSA. These acts, like the sections of the IPC, can also provide indirect support in combating acts of terrorism, even though they, by themselves, may not constitute acts of terrorism. Some of these acts are the Passport (Entry into India) Act. Earlier the punishment was only three months imprisonment and fine. Now, under Section 3 of that Act, term of imprisonment has been extended upto five years and / or fine upto Rs. 50,000 (MHA *A.R., 2001-02*, p. 124).

Smuggling has been a major component of economic crimes of NSA. The Sea Customs Act, 1879 has been amended several times. A consolidated *Customs Act 1962*, was further amended in 2007. The Customs Act is applicable in adjacent sea space also. As per Section 2 of that act, conveyance includes vessel also. Under Section 28, Indian Customs Water means waters extending into the sea upto the outer limit of the contiguous zone of India. Provision of 33 (1) dealing with contiguous zone in UNCLOS-III is unclear. It says that the coastal state 'may exercise the control necessary to prevent infringement of the customs, fiscal, immigration or sanitary laws and regulations "within its territory or territorial sea". But, not only India's Customs Act but also MZI Act, 1976, Section 5, Sub-section 4 (a) dealing with contiguous zone, clearly gives Government of India full jurisdiction in these matters over the entire contiguous zone extending upto a maximum distance of 24 n. miles from the base line. Contiguous zone includes any bay, gulf, harbour, creek or tidal river. Thus, Customs Act allows the enforcement agency to exercise jurisdiction in this field in the waters extending from any part along the shore upto the maximum distance of 24 n. miles from the baseline, under the Customs Act, 1962, MZI Act, 1976 as also UNCLOS-III.

Sections 39 and 111-119 of the Customs Act define crimes that constitute smuggling. Though smuggling activities fall under those of NSA, it should not be forgotten, at least in the case of India, that terrorist-related material as also men are often brought to the Indian coasts by smugglers. Thus, smuggling and maritime terrorism are closely interrelated. One wonders if India's Customs Act has not taken this aspect of the nexus between terrorism and smuggling into account and expanded its related operational framework. The Customs Act also needs to be analysed along with the provisions of the Marine Wing of Customs and also the Coast Guard Act, 1978 which defines the duties of the Coast Guard in that context. This aspect will be dealt with in details in Chapter V that deals with maritime enforcement agencies of India.

Not only NSA but also terrorists depend upon illegal transfer of funds for their criminal activities. After 9/11, Security Council in its Resolution 1373 of September 28, 2001, had urged Member States to enact laws to give effect to that resolution. Indian Government had, much before that, passed enactments so as to curb the linkage between foreign exchange and smuggling. It passed the Conservation of Foreign Exchange and Prevention of Smuggling Activities Act in 1974 (Manohar and Chitley, *AIR Manual* vol. 45, 1988, p. 584). CFEPSA has been updated and amended several times. Though it primarily aims at containing the criminal activities of NSA, it can also become an important tool in containing acts of maritime terrorism. The Anti-Money Laundering Act of 2008, that amended the earlier Act of 2002, also strengthened the hands of enforcement agencies in monitoring and checking the flow of money to the terrorists.

Maritime Zones of India (MZI) Act, 1976

Indian Parliament passed the Territorial Waters, Continental-shelf, Exclusive Economic Zone and Other Maritime Zones Act (Act No. 80 of May 28, 1976). It came into force in August 1976. The full text was published in *The Gazette* of India Extraordinary, Part II, Section 1, No. 121 of August 26, 1976. (Manohar and Chitaley, vol. 43, 1988, pp. 591-97). Section 5 dealing with contiguous zone and Section 7 dealing with EEZ became operational since January 15, 1977, following the notification in the Extraordinary Gazette of India [GSR 16 (E)]. The Ministry of External Affairs is the nodal ministry for the Act.

As analysed in Chapter I, Maritime Zones of India Act of 1976 had defined various maritime frontiers of India in its adjacent sea space. The Act also defines India's jurisdiction over the economic resources. The 'high seas' as defined under Article 86 of UNCLOS-III (beyond outer limits of EEZ) does not come under the purview of this Act. Since MZI Act was passed in 1976, long before UNCLOS-III was approved in 1982, it differs in some crucial 'security related' issues from the provisions of UNCLOS-III. India ratified UNCLOS-III in 1995 but did not amend MZI Act of 1976 in the light of provisions of UNCLOS-III. It has also not passed an act giving legal validity to UNCLOS-III.

Some Indian legal experts have argued that since provisions of MZI Act 1976 of India were not incorporated in UNCLOS-III "there was an obligation to modify these provisions after India formally ratified the Convention (Sharma, 2005, p. 379). While the point made by the expert has merit, it also needs to be noted that UNCLOS-III was approved in 1982 when terrorism was already an emerging threat to national and international peace and security. But, it had failed to make any provision in the context of this security-related challenge posed by NSA and terrorists. Thus, it had already become out-dated in that context when it was signed in 1982. The other point worth noting is the supremacy of national laws and provisions of the Constitution, *vis-à-vis* international conventions, under Indian legal and judicial system.

Attempt will be made to analyse sections of MZI Act, 1976 to see if that act provides not only for maritime security but also for instituting criminal action against NSA and terrorists in various maritime zones like territorial sea, contiguous zone, continental-shelf and EEZ and how they compare and contrast with various articles of UNCLOS-III and other conventions like SUA Convention, 1988. Section 4 (1) of MZI Act provides for freedom of navigation in its territorial waters to all foreign ships. It, however, says that this right of innocent passage is not fully applicable to foreign warships and submarines. Under Section 4 (2), they may enter or pass through the territorial waters after giving prior notice to the Central Government. In that case, submarines shall also navigate on the surface and show their flag. This contrasts with Article 17 of UNCLOS-III which makes no difference between warships and other vessels. Article 20 of UNCLOS-III, however, stipulates that submarines navigating in the territorial sea are required to navigate on the surface and show their flag.

As per Section 4 (1) of MZI Act (in the explanation), passage is innocent so long as it is not prejudiced to the peace, good order and security of India. While this explanation is similar to Article 19 (1) of UNCLOS-III, Article 19 (2) of UNCLOS-III lists 12 reasons when it is not deemed to be innocent. It provides a fairly wide coverage even of undesirable activities of NSA and terrorists.

Innocent passage through the territorial waters of another state in times of non-hostility is a time honoured concept. That facility (or right?) is essential for promoting maritime trade among states. No one will seriously object to it as long as foreign flag vessels follow rules and regulations of the coastal states which are often designed to ensure a safe passage through waters which are normally crowded with various types of vessels. New developments like the ISPS Code have also supported this arrangement. There is no reason why a vessel should deliberately deviate from its intended path so as to pass through the territorial waters of another state unless there are compelling reasons. If it does so the action is bound to raise doubts about its intentions. This applies to warships as well. Visits of foreign warships are often a formal affair for which preparations are made well in advance. There is no reason why eyebrows should be raised by legal experts while reading Section 4 (2) of MZI Act, 1976.

Section 5 of MZI Act deals with India's contiguous zone. Its sub-section 4 (a) empowers the Central Government to take measures in relation to the *security* of India. Sub-section 4 (b) empowers the government to take measures in relation to immigration, sanitation, customs and other fiscal matters.

Section 5, Sub-section 4 (a) has been criticised by some as going beyond the provisions of UNCLOS-III. In fact, it will be more appropriate to say that those who had negotiated the final text of UNCLOS-III had, for various reasons, ignored the security considerations of the coastal states when they approved the final text of UNCLOS-III in 1982, six years after Indian Parliament had passed the MZI Act. Every country has a right to define its security zone. Probably, a misinterpretation of Section 5, Subsection 4 (a) led one scholar to conclude that India had stipulated 24 n. miles as a 'military warning zone' (Valencia, 1997, p. 275). No such zone has been established so far. However, no one can prevent India from creating such a zone which is also co-terminous with its contiguous zone. MZI Act, under section 5, Sub-section 2, even allows for altering, through notification in the *Official Gazette*, the limit of the contiguous zone. It may do so especially in the context of Section 5, Subsection 4 (a), in future in the light of its new approach to the question of maritime threat to homeland security posed by terrorists. Critics also fail to differentiate between the concept of 'defence' *vis-à-vis* other state actors and 'security' in the context of NSA and terrorists.

In the Statement of Objects and Reasons, appended to the MZI Act, 1976, the powers asserted in and in relation to the contiguous zone have been characterised as 'jurisdiction' in matters related to the security of India, immigration, sanitation, customs and other fiscal matters. Any enactment (made in that context) extended to the contiguous zone shall have effect as if the zone was a part of the territory of India. In short, according to P. Chandrashekhar Rao, the contiguous zone will be deemed to be part of the territory of India for purposes of the enforcement of the relevant Indian laws" (Rao, 1983, p. 298). Rao also added that till 1983, no Indian enactment had been extended to cover the contiguous zone, except by implication, the Coast Guard Act, 1978. One wonders if there is any enactment that clearly spells out contiguous zone as India's 'security' zone as per Section 5, Sub-section 4 (a) of MZI Act. If not, it is high time that it be done speedily.

According to O.P. Sharma, India did not mention 'security' as one of the purposes for which a contiguous zone was being claimed either in the general statement made by the leaders of the Indian Delegation at the Caracas Conference or in the formal proposal sponsored along with 13 other states (Sharma, 2005, 376). P. Chandrasekhar Rao had raised a very pertinent point in that context. According to him, "It can scarcely be contemplated that a State must remain passive while acts prejudicial to its security are mounted just across its territorial sea (Rao, 1983, p. 334). Not only India but other states of South Asia have also inserted 'security' related sections under contiguous zones in their respective maritime zones act. It is mentioned under Section 4 (2a) of Territorial Waters and Maritime Zones Act, 1974 of Bangladesh, Section 4 (1a) of the Maritime Zones Law No. 22 of 1976 of Sri Lanka, Section 4 of the Territorial Waters and Maritime Zone Act of 1976 of Pakistan and Territorial Sea and Maritime Zones Law of 1977 of Burma (Myanmar), (*Regional compendium of Fisheries Legislation; Indian Ocean Region, Legislation Study No. 42, vol. 1*, F.A.O., Rome 1987).

Article 33 (1a) of UNCLOS-III, unlike Section 5, Subsection 4 (b) of MZI Act, lacks precision. As per the MZI Act, the Central Government may exercise such powers and take such measures *in* or in relation to the contiguous zone as it may consider necessary with respect to immigration, sanitation, customs and other fiscal matters. By contrast, under Article 33 (1a) of UNCLOS-III, the coastal state *may* exercise the control necessary to prevent infringement of its customs, fiscal, immigration or sanitary laws and regulations 'within its territory or territorial sea'. While UNCLOS-III has created a grey area in its interpretation of rights of a coastal state in its contiguous zone, there is no such confusion under MZI Act, 1976.

Sea space beyond territorial waters is considered to be the high seas in which all states are supposed to exercise freedom of the high seas. However, under UNCLOS-III as also MZI Act, India is entitled to a degree of *sovereign jurisdiction* in the sea space that is covered under the EEZ, which till now is also the outer limit of India's continental-shelf. India has the right to impose its jurisdiction as far as exploration and exploitation of living and non-living resources in this sea space, adjacent to its coast, is concerned.

It will be useful to examine the extent of a coastal state's jurisdiction especially in the context of provisions against criminal activities of NSA and terrorists in the context of continental-shelf and the EEZ. While UNCLOS-III discusses them separately, MZI Act of 1976 discusses them together in Sections 6 and 7.

India's jurisdiction in its continental-shelf has been provided under Section 6, Subsection 3 and Section 7, Subsection 4. The Central Government has the 'sovereign rights' for the purposes of exploration, exploitation, conservation and management of all resources, as also 'exclusive rights and jurisdiction' for the construction, maintenance or operation of off-shore platforms. This right has been duplicated under Article 77 (1) of UNCLOS-III. Section 6, Sub-section 5 (b) as alsoSection 7 Sub-section 4 and 6 authorises the Central Government to make provisions in respect to the exploration, exploitation and protection of the resources as well as the safety and protection of off-shore installations in the designated area in the continental-shelf. Explanations accompanying section 6 (5) and section 7

(6) add that the state through notification may provide for the regulation of entry into and passage through the designated area of foreign ships by the establishment of fairways, sea lanes, traffic separation schemes or any other mode of "ensuring freedom of navigation which is not prejudicial to the interest of India." This provision under MZI Act is constrained by Article 60 (7) of the UNCLOS-III. Under it, the state may not construct artificial installations in areas where interference may be caused to the use of recognised sea lanes essential to international navigation.

UNCLOS-III does recognise the right of the coastal state to ensure 'safety' of these off-shore installations under Article 60 (4 and 5). Normally safety zones around these installations are not to exceed 500 metres "except as authorised by generally accepted international standards or as recommended by the competent international organisations." A very vague formulation indeed. According to Vice-Admiral G.M. Hiranandani, India had argued that considering the size and speed of modern tankers and the time taken to stop or divert such huge vessels, a 500-metre safety zone was inadequate. According to him, India's concern was partly met under Article 60 (5) as noted before (Hiranandani, 2003, p.196). UNCLOS-III, while determining these 'safety' zones had taken into account the possibility of navigational error which can be avoided if traffic lanes are designated in the zone.

But, does this 500-metre safety zone protect the high value targets from acts of terrorism? Even a fishing trawler with a speed of 10 knots per hour can cover that distance in less than two minutes, hardly the time to take effective countermeasures unless they are mounted on the installation itself. These safety zones, however, inadequate they might be, as well as traffic separation scheme and designated sea lanes in these specific areas, under MZI Act as also provisions of UNCLOS-III, extend India's criminal jurisdiction and security-related concerns well beyond its territorial waters into what is part of the high seas. Has India passed laws appropriate for the security of its high value targets, located on the high seas?

MZI Act of 1976 needs to be looked at more carefully to find if it has provisions that can help strengthen the security/protection of the structures there. Section 5, Sub-section 5 (a) mentions that the Central Government may declare any area of the continental-shelf and its super adjacent waters to be a 'designated area' for exploitation. Section 5, Sub-section 5 (bii) empowers the Central Government to make such provisions as it may deem necessary with respect to the *"safety* and *protection"* of off-shore islands, terminals etc in such designated areas. It is important to underline the fact that unlike Article 60 (paras 4 and 5) of UNCLOS-III that refers only to 'safety' zone in the continental-shelf, MZI Act under section 5, sub-section 5(bii), includes not only safety but also protection of the structures constructed on the continental-shelf. The explanation accompanying that section also says that the state may provide for the 'regulation of entry into the passage through the designated area for foreign ships by the establishment of fairways, sea lanes, traffic separation scheme or any other mode of ensuring freedom of navigation "which is not prejudicial to the interest of India". Thus, that act, while complying with the norms of freedom of the high seas, also provides the framework for ensuing safety and protection (security) of these off-shore installations.

One needs to know if enactments like IPC/CrPC and UAPA have been formally extended to cover off-shore platforms on the continental-shelf as well or their application is restricted to territorial waters only. The SUA Act, 2002, however, has that provision. Under Section 1, Sub-section 2, the Act extends to the whole of India, including the limit of the territorial water, the continental-shelf, the EEZ or any other maritime zone (i.e. contiguous zone also as per Section 2 of MZI Act 1976). Section 1 (3c) specifically refers to fixed platforms on the continental-shelf. Offences are listed under Section 3.

MZI Act, in Sections 6 and 7, combined features dealing with the continental-shelf and the EEZ. Section 7, Sub section 4(a) of that act gives India the 'sovereign rights' for exploiting living resources in its EEZ. Subsection 4 (d) gives India exclusive jurisdiction to preserve and protect the marine environment and to prevent and control marine pollution. Under Sub-section 5, Indian citizens are free to fish unhindered in Indian EEZ but not foreigners. As will be analysed subsequently, fishing by foreign vessels was regulated by the Maritime Zones of India (Regulation of Fishing by Foreign Vessel) Act of 1981. There were no norms for regulating fishing by Indian fishermen in EEZ. An attempt is being made to correct it. The draft of Marine Fisheries (Regulation and Management) Bill, 2009, had provisions that sought to regulate fishing by Indian fishermen in these waters. The draft bill was opposed by the fishermen of the coastal states of India since it was seen as encroaching upon the traditional rights of these fishermen. Article 73 of UNCLOS-III not only collaborates sections 6 and 7 of MZI Act but also allows for enforcement action by the coastal state for violation of its laws, dealing with EEZ. That includes boarding, inspection, arrest and judicial proceedings.

Though MZI Act 1976 does not mention it specifically in relation to EEZ, but section 11 provides for imprisonment upto a maximum of three years, or a fine, or both, for those who contravene any provision of that act. Under section 15 sub-section 3(c), the Central Government had to make rules for implementing the provisions of that act, concerning the EEZ. Government of India enacted the Maritime Zones of India (Regulation of Fishing by Foreign Vessels) Act, 1981 to give effect to that provision. The Coast Guard, under Section 14, Sub section 2 (e) of the Coast Guard Act, 1978, is entrusted with the task of enforcing provisions, related to EEZ under MZI Act, 1976 as also MZI (Regulation of Fishing by Foreign Vessels) Act, 1981. Since both these acts predated UNCLOS-III, 1982, their provisions do differ, especially on issues of trial and punishment.

Article 73 of UNCLOS-III sets different norms. Under Article 73 (2), arrested vessels and their crews shall be promptly released upon the posting of 'reasonable' bonds or other security. Article 73 (3) stipulates that coastal state's penalties for violation of fisheries laws and regulations in the EEZ "may not include imprisonment in the absence of agreements to the contrary, by the states concerned etc.

To regulate fishing by foreign vessels in India's EEZ, Government of India passed Maritime Zones of India (Regulation of Fishing by Foreign Vessel) Act, 1981 (Act No. 42 of 1981). That Act came into force on November 2, 1981. It provides for issuing of licence to foreign fishing vessels, under stipulated conditions, to fish in India's EEZ. Reflecting the involvement of diverse ministries in India's maritime affairs, this bill was piloted in the Parliament by the Ministry of Agriculture since fishing in EEZ comes under the jurisdiction of that ministry; yet another illustration of the so-called continental mindset of Indian bureaucracy and law makers. (For the text of the Act see Manohar and Chitaley, vol. 33, 1988, pp. 800-803).

The act not only provides the framework for obtaining the licence for fishing in Indian waters but also stipulates conditions when it is violated. It also entrusts enforcement agencies responsible for prevention of violation of this act, with necessary powers, as also gives details of the method of enforcement and penalties for those who violate the provisions of that act. Under Section 7 and Section 22 (3) of the act, a foreign fishing vessel, not having the licence to fish in India's EEZ, is deemed to have violated the act if it is found within any maritime zone of India and if its fishing gear is not stowed in the prescribed manner or if fish is found on board such vessel. It shall be presumed, unless the contrary is proved, that the said vessel was fishing within that zone.

Chapter III of the act deals with powers of search and seizure. Under section 9 (1), any officer of the Coast Guard or such other officer of Government, as may be authorised by the Central Government, is authorised for the purposes of ascertaining whether the act is being violated or not. The person who authorises can, even without a warrant:

(a) Stop or board a foreign vessel in any maritime zone of India and search such vessels for fish and for equipment used or capable of being used for fishing;

(b) To require the master of such vessel to produce any licence, permit, log book etc and examine those documents as also any catch, fishing gear or other equipment etc. Section 9 (2) empowers that officer, if the vessel had violated provisions of the said act, to seize and detain such a vessel including its cargo, required the master of the vessel to take the vessel to specified port and arrest those who had committed the offence. Chapter IV, Section 10, has provisions for trial and punishment for the violation of the act. Violations in the territorial waters of India are punishable with imprisonment of a term not exceeding three years or with fines not exceeding rupees fifteen lakhs or with both. In case where such contravention takes place in any area in EEZ (beyond the territorial waters limit) the person can be fined to a maximum of Rupees ten lakhs. Section 23 of the act provides a legal cover to the enforcement agency. Under section 23(1), no suit, prosecution or other legal proceeding shall lie against any person for anything which is in good faith done or intended to be done in pursuance of the provisions of this Act. Section 23 (2) offers similar cover to the Government. Thus, Section 23 of the Act provides a legal cover that protected them in the context of Article 106 of UNCLOS-III (liability for seizure without adequate ground). It needs to be noted this act of 1981 pre-dated UNCLOS-III of 1982.

A draft of Marine Fisheries (Regulation and Management) Bill was introduced in 2009 for discussion. This draft bill sought to regulate marine fishing in Indian waters, including territorial waters. If and when approved, it will override/replace/amend some of the provisions of the MZI Act 1976 as also MZI (Regulation of Fishing by Foreign Vessels), 1981. The draft bill defines Indian vessels as vessels that have a 51 per cent share capital held by Indians. It also says that not only ownership but also control of operations should also be the consideration. The draft bill under Section 4, Sub-section 4.1, said that all fishing vessels fishing in territorial waters and beyond it will have to obtain fishing permits.

Fishing is segmented as per the size of vessels. All vessels below 20 metre and Indian owned would have preferable access to the EEZ, along with categories of vessels registered under states but habitually fishing in territorial waters and adjacent EEZ for shark, tune(tuna) etc. Vessels below 20 metres are recommended to be brought under the fisheries department of coastal states but will be subject to obligations under Fisheries Act, 2009. Permits would be issued by Central Government but through the state's administration.

The act noted that Indian vessels above 20 metres and foreign vessels of any size should be seen in a different context. It is said that larger vessels should be given permission to operate in EEZ only after progressively exhausting the fishing opportunities to those below 20 metres. Such an approach is likely to hinder India, developing a fishing fleet of larger size that can help India exploit fishing in deep waters even in its own EEZ. leave aside sea space beyond it. One wonders how such a narrow focus on fishery can prepare India to compete in the years to come, even with Asian fishing states like Korea, Japan, Taiwan etc, leave aside European states who have virtually monopolised the offshore and deep sea fishing in the Indian Ocean region (Biswas, 2009, pp. 129-43).

The draft Fisheries Bill, 2009, introduces a concept of allowing neighbouring maritime states to have access to fishing in adjacent Indian EEZ. That step was sought to be rationalised under Article 24 (b) of 1995 UN Fish Stock Agreement that recognised the need for access to fishing by small-scale and artisanal fishermen as well as indigeneous people in developing states. Under section 20 of the draft bill, artisanal and small-scale fishers and fishing vessels from neighbouring countries would be preferentially considered before extending fishing opportunities to larger vessels even of Indian origin. It is suggested that they be granted right to fish in specified areas of Indian EEZ, adjacent to maritime boundaries on the basis of reciprocity *or* long and mutually recognised usage. Can the Wedge Bank in the Gulf of Manar or the Andaman Sea be considered as such areas? This arrangement will be based upon bilateral negotiations. This privilege to fish in Indian EEZ cannot be passed on to a third party.

The draft bill also has provisions on penalty and punishment for violation of the provisions of this bill. Punishment for foreign as also Indian fishermen for violating the act is the same. It can be maximum imprisonment upto three years. While MZI Act 1976 and MZI (Fisheries) Act 1981 has provisions for foreigners, Indians are left out. Thus, this provision also adversely affects the interests of Indian fishermen as also violates provisions of MZI Act, 1976. No wonder, the draft bill has attracted criticism from almost all sections of Indian fishermen as also from some states like Kerala that have seen it as an infringement of the exclusive rights of the coastal state to regulate fishing in territorial waters. This bill, though well intentioned, also poses problems of maritime security in the context of terrorism, because it provides means to the terrorists to employ fishing boats of neighbouring states to operate in Indian EEZ and sea space almost adjacent to the sea coast along the outer limit of the territorial waters.

Acts Targeting Terrorism

India has passed several laws that enable enforcement agencies to target those who indulge in acts of terrorism. As noted, events of 9/11 gave a new thrust to India's own war on terror. But, acts were passed even before that. These acts can be analysed under three broad categories. Acts that enable enforcement agencies to target terrorists though they were not meant to be terrorist-specific when they were enacted. They include Explosive Substances Act, the Customs Act, Passport Act, the MZI Act, the Navy Act, the Coast Guard Act etc. The second category of acts are those that are based primarily upon a state's own perception of the threat and are terrorism-specific. They included Prevention Detention Act, 1950, Unlawful Activities (Prevention) Act (UAPA), National Security Act, 1980, TADA 1987; POTA 2002 etc. The third category of acts are those that were enacted so as to give domestic legitimacy to several international conventions on terrorism to which India was a party. They include the SAARC Convention Act of 1993 and its Additional Protocol in 2004, SUA Act, 2002 and WMD Act, 2005. Some of these are specific to maritime terrorism.

At least three sections of the MZI Act, 1976 are terrorism-specific since they emphasise the aspect of maritime security/protection. These words are often seen by some experts as contrary to the ethos of UNCLOS-III. But it must be noted that 'security' is not 'defence' *vis-à-vis* other state actors. Security has a wider scope in the context of the coastal state and also includes social, economic and political facts. Now, terrorism is recognised as an intrinsic part of threat to national security. As examined, MZI Act, 1967, in Section 4 Sub-section 1(a) and its explanation, while dealing with the question of innocent passage through the territorial waters, emphasises security of India as a major variable, determining the right of innocent passage. Section 5, Subsection 4(a) deals with 'security of India' in India's contiguous zone. Section 6 Sub-section 5 (bii) and the related explanations deal with safety and protection of off-shore platforms in India's continental-shelf. While these sections enable India to take appropriate measures, those measures and related laws are as yet not clearly spelled out, thereby leaving a legal grey area that can be exploited by a defence lawyer. This theme will be discussed in greater details when examining SUA Act 2002 and WMD Act 2005.

The Navy Act, 1957

The Navy Act of 1957 in often quoted in the context of piracy. But, if one reads the full text of Section 3 (7) of Chapter I of the Navy Act, the definition of the term 'enemy' reads as follows, "enemy includes all armed rebels, armed mutineers, armed rioters and pirates, *and any person in arms against whom it is the duty of any person subject to naval law to act"*. (Manohar and Chitaley, vol. 36, 1988, p. 8). That section not only empowers the Indian Navy to act against the pirates but also against all those elements on the high seas that are deemed as enemies of mankind, i.e. any person in arms against whom it is the duty of any person, subject to naval laws, to act. That would include the hijackers as well as maritime terrorists.

Enforcement measures taken by the Navy on the high seas against such elements (other than pirates) are also strengthened by the provision in the Indian Constitution. Item 21 of List I (Union List) of the Seventh Schedule of the Indian Constitution gives the Union Government and by implication, the Navy, jurisdiction over "piracy and crimes committed on the high seas or in the air; offences against the law of nations committed on land or the high seas or in the air." Terrorism is now accepted as a crime under the new *de facto* international law that is emerging after 9/11. Thus, the Navy Act of 1957 as well as Item 21 of List I of the Seventh Schedule of the Indian Constitution offers adequate legal basis for action taken against non-flag vessels operating against shipping in the western part of the Indian Ocean.

Unlike the Navy Act, 1957, the Coast Guard Act of 1978 does not include specific reference either to piracy or acts of terrorism. The main reason for it is that the Coast Guard was formed primarily in the context of enforcement of provisions of MZI Act, 1976. Hence, the Coast Guard Act does include provisions dealing with safety/protection, primarily in the context of NSA, like those indulging in illegal fishing in Indian waters or indulging in smuggling (contiguous zone). It is also entrusted under Chapter II, Section 4 with the task of ensuring the *'security'* of the maritime zones of India, with a view to the protection of maritime and other *national interests* in such zones. The word 'security', however, does not figure in Chapter III that defines duties and functions of the Coast Guard, though the second half of section 4 of Part II is retained in Section 14 (1). There are also references to safety and protection in Section 14 (2a) that deals with the safety and protection of offshore installations in the continental-shelf. Section 12 (2e) however, provides it with an open-ended role by saying that its duty is "enforcing the provisions of such enactments as are for the time being in force in the maritime zones". As noted earlier, provisions of IPC and CrPC as also other acts are expected to cover the EEZ of India.

Chapter XII, Section 121, while defining powers and duties conferrable and imposable on members of the Coast Guard under Sub-section 1(i) lists various Acts of Government of India under which the Coast Guard can take action. It is surprising that the Unlawful Activities (Prevention) Act (UAPA), that is often quoted in the context of acts of terrorism, was not specifically listed there though it was enacted in 1967. However, that Sub-section does mention that the Coast Guard can act under 'any cognizable offences punishable under any other Central Act".

Acts specific to Terrorism

Government of India was shy of using the term 'terrorism'. Hence, though UAPA, 1967 had provisions against acts of terrorism, its title, Unlawful Activities (Prevention) Act (UAPA), did not mention that word. UAPA will be analysed in depth in subsequent pages. However, Government of India had passed and subsequently repealed several acts that touched upon acts of terrorism. Some of them specifically mentioned terrorism. The Prevention Detention Act, 1950, authorised only for 'preventive' detention in the context of defence of India, adverse impact upon relations with foreign powers and 'security' of India. It also did not specifically mention threats posed *via* the sea space. National Security Act, 1980, (Act No. 65 of 1980, December 27, 1980) almost duplicated the Prevention Detention Act, 1950. Preventive detention under that act could extend upto a period of 12 months (MHA, *A.R., 1993-94*, p. 13).

The Terrorist and Disruptive Activities Act (TADA), 1987 was probably the first act passed by the Indian Parliament that specifically mentioned terrorist activities *per se*. Section 2 of the act not only targeted terrorists but also those who abetted, helped, assisted them or offered them financial assistance. Part II, Section 3(1) described terrorists and disruptive activities as an attempt to overawe the government or to strike terror in the hearts of the people or sections of the people or to alienate a section of the people by the use of bombs, dynamites, or other explosive devices or inflammable substance or firearm or poison, noxious gas etc. Section 28 empowered the enforcement authorities to enter into and search any vehicle, vessel, or aircrafts in any place and seize and detain persons involved in these activities. It is important to note that TADA, 1987, not only specifically identified terrorism as a threat but also authorised the enforcement agencies 'to enter any *vessel*' and detain the persons suspected of being involved in these activities. It must be remembered that this aspect of maritime terrorism was incorporated in an Indian Act even before the SUA Convention of 1988.

TADA was replaced by POTA 2002. The Prevention of Terrorism Act (POTA) replaced the Prevention of Terrorism Ordinance (POTO) of 2001. The bill was passed by a joint session of the Parliament under Article 108 of the Indian Constitution. It got the assent of the President on March 28, 2002. It was a controversial act and was repealed by an Act of the Parliament in September 2004. Like the TADA, it also provided for prevention of terrorist related act including funding. It was partly in response to the Security Council Resolutions 1368 and 1373 of September 2001, under which all UN Members were obliged to take steps to curb terrorist activities and related issues of funding.

Under Section 3 (2), POTA, 2002, provided for stringent punishment for the crimes related to terrorism. It recommended life imprisonment, even death, as also fines if the act led to the loss of life. In any other case, the punishment could be imprisonment from five years to life term as also fine. Others who had helped in that process were also accorded similar punishment. Section 4 mentioned that if any person was found to be in unauthorised possession of arms or ammunition (Arms Rule, 1962) in any area specifically notified by the state in that context (or of bombs or other hazardous explosive substance) he shall be guilty of terrorist act and could be punished with term upto life imprisonment and/or fine. This concept of presumed to be guilty till proved otherwise went against the general ethos of legal systems in India till then. Legal experts like Fali S. Nariman criticised it (Nariman, 2002.). The major concern was that provisions of that act could be/would be misused by state authorities. TADA and POTA, while focussing upon acts of terrorism, had tried to facilitate the work of the enforcement authorities by going beyond the normal framework of Law of Evidence and Criminal Procedure Code, while dealing with these cases. Hence, they were often criticised by human rights activists who argued that they would be used for political ends (Mani, 2002).

While TADA and POTA have been replaced, largely for political reasons, the Unlawful Activities (Prevention) Act (UAPA), 1967, has not only survived but has been amended after the events of 26/11 in Mumbai to give it more powers. Unlike TADA and POTA, even amended UAPA does not mention the term 'terrorism' in its title, though it has now become the basis for handling most of those issues. Though it does not use the term 'terrorism' *per se*, acts of violence mentioned in Section 15 of UAPA does list what can be described as acts of terrorism.

The Unlawful Activities (Prevention) Act (UAPA), 1967 came into force on November 30, 1967. Though the title of the Act does not mention the term 'terrorism', Section 2, Sub-section 1, para k, mentions that terrorism has the meaning attached to it, in Section 15 which defines acts of terrorism. According to that section whoever, with intent to threaten the unity, integrity, security or sovereignty of India or to *strike terror* in the people or any section of the people in India, or in any foreign country, does any act by using bombs, dynamite or other explosive substances or inflammable substances or firearms or other lethal weapons or poison or noxious gases or other chemicals or by any other substance (whether biological or otherwise) of a hazardous nature, in such a manner as to cause, or likely to cause, death or injuries to any person or persons or loss of or damage to or destruction of property or disruption of any supplies or services essential to the life of the community in India or in any foreign country or causes damage or destruction of any property or equipment used or intended to be used for the defence of India or in connection with any other purposes of the Government of India, any State Government or any of their agencies, or details any person or threatens to kill or injure such persons in order to compel the Government of India or the Government of a foreign country or any other person to do so or abstain from doing any act, commits a terrorist act.

Section 16 prescribes punishment for such acts. If the act results in the death of any person, the punishment can be life imprisonment or even death or fine. In any other case, the punishment can range from imprisonment for a minimum period of five years and to a maximum of life imprisonment as also fine. Under Section 17, whoever raises funds for that act shall be punished with imprisonment ranging from five years to life imprisonment and fine. Sections 18-23 deal with details of punishment for crimes associated with acts of terrorism. Section 35 mentions that the Government should identify terrorist organisations. The Annual Report, 2007-08, of the Ministry of Home Affairs, in Annexure –VI lists such organisations. The list includes not only Indian but also foreign organisations.

After the repeal of POTA, in 2004 and the rise in acts of terrorism in India, there was a demand for a new act to tackle the threat posed by terrorism. But the government succumbed to the criticism that a stronger law would be misused for political purposes against the opposition as also the minority community. However, the events of 26/11, when Mumbai was targeted by foreign terrorists, raised a public outcry which, in a way, paved the ground for amending the UAPA, 1967, so as to provide it with sharper teeth. The amended UAPA was introduced in the Parliament in December 2008 and was quickly passed. It also received the assent of the President by the end of December 2008. It was a legal response to 26/11 in India.

The amended UAPA incorporated several points of the TADA and POTA that had been repealed earlier. Under TADA and POTA, confession before the police was valid. That was not incorporated in the amended UAPA. However, the Maharashtra Control of Organised Crime Act (MCOCA) has that provision. The amended UAPA incorporates several provisions that were similar to those that were repealed earlier. The new definition of terror includes attack on public functionaries. The amended act has increased the period for which the accused can be held under police custody from 15 to 30 days. Also the suspect can be held without charge for 180 days instead of 90 days. This applies only the Indians. Foreigners can be held for a period till they are proved innocent. The procedure for granting of bail by the court is also made more tough with the judge given limited choice for granting bail. The Court can reject the bail if it is satisfied that the allegations are *prima facia* true. The act also incorporates provisions of presumption of guilt till proven innocent.

The amended act also enhances punishment for those associated with acts of terrorism. Those using explosives, fire arms, lethal weapons, poisonous chemicals, biological or radiological weapons even with the intention of aiding, abetting or committing terror acts shall be punishable with imprisonment upto a maximum period of 10 years. Any one in India or in a foreign country, who directly or indirectly raises or collects funds or provides funds for a terrorist act, shall be punishable with imprisonment extending from five years to life term. There is also the provision for freezing, seizing and attaching funds held by individuals or entities engaged in or suspected to be engaged in acts of terrorism. In that case, the credit or debit cards so seized can be used as evidence. In response to the resolutions of the UN Security Council of September 2001, dealing with terrorism, the amended act has a provision under which all those terrorist outfits that have been listed by the UN, as terrorist organisations, shall be banned in India as well. This is over and above the terrorist organisations that have been banned by the Government of India.

Despite the new clauses that have been introduced in the amended UAPA, many legal experts are still not satisfied. The then Chief Justice of India, K.G. Balakrishnan, on the eve of his retirement, while commenting upon the acquittals in the cases of 26/11 Mumbai terror attacks, said that more stringent laws were needed to sufficiently enable probe agencies to crack complex terror cases, especially when conspiracies are hatched in foreign lands and evidence collecting is tough. (Mahapatra, 2010). Another fact that needs to be underlined is that these acts focus more on prosecution of persons arrested. Few of its sections help in the preemption of terrorist acts. While it is relatively difficult to preempt terrorists from launching their attacks on land, it is relatively easier to interdict and preempt them in adjacent water spaces comprising of multiple maritime security zones. Also, despite the fact that the amended UAPA was the result of terrorist attacks on Mumbai, there is hardly any reference on combating maritime dimensions of terrorism.

Acts passed to implement conventions and UN resolutions

The Parliament also passed laws so as to give effect to various international conventions as also UN resolutions which were ratified by it so as to provide the needed legal framework for their implementation in India. These include Suppression of Unlawful Acts Against Safety of Civil Aviation Act, 1972 in response to Montreal Convention of September 28, 1971 on that subject. India passed SAARC Convention (Suppression of Terrorism) Act, 1993 (Act No. 36 of 1993). That was in response to the SAARC Convention signed at Kathmandu on November 14, 1987 and ratified on August 22, 1988. (Text Manohar and Chitaley, vol. 41, 1988, pp. 529-30). That convention included acts of terrorism approved earlier under various international conventions like the Hague Convention of December 16, 1970 on unlawful seizure of aircrafts, Montreal Convention of September 13, 1971 on safety of civil aviation, Convention on Crimes Against Internationally Protected Persons, including diplomats signed in New York on December 14, 1973 etc. The SAARC Convention also listed other crimes like manslaughter, kidnapping, hostage taking and offences related to arms, weapons, explosives etc. It had also recommended various types of punishment for various offences. The SAARC Convention had to be put as an Act of the Parliament to give it legal validity.

After the events of 9/11, in pursuance of the Security Council Resolution 1373 of September 28, 2001 that, among other things, focussed upon restricting funds to terrorist organisations, SAARC signed an additional protocol to the SAARC Convention of 1988. It was approved on January 6, 2004 (Text of the Additional Protocol, *Strategic Digest*, 34(3), March 2004, 323-28). Though these are important conventions, they do not directly address the issue of maritime terrorism. That issue was the focus of SUA Convention, 1988 as also Security Council Resolution 1540 (2004) and UN Convention on WMD terrorism (2005). These have been discussed in details in Chapter III. In that context, Indian Parliament passed two bills; the SUA Bill, 2002 and WMD Bill, 2005.

The SUA Act, 2002

The SUA Act or The Suppression of Unlawful Acts Against Safety of Maritime Navigation and Fixed Platform on Continental-Shelf Bill, was passed as an Act of the Parliament (Act No. 69 of 2002) and came into force on December 20, 2002 after it was assented to by the President. In keeping with the Indian tradition of distributing issues of maritime affairs among different ministries, the Ministry of Shipping is the nodal agency for this act. Sri Vedprakash P. Goyal, while introducing the bill on July 10, 2002, said that it was in response to the Convention for the Suppression of Unlawful Acts Against the Safety of Maritime Navigation (SUA Convention) of 1988 and the accompanying Protocol for the Suppression of Unlawful Acts Against the Safety of Fixed Platforms located on the Continental-shelf, 1988.

India had already ratified both, the SUA Conventions as also the associated Protocol. Shri Goyal said that a separate legislation was considered necessary for the purpose of ensuring an effective and smooth implementation of the provisions of that Convention and the associated Protocol. Thus, India's SUA Act, 2002, combines the essence of the SUA Convention of 1988 as also associated Protocol on off-shore platforms. One wonders why India took twelve long years to pass an act that was specific to maritime terrorism.

SUA Act, 2002, as per Section 1 (2), extends to the whole of India, including the limit of its territorial waters, the continental-shelf, the exclusive economic zone of India within the meaning of Section 2 of the Territorial Waters, Continental-shelf, Exclusive Economic Zone and other Maritime Zones Act, 1976. Its effective jurisdiction is, however, limited under Section 1, Sub-section 3 (b) and (c) to ships in India's territorial waters and on fixed platforms in the continental-shelf. Interestingly, reference to fixed platforms in continental-shelf that is mentioned in Section 1 Sub-section 3 (c) is not listed under Section 3, Sub-section 4 (a) which refers to crimes committed. While it refers in Section 3 (4a ii) to ships in the territorial waters, there is no mention of fixed platforms in India's continental-shelf. This lacuna, if one does exist, needs to be corrected if any confusion in its implementation has to be avoided.

SUA Act combines the features of SUA Convention, 1988 and associated Protocol on fixed platforms on the continental-shelf. The SUA Act applies to acts of violence, committed in the context of off-shore platforms as well. SUA Act, 2002, lists offences that come under that Act.

Chapter II, Section 3, not only lists those offences but also prescribes punishment for those offences. Attempt will be made to list offences committed *vis-à-vis* a ship and *vis-à-vis* off-shore platforms, separately though they are grouped together in this act.

Acts of violence against ships

Section 3 (1):

(a) Act of violence against person on board a ship which is likely to endanger safe navigation. Prescribed punishment is imprisonment upto 10 years and fine.

(b) Destroys a ship or causes damage to a ship or cargo of the ship in a manner likely to endanger safe navigation of the ship. Punishment prescribed is imprisonment for life.

(c) Seizes or exercises control over a ship by force or threatens/ intimidates to do so. Prescribed punishment is imprisonment for life.

(d) Places or causes to be placed on a ship by any means whatsoever, a device or substance which is likely to destroy that ship or cause damage to the ship or its cargo, which endangers or is likely to endanger the safe navigation of that ship. Prescribed punishment is maximum imprisonment upto 14 years.

(e) Destroys or damages maritime navigation facilities or interferes with their operation if such an act is likely to endanger the safe navigation of a ship. The act prescribes punishment of imprisonment upto 14 years.

(f) Communicates information which is known to be false thereby endangers the safe navigation of a ship. For it, punishment is imprisonment upto 14 years and also a fine.

(g) In the course of commission, or in attempt to commit any of the offences specified in clauses (a) to (f);

    (i) causes death to any person; punishment is death;

    (ii) causes grievous hurt; punishment is imprisonment upto 14 years.

(iii) causes injury; punishment is imprisonment upto ten years;

(iv) seizes or threatens a person; punishment is imprisonment upto 10 years;

(v) threatens to endanger a ship; punishment is imprisonment upto 2 years.

Under Section 3 (2) of SUA Act, whoever attempts to commit or abet the commission of an offence, punishable under Section 3, Sub-section 1, shall be deemed to have committed such an offence and shall be punished with the punishment provided for such an offence. Under Sub-section 3, whoever unlawfully or intentionally threatens a person to compel that person to do or refrain from doing any act or to commit any offence specified in clause 1, (b) or (c) of Sub-section 1 and if such threat is likely to endanger the safe navigation of a ship, the person shall be punished with the punishment provided for such offences.

Acts of violence against fixed platform

Since these offences are listed alongside offences against a ship, they carry similar punishment. These offences are also listed under Section 3 of the act. As per Section 3, Sub-section 1, whoever unlawfully and intentionally:

(a) commits an act of violence against a person on board a fixed platform which is likely to endanger the safety of the fixed platform, the punishment is imprisonment upto 10 years and fine.

(b) destroys a fixed platform or causes damage to a fixed platform; punishment is imprisonment for life.

(c) seizes or exercises control over a fixed platform by force or intimidation; punishment is imprisonment for life.

(d) places or causes to be placed on a fixed platform, a device or substance that is likely to destroy that fixed platform or cause damages to it; punishment is imprisonment upto 14 years.

(e) in the course of commission of or in the attempt to commit any of the offences specified in clauses (a) to (d), in connection with the fixed platform:

(i)   causes death to any person, the punishment prescribed is death,

(ii)   causes grievous hurt to any person; punishment is imprisonment upto 14 years,

(iii) causes injury to any person; punishment is imprisonment upto 10 years,

(iv) seizes or threatens a person; punishment is imprisonment upto 10 years,

(vi) threatens to endanger a fixed platform; punishment is imprisonment upto 2 years.

(vii) Punishment prescribed in the case of offence against ship under Section 3 Subsection 2 as also Subsection 3 also applies in case of offences against fixed platform on the continental-shelf.

SUA Act, 2002, under Section 4, Sub-section 1, provides the mechanism for powers of arrest, investigation and prosecution by a police officer as also by any gazetted officer of the Coast Guard or any other gazetted officer of the Central Government as notified in the *Official Gazette* under the Criminal Procedure Code (CrPC). Under Sub-section 2, officers of police as also other officers of the Government are hereby required and empowered "to assist the officer of the Central Government referred to in Sub-section 1 of Section 4. Section 5 provides the mechanism for a speedy trial. Towards that end, the State Government shall, with the concurrence of the Chief Justice of the High Court, specify a court of session to be a Designated Court which shall, as far as practicable, hold the trial on a day-to-day basis. Under Section 8, no person accused of an offence punishable under this act shall, if in custody, be released on bail unless the court is satisfied that there are reasonable grounds for believing that he is not guilty of such offence and that he is not likely to commit any offence while on bail.

The Act provides for the presumption of guilt as to offences under section 3 (1). Under section 13, the Designated Court shall presume, unless the contrary is proved, that the accused had committed such offence under the following conditions:

(a) that the arms, ammunition or explosives were recovered from the possession of the accused and that there was reason to believe that such arms, ammunition or explosives of similar nature were used in the commission of such offence,

(b) that there is evidence of use of force, threat of force or any other form of intimidation caused in connection with the commissioning of such offence,

(c) that there is evidence of an *intended threat* of using bomb, fire arms, ammunition, or explosives or of committing any form of violence against the crew, passenger or cargo of a ship or fixed platform located on the continental-shelf of India.

As per the provision of Article 11 of the SUA Convention, 1988, SUA Act of 2002 also provides for extradition under Section 9. SUA Act of 2002 also provides legal protection to enforcement agencies *vis-à-vis* Article 106 and Article 110 (3) of UNCLOS-III dealing with liability for seizure without adequate grounds. Under Section 14 (1) of SUA Act, no suit, prosecution or other legal proceedings shall lie against any person for anything which is in good faith done or intended to be done in pursuance of the provisions of this act. Sub-section 2 protects the Government action in that context.

Though SUA Act of 2002 was passed in response to international obligation under Article 5 of SUA Convention, 1988, yet it must be realised that it is also probably the first comprehensive legislation that deals with two crucial aspects of maritime terrorism; those dealing with crime related to ships and those related to off-shore platforms. It will make it much easier for the enforcement agencies not only to implement the provisions of the act but for the judicial process to be completed as rapidly as possible. This act does not pronounce punishment that is greater than what is normally prescribed under amended UAPA or even TADA or POTA but the act defines very clearly the offences and their punishment. Though Section 1 (2) quotes MZI Act 1976, yet it retains the limitations of SUA Convention of 1988 and of UNCLOS-III in the context of ship-based offences by restricting action within the limits of India's territorial waters. That limitation is also reflected in India's WMD Act of 2005. The act also does not specify conditions under which maritime enforcement authorities can preempt the crime in India's multiple maritime security zones though Section 14 (1) does provide some protection *vis-à-vis* "wrongful seizure". But is that adequate?

WMD Act, 2005

Though there always were apprehensions that terrorists might employ WMD-related material in their criminal acts, that fear became the matter of prime concern after the events of 9/11. As noted in Chapter III, USA had been pushing for action in that context and had the support of Russia in that drive since Russia, along with several pro-US states had sponsored PSI in 2003. They had also pushed for the Security Council Resolution 1540 (2004) of April 28, 2004, dealing with non-proliferation of WMD and its delivery system. While the US-led coalition was pursuing its agenda, UN General Assembly had been debating the issue. It passed a resolution by consensus on April 13, 2005. The resolution subsequently became International Convention for the Suppression of Acts of Nuclear Terrorism. It was opened for signature from September 14, 2005. India ratified it in July 2006.

The Weapons of Mass Destruction and their Delivery Systems (Prohibition of Unlawful Activities) Act of India (WMD Act), 2005 was passed by the Parliament in May 2005. Thus, it was influenced by the mandatory Security Council Resolution 1540 (2004) as also by the General Assembly's resolution of nuclear terrorism of April 13, 2005. Security Council Resolution 1540 (2004) was passed under Chapter VII of UN Charter. Hence, it was mandatory on the part of Member-States to implement its provisions as per Article 2 of that resolution. That meant that States had to enact appropriate laws that would prohibit any NSA or terrorist from manufacturing, acquiring, possessing, developing, transporting, transfering or using nuclear, chemical or biological weapons and their means of delivery. The then Foreign Minister of India, Shri Natwar Singh, in his statement in Rajya Sabha on May 13, 2005, while introducing the bill, mentioned that point. But, a closer reading of India's WMD Act, 2005 reveals that it is nearer to the General Assembly's resolution on nuclear terrorism of April 13, 2005 than Resolution 1540 (2004) of the Security Council.

Security Council Resolution 1540 (2004) had targeted not only terrorists but also state actors. India, Pakistan and Malaysia (speaking on behalf of the NAM), had objected to State Parties being targeted under that resolution. Natwar Singh, in his statement in the Rajya Sabha on May 13, 2005, made India's official position, as a nuclear-weapon power, very clear while presenting that bill. (For the text of Natwar Singh's speech see Singh, 2006, pp. 214-16) India's position as nuclear weapon state and its relevance to the WMD Act, 2005 was also made specific in Section 3 Sub-section 5 of the Act which states that provisions of this act shall apply to export, transfer, re-transfer, transit and trans-shipment of material, equipment or technology of any description as are identified, designated, categorised or considered necessary by the Central Government, as pertinent or relevant to India as a Nuclear Weapon State, or to the national security of India, or to the furtherance of its foreign policy or its international obligations under any bilateral, multilateral or international treaty, covenant, convention or arrangement relating to weapons of mass destruction or their means of delivery, to which India is a Party.

As per Section 3 (1), it extends to the whole of India including its Exclusive Economic Zone. Under Section 3, Sub-section 2, every person shall be liable for punishment under this Act of which he is held guilty in India. Section 3, Sub-section 3 says that the act shall apply to a person who has committed offence even beyond India. Sub-section 4 says that the provision of the act shall apply to citizens of India in and outside India, companies or bodies corporate, registered or incorporated in India or having their associates, branches or subsidiaries outside India, any ship, aircrafts or any means of transport registered in India or outside India, wherever it may be, foreigners while in India, and persons in the service of the Government of India, within or beyond India.

The act does not 'ban' movement of material. But, under Section 5 of the act, the Central Government may identify, designate, categorise or regulate, the export, transfer, re-transfer, trans-shipment, or transit of any item related to relevant activity in such manner as may be prescribed. Thus, the state's sovereignty is fully protected.

Section 8 deals with prohibitions related to WMD. Under Section 8 Sub-section 1 and 2, no person shall *unlawfully* manufacture, acquire, possess, develop or transport a nuclear weapon or other nuclear explosive devices and their means of delivery or transfer control over them. Section 8, Sub-section 3 and 4 deal with biological weapons and 8 (5) deals with missiles specially designed for the delivery of WMD. Section 9 is very specific on prohibiting the transfer of WMD-related material to NSA or terrorists. Transfer to NSA is allowed only by persons acting under lawful authority of India. Thus, this act differentiates between NSA *per se* and terrorists.

Section 10 prohibits any person from transferring WMD-related material so that it could be used to intimidate others. As per section 11, no person shall export any material, equipment or technology knowing that such material, equipment or technology is intended to be used in the design or manufacture of WMD or its missile delivery system. Section 12 prohibits brokering of any of these materials. As per Section 13, no item notified under this act shall be exported, transferred, re-transferred, brought in transit or trans-shipped except in accordance with the provisions of this act or any other relevant act. Thus, Sections 10 to 13 are specific to WMD-related terrorism.

India's WMD Act, 2005, has prescribed punishment for violation of the provisions of the act. Under Section 14, for violation of provisions of Section 8 or 10 of the act, punishment will be imprisonment extending from 5 years to life imprisonment as also fines. Section 15 prescribes the same punishment for violation of Section 9. Punishment for unauthorised export (Section 16) is a fine ranging from rupees three lakhs to twenty lakhs. Punishment for repeating the offence is imprisonment from six months to five years and fine. If the offence is committed by a company, all those who were in charge of or responsible for conducting that business are to be held responsible, proceeded against and punished accordingly. Section 24 offers legal protection to those who might have taken action under this act, under the concept of acting in good faith. WMD Act, 2005, has no section dealing with extradition, though section 3 (3) targets any person who commits an offence beyond India which is punishable under this act.

Interestingly, WMD Act, 2005, though claiming jurisdiction under section 3 (1) to whole of India 'including its EEZ', has no provision of enforcement in any of its maritime zones beyond the territorial waters. Section 4 (b), while dealing with the question of transit, clearly states that it "does not include a conveyance in innocent passage through Indian territory, Indian territorial waters or Indian airspace of a foreign conveyance carrying goods. By allowing innocent passage to foreign vessels carrying WMD-related material, the Act has restricted the application of its provisions to Indian ports, or airports or border check posts. This slavish acceptance of the outmoded UNCLOS-III needs to be reassessed. While UNCLOS-III recognised piracy, drug trafficking and transport of slaves as crimes on the high seas, it will be preposterous to claim that WMD-related terrorism does not make wider, the category of crime against humanity. While framing the WMD Act, 2005, India has followed the spirit of UNCLOS-III too literally even in the case of transit through its territorial waters. It has ignored section 5 (4a) of its MZI Act, 1976, that has defined the contiguous zone as its security zone. It is time that Indian law makers get rid of their UNCLOS-III phobia and enact laws keeping in view not only present realities but also the fast changing nature of maritime crimes. It seems that law makers of 1970s were far more conscious of their responsibility to the state's security than those of the present day.

India: State Practices

India had always paid due respect to the spirit of UNCLOS-III, 1982, though it ratified it only in 1995. It has, however, not hesitated, whenever necessary in the interest of security of India or its allies, to pursue a path of violence. These form a precedent in India's state practices. While doing so, it even seemed to have bypassed the norms as laid down by UNCLOS-III. The sinking of *MV Progress Light* in 1988 and of *M.V. Ahat* in 1993 as also of the Thai fishing trawler in the Gulf of Aden in 2008 and other pirated vessels in 2011, were some of the examples of that state practice.

Other examples of India's pragmatic approach to its maritime security, especially after 9/11, relate to its role in multi-lateral state initiatives like the PSI, RMSI, the Petersburg Initiative and ReCAAP. India has not formally joined US-led PSI and RMSI, because they target not only NSA and terrorists but also the so-called state of proliferation concern. India thought that as a non-NPT state and as a nuclear weapon power it could also be targeted. But, in practice, Indian Navy has been conducting joint exercises with navies of states that have promoted PSI and RMSI. These exercises include manoeuvres related to compatibility for initiatives like PSI and RMSI, that are not backed by any UN sanction and which have not been formally approved of by India. India has also agreed to join the Petersburg Initiative of 2006, initiated by Russia and USA. India is also an important component of Japan-led ReCAAP that is a multi-lateral effort to combat acts of piracy around the Malacca Straits. Thus, India too has contributed by its state practices towards the evolution of *de facto* maritime international law that goes beyond the limits set by UNCLOS-III and which is more in tune with new requirements of maritime security as also regional and international peace.

Unilateral efforts - Operation Cactus

A group of opposition leaders from the Maldives hired mercenaries to overthrow the government led by President Abdul Gayoom. In November 1988, reportedly 200 members belonging to Sri Lanka's Tamil militant group People's Liberation of Tamil Elam (PLOTE) reached Male, the capital of the Maldives, in fishing boats and attempted to overthrow the government of President Gayoom. The attempt was ill prepared. Mercenaries, upon their landing in Male on November 3, failed to capture the main security base in Male. They also had not occupied the airstrip in the nearby island. President Gayoom went into hiding and requested the Government of India for help. Other states were also so requested. India responded quickly.

Process to launch military operation (*Operation Cactus*) to rescue the legitimate government in Male from threat posed by foreign mercenaries was quickly put into effect. While preparations were being made to send force by using large *Il-76* transport aircrafts of the Indian Air Force, Indian Navy had dispatched its long-range MR aircrafts, *Tu-142*, to check if the airfield was safe for the landing of the Indian transport aircrafts. Indian Navy also deployed its warships as well as *Il-38* MR aircrafts to help in the operation. Thus, Indian Navy was engaged in *Operation Cactus* right from its inception till its conclusion.

Once Indian troops reached Male, mercenaries and those who had employed them, knew that the game was up. Some of the mercenaries hijacked a commercial vessel, *M.V. Progress Light,* that was in the port. They boarded it along with some important hostages from the Maldives and left the port. Indian Navy had no warship in Male at that time. Hence, *M.V. Progress Light* was able to reach the high seas. It was soon tracked by the Navy and warships that carried helicopters and were dispatched to intercept it on the high seas. The aim was to force the hijackers to stop and surrender the ship before it entered the territorial waters of Sri Lanka. Indian aircrafts, in a bid to scare the hijackers and to force them to stop, dropped depth charges as also fired rockets near the vessel. When the hijackers persisted in sailing towards territorial waters of Sri Lanka, *M.V. Progress Light* was fired upon and boarded in the early hours of November 6, 1988. The vessel was badly damaged in the process and though it was towed towards Male, it could not be saved and sank before it could reach the port. However, 20 hostages, 40 hijackers and the crew were rescued and taken back to Male (Roy, 1995, p. 370; Roy-Choudhury, 1995, p. 54, Singh 1990, pp. 32-5 and Hiranandani, 2003, pp. 14-15). This was probably the first case when Indian Navy had, in 'peace time' engaged and sunk on the high seas, a foreign vessel that was hijacked by NSA

India's response during *Operation Cactus* was in keeping, not only with the clauses of UNCLOS-III, but also with the General Assembly's resolution of December 7, 1987 that had voiced deep concerns at the use of mercenaries in contravention of fundamental principles of international law. That resolution was approved by 127 votes to 10 votes, while 19 had abstained. Interestingly, ten countries that had voted against UN General Assembly resolution included Belgium, France, West Germany, Italy, Japan, the Netherlands, Portugal, UK and USA. One wonders as to why the NATO members and Japan should have voted against that resolution. It needs to be noted that using mercenaries as proxies for their policy of destabilisation of regimes in Africa was a fairly common practice pursued by some European states and South Africa at that time. Indian action in the Maldives was thus an important step in upholding the General Assembly resolution on hijacking.

Operation Cactus also offers an insight into the use of force in the context of suppressing acts of violence on board a vessel. As noted, opposition leaders and some mercenaries had tried to escape from the Maldives by hijacking *M.V. Progress Light*. They also had held hostages on board the vessel. The vessel was intercepted on the high seas and force was used as a last resort by the Indian Navy to rescue the hostages, apprehend the culprits and bring the vessel back to Male. In that process, the ship was badly damaged and sank while it was being towed back to Male. Was Indian action compatible with the provisions of UNCLOS-III, traditional international law and UN Charter?

That drama on the high seas raised three points. Was it a case of piracy or only of hijacking? Did UNCLOS-III provide for legal action against act of hijacking *per se?* Indian action was not of 'hot pursuit' but of interception on the high seas. Was it legal under the terms of UNCLOS-III? Obviously, it was not a case of piracy since it did not meet any of the three criteria of piracy as defined under UNCLOS-III; use of two ships, attack on the high seas and object of private gain. Though it was a criminal act, UNCLOS-III had no provision for action against hijacking of ships. It was not a question of hot pursuit since no warship, either of the Maldives or of India had initiated the pursuit from within the territorial waters of the Maldives. The vessel was intercepted on the high seas while it was proceeding towards the territorial waters of Sri Lanka. It was intercepted before it could reach there.

Use of force by Indian Navy *vis-à-vis* the hijacked vessel, however, can be held valid only under Article 110(d) of UNCLOS-III which authorises any warship to intercept a vessel without nationality that is operating on the high seas. *M.V. Progress Light* had lost its nationality the moment it was hijacked by unauthorised persons. Thus, *Operation Cactus* of 1988 provides an example of India's state practice under UNCLOS-III *vis-à-vis* vessels hijacked by unauthorised persons. These vessels then become 'stateless' and hence warship of any state can intercept them even when they are not indulging in acts of piracy on the high seas. This case study is of vital importance in the present context of tackling the problem of 'piracy' by non-state vessels in Western Indian Ocean region and South Arabian Sea.

M.V. Ahat

M.V. Ahat, a small ship carrying an important LTTE leader as also war material, was intercepted by Indian maritime enforcement forces in January 1993, near Chennai. Request for boarding was refused and the LTTE cadre on board set the vessel on fire which caused it to sink. To understand this episode one needs to go into the background of the event as also to analyse the legal implications of Indian action.

India and Sri Lanka had signed a bilateral accord in 1987, which among other things, included clauses that amounted to a bilateral military cooperation. India had sent the Indian Peace Keeping Force (IPKF) to Sri Lanka to contain the LTTE. (For details of 1987 Accord and the role of IPKF see Hiranandani, 2003, pp. 143-152). IPKF, however, had to be deinducted due to change in domestic politics as also because of the temporary patchup between LTTE leader Prabhakaran and Premadasa, the then President of Sri Lanka. Despite the deinduction of the IPKF, the 1987 Accord was not formally abrogated by either party. Since there was no time limit for the Accord, legally speaking it remains in force even today. Thus, India was legally bound to help Sri Lanka *vis-à-vis* its Tamil militants.

Indian establishment had seen LTTE as a possible threat to its national security and territorial integrity because of its ethnic base in Sri Lanka as also strong support base in Tamil Nadu. Moreover, Indian intelligence had suspected that LTTE had links with anti-India terrorist groups in Kashmir like the *Harkat al-Mujahideen*. Reportedly, it also had the support of Pakistan's ISI. That linkage continued. Shivraj Patil, Home Minister, told the Parliament as late as May 2007 that there was enough evidence to suggest that there was a coordination between the LTTE and the J & K militants (*The Times of India,* New Delhi, May 16, 2007).

According to B. Raman, members of India's Research and Analysis Wing (RAW) had intercepted the communication to the effect that the LTTE was attempting to smuggle a consignment of arms and ammunition *from Karachi* to the LTTE-controlled area in the Northern Province of Sri Lanka. According to B. Raman, those arms and ammunition had been given to the LTTE by Pakistan's *Harkat al-Mujahideen*, with the complicity of the ISI. The movement of the ship carrying the consignment was continuously monitored and it was ultimately intercepted by the Indian Coast Guard. Before the ship could be 'captured', its crew set fire to it as a result of which it sank. While the arms and ammunition carried by it could not be seized, some of the crew members were captured alive. Their interrogation revealed the links between the LTTE and Pakistan, (Raman, 2007, p. 249).

At the time the incident took place, it was presumed that the ship, a 400-ton vessel registered at Son Lorenzo, was coming from South-East Asia because LTTE was known to be procuring equipment from there. However, account given by B. Raman must be accepted as more authentic. One, however, wonders about the presence of *M.V. Ahat* off Coromondal coast when it was supposed to off-load its cargo along the northern coast of Sri Lanka where the Sea Tigers would have offered it naval protection. The only plausible explanation for the presence of *M.V. Ahat* far north of its proposed destination could be that the LTTE believed it safer to land the cargo off Coromondel coast and then to tranship it *via* the Palk Strait, to its bases in the northern part of Sri Lanka. If so, it meant that LTTE had a much wider network of supporters in Tamil Nadu than was anticipated.

M.V. Ahat also carried on board Kittu, an important LTTE leader. The sinking of the vessel raised several political and legal questions in India. Mr. P. Nedumaran, leader of the Tamil National Movement, filed an *habeas corpus* petition. He argued that the Indian Government had no right to arrest the crew of the vessel or to stop the ship in 'international waters'. He also said that the Indian Government was aware of the presence of Kittu on board the ship. The petition also said that the vessel was 'dragged' into Indian waters and then set on fire.

The Defence Ministry submitted a counter affidavit in which it denied that it had arrested nine crew members of *M.V. Ahat* in 'international waters'. It even said that the name of the ship itself was false. According to the Defence Ministry, Indian Navy had spotted the ship 440 n. miles south-east of Madras (Chennai) at 00.45 hours on January 16, 1993. That vessel had displayed the 'not under command' signal indicating that it had mechanical problems. However, the Navy found out that the signal was displayed to mislead other ships. The counter-affidavit of the Defence Ministry said that the ship was "escorted" to Indian territorial waters on January 16 and asked to surrender so that a search could be carried out. It argued that the crew refused and the LTTE cadre set fire to the ship to conceal the cargo. They also forced the crew to jump into the water where they were rescued by the Navy. It also quoted Jayachandran, the master of the ship, as saying that Kittu had consumed cyanide and had died on board. The Ministry also denied that it knew about Kittu's presence on board the ship. It said that the ship had allegedly departed from Singapore on January 8, 1993. This differs from the data provided by B. Raman, as noted earlier.

Though the matter was closed at that time, the question whether Indian action was legally justified, remained unanswered. Was Indian action justified under India's MZI Act, 1976 and UNCLOS-III of 1982? India had ratified it only in 1995. Several legal questions arise. Was *M.V. Ahat* first intercepted on the high seas or was it dragged/escorted to territorial waters? Did *M.V. Ahat* have the freedom of the high seas and right of innocent passage in the territorial waters of India? Did India have the right to intercept/board it on the high seas and/or the territorial waters?

Article 87 of UNCLOS-III guarantees freedom of navigation on the high seas. To that extent, *M.V. Ahat* had that right. However, Article 110 (1) allows a warship to interfere with this freedom if its action was derived from power conferred by the treaty. In such a case, boarding is justified. In that context it will be relevant to refer to India-Sri Lanka Accord of July 29, 1987, especially Article 2, para 16 (b), which obliges India to offer help, even military help, to Sri Lanka *vis-à-vis* the threat posed to it by Tamil militants. It, therefore, amounted to a military cooperation agreement *vis-à-vis,* the LTTE (Singh, 1990, p. 27). Thus, vessels of the Indian Coast Guard as also Indian Navy had every right to intercept and board *M.V. Ahat* even on the high seas when there was adequate ground to suspect that it was involved in militarily supporting the LTTE.

India retained the right to intercept and board *M.V. Ahat* even in the territorial waters where it was allegedly dragged/escorted. Vessels do enjoy right of innocent passage in the territorial waters under Article 17 of UNCLOS-III as also section 4 of MZI Act, 1976. Yet Article 19 (1) of UNCLOS-III as also section 4 (1) of MZI Act, define passage as innocent so long as it is not prejudicial to the peace, good order or security of the coastal state. Surely a ship carrying weapons as also LTTE cadres did not merit freedom of passage in India's territorial waters. Thus, whether *M.V. Ahat* was intercepted on the high seas or in the territorial waters, action of Indian maritime enforcement agencies had violated neither international law nor the national law (MZI Act, 1976).

Anti-piracy operation in Indian Ocean

Operations against *M.V. Progress Light* and *M.V. Ahat* were one time affairs, close to the Indian coast. By contrast, anti-piracy/hijacking patrol in Western Indian Ocean region since mid-October 2008, has introduced a new element of sustained power projection against NSA in waters further away from the Indian coast. These waters, especially in the Gulf of Aden and off the coast of Horn of Africa, had become a happy hunting ground for some regional gangs who had been indulging in capturing ships on the high sea and holding the ship, its cargo as also the crew for ransom. Prabhakaran Paleri coined the term 'protectionist piracy' (Paleri, 2006, 229) to designate this curious mix of piracy, hijacking and demand for ransom. It was further compounded by the fact that the littoral along the Horn of Africa has become *res nullis* for almost two decades if not more.

The sea space of North-West Indian Ocean is of strategic significance for India. Reportedly, in 2008, Indian exports worth $60 bn and imports worth $50 bn passed through that region. On an average, about 24 Indian flag ships pass through this area every month. These are ships manned by Indian crew. (*Hindu*, March 23, 2009). Indian cargo is also carried by foreign flag vessels. All these need a safe passage.

Reportedly, the Indian Navy had been seeking permission from Government of India for stationing warships in the area to offer protection to Indian flag ships as also to Indians who were often employed as crew in many foreign-owned ships. The capture on September 15, 2008 of a Japanese-owned and Hong Kong registered ship, *MV Stolt Valor*, with a crew of 22 of whom 18 were from India, probably marked the turning point. The ship was taken to a port on the Somali coast and ransom was demanded for its release. The ship was released on November 16, 2008 after the ransom, reportedly $1.25 mn, was paid.

INS Tabar, a very modern and highly sophisticated missile-armed frigate, that had been recently acquired from Russia was dispatched to the region and began operating there reportedly since October 20, 2008. Indian Defence Minister A.K. Antony said on November 26, 2008 that the Indian Navy would provide 'security cover for Indian cargo ships passing by the Somali coast. He said that all ships carrying Indian flag would be given protection in the Indian Ocean (*Hindu,* November 27, 2008).

On November 11, 2008, *INS Tabar* was able to prevent capture of *M.V. Jag Arnav,* a 38, 265-ton bulk carrier belonging to Great Eastern Shipping Company that was being threatened about 60 n. miles east of Aden. When informed of the threat, a helicopter from *INS Tabar* scared away those who were threatening the ship. *INS Tabar* was reportedly 25 n. miles away.

The 'success' of November 18 probably became a cause for a grim tragedy. *INS Tabar* noticed one trawler and two speed boats about 285 n. miles south-west of Salalah. It believed them to be pirate vessels especially when there were men armed with assault rifles and RPG on the deck of the trawler. *INS Tabar* ordered them to stop and to allow boarding for inspection. Men on board the trawler not only refused to do so but also threatened to blow up *INS Tabar.* The stand-off continued for two hours. Probably, the men on board the trawler would have fired shots to desist the team from *INS Tabar* from boarding. In reply, *INS Tabar* opened fire with the result that the trawler caught fire and sank. One speed boat managed to escape while the other was found abandoned.

The matter took a serious turn when it was realised that the trawler, which was considered a 'mothership', was a Thai trawler that had been captured by the Somalis the same day. The Thai crew of the trawler would have been in the hold of the ship when it was fired upon and sunk. Indian Navy said that they had no information about it. Pirates on board the 'mother ship' were in radio contact with *INS Tabar.* They also did not report about the Thai crew imprisoned and in their hold. If they had been displayed on the deck, it is possible that *INS Tabar* would have resorted to other options. Also, soon before *INS Tabar* had intercepted the 'mother ship', a very large crude carrier, carrying crude from Saudi Arabia to USA, was captured by the pirates. All these factors would have influenced the decision to engage the pirate vessel which led to its sinking.

The capture of the Thai trawler had been reported by the Piracy Reporting Centre of IMB, Kuala Lumpur. Indian Navy that was specifically operating in a 'pirate infested area' in anti-piracy operations claimed that it was unaware of that. It even reportedly blamed the Indian Coast Guard which is the nodal agency in India on piracy under ReCAAP for not reporting the matter to *INS Tabar* . Thai Foreign Ministry also reportedly had sought clarification from the Indian Navy on its rules of engagement in sinking the pirate ship. It is not known how the diplomatic row was sorted out. To say the least, it was a game of passing the buck.

INS Tabar was replaced by *INS Mysore.* It thwarted an attempt by the pirates to capture Ethiopian ship *MV Gib,* 150 n. miles off Aden. *M.V. Gib* sent the signal that it was being targeted. *INS Mysore* sent a *Cheetah* armed helicopter with four marine commandos and speeded up towards the scene of the crime. Heavy machine-gun fire across the bow was enough to force them to surrender. INS *Mysore* was able to arrest 23 persons of whom 12 were Somalis and 11 were from Yemen. Ten assault rifles, one RPG with two rounds, a few granades and a GPS was recovered.

Ships of the Indian Navy continue to operate in these waters. Indian Navy had carried out these operations on its own though there were about 20 foreign warships, mostly from the NATO countries, operating in the region. India had not formally joined in the operations of US-led coalition in these waters. However, there are instances when it had coordinated its actions with warships of other states. On April 29, 2009, *INS Nirdeshak*, a hydrographic survey ship, which operates a *Chetak* helicopter from its deck as also carries interceptor boats, was able to save an Italian cruise liner from being hijacked near Seychelles. Its efforts were coordinated with those of the Spanish frigate *Numancia* and a French MR aircrafts. The culprits were arrested and handed over to authorities in the Seychelles for legal action. In July 2009, warships of the Indian Navy and of the French Navy coordinated their efforts to rescue an Indian *dhow MV Nafeya* from Porbundar and its crew members. They were taken hostage on July 10, 2009 by seven hijackers, armed with assault rifles and RPG near the Puntland in north-east Somalia. The *dhow* was captured while returning. It was converted into a mothership and an attempt was made by pirates on board to capture *MV Elephant*, a Liberian tanker. The French and the Indian warships used standard operating procedures not only to prevent that hijack but also to force the hijackers to abandon the vessel and the crew near the coast of Somalia on July 15. The *dhow* proceeded towards Mukkalla in Yemen (*The Hindu*, September 17, 2009). Was that a prelude to a *de facto* cooperation between Indian Navy and other navies operating in the region?

Indian Navy and the Coast Guard conducted strong anti-piracy measures in the waters of South Arabian Sea, since January 2011 when pirates began to expand the zone of their operation, to target the SLOC, linking the Horn of Africa/Persian Gulf to South-East Asia and the Pacific. Their action not only threatened freedom of navigation in that SLOC but also posed a threat to India's island territories as also its Arabian Sea coast.

On January 28, 2011, Indian Navy intercepted a pirated ship north of Minicoy Island. 15 pirates were apprehended. On February 5, Thai fishing vessel *Prentalay-11* was seized 100 n. miles off Kavaratti. 28 pirates were apprehended and 24 Thai fishermen rescued. On March 12, ship of the Indian Navy intercepted *Vega-5*, a Mozambique-flagged fishing vessel, 600 miles from the Indian coast. 13 sailors were rescued while 60 pirates were arrested. Many of them were reportedly children.

These events caused serious concern in Indian decision-making circles. The Cabinet Committee on Security formalised the basis for a pro-active policy. That included standard operating procedure, rules of engagement appropriate to the threat, new law on piracy etc. Thus, India is chartering new paths in state practice on maritime security on the high seas in its adjacent sea space.

It is some surprise that while navies of distant countries have sent their warships to protect SLOC in this region, navies of the regional powers, especially the GCC states, are keeping aloof. Indian Navy has been suggesting for some time for such a coordinated effort to curb the menace but without any satisfactory result so far.

Operations of ships of the Indian Navy in these waters, especially the sinking of the Thai trawler, in 2008, raise some pertinent questions on India's state practice in this regard. To what extent was Indian stand on the sinking of the Thai trawler legal and, more so, reasonable? India's Minister of External Affairs, Pranab Mukherjee, while defending the action, told the media, "We deeply condole the loss of lives. But, it has to be kept in mind that the trawler was under the command of pirates. As per international law and practice, the vessel is sunk if the pirates do not surrender. It (the firing) is perfectly within our rights and as per international law (*The Hindu*, November 27, 2008). Some retired high ranking officers of the Indian Navy, on TV, quoted 'rules of engagement' to justify the sinking of the Thai trawler. But, even under the rule of engagement, was there any comparison between a few armed men on board a captured trawler equipped with short range RPG and assault rifles and a frigate armed to the teeth with most modern weapons? Did such an asymmetry in capability justify sinking of that vessel as a 'reasonable' response?

There is no doubt that offences that were committed in that region fulfilled all the legal norms to be equated with acts of piracy. Two or more ships were involved. Crime was committed on the high seas. Reason was private gains. But there were other aspects of the crime that made it different from piracy *per se*. The act was committed for extracting ransom. Thus, it qualifies for a new crime; hijacking on the high sea for ransom. Once the amount was negotiated and paid, the ship, its cargo and the crew were released almost unharmed. Unfortunately, UNCLOS-III has provision for piracy but not for hijacking for private gains. Hence, this crime is also labelled as piracy and the norms that are applied to piracy are applied to this new type of maritime crime.

Vessels used in this crime and persons on board also violate another basic norm of international law. These vessels are operated by NSA and hence do not fly the flag of any recognised state. Thus, these vessels are violating Article 110 (1d) of UNCLOS-III. Under that clause, a warship has a right of visit *vis-à-vis* a ship without nationality. Thus, these unauthorised vessels on the high seas can be intercepted and seised(seized?) even if they are not involved in any criminal activity like piracy or hijacking at the time of visit. Punishment for violating Article 110 (1d) of UNCLOS-

III normally would differ from state to state. If the navies operating in this region act under Article 110(1d), rather than under norms of piracy, they will be able to eliminate the presence of these unauthorised vessels in the area and thus, indirectly reduce the incidence of piracy/hijacking in these waters. The UN Security Council can even pass a resolution authorising such seizure and the follow up action under Chapter VII of the UN Charter so that it becomes mandatory for all warships operating in the region.

India: State practice in multilateral efforts

As noted in Chapter III, India had certain reservations in formally joining the US-sponsored PSI (and related RMSI) since it felt that they, at least on paper, could challenge its status as a non-NPT nuclear weapon power. But, Indian Navy did participate in several bilateral and multilateral naval exercises with states like USA, Russia, Japan, Singapore etc. that among other things, include the essence of PSI. India, was however, more forthcoming in joining the Petersburg initiative that was jointly proposed by Bush and Putin. This new initiative targeted only NSA/terrorists and not state actors. Also, it dovetailed with UN Convention on WMD Terrorism of 2005 and India's own WMD Act, 2005.

India is already very actively involved in ReCAAP that was sponsored by Japan and seeks to evolve regional mechanism to meet the challenge of piracy in South-East Asia and the Pacific coast of Asia. As yet, there is no parallel initiative to combat acts of piracy/hijacking in West Indian Ocean region. India has deployed its warships to meet the challenge and will surely welcome any cooperative initiative that involves regional states as well as is authorised by the UN.

Constitutional constraints: Centre-State relations

One factor that is obvious in the context of India's legal and constitutional constraints in combating criminal activities of NSA and terrorists along its adjacent waters is the insignificant role given under the Constitution to India's coastal states in maritime affairs, including security in their adjacent waters. Now that Indian decision makers, both at the union level as also the state level, are keen to have a fresh look at the entire framework of homeland security in the context of threats posed by terrorism *via* adjacent sea space, the legal and constitutional framework and related enforcement agencies and procedure in these waters need to be re-examined and means found to correct the present imbalance so as to enable coastal states of India to contribute effectively towards maintenance of peace and order in the adjacent water space as well.

Though Indian Constitution emphasises the federal principle, which implies equitable distribution of power and responsibility between the Union Government and the states, the Constitution gives the Union Government almost exclusive jurisdiction over all aspects of maritime affairs with a very limited exception for fishery activity in territorial waters and non-major ports.

The result of this inbuilt constraint was that though coastal states were facing threats from NSA and terrorists *via* their adjacent sea space, they had practically no say in matters related to maritime security. This was true in Tamil Nadu *vis-à-vis* Tamil militancy in Sri Lanka, and also in Maharashtra about smuggling of RDX, preceding the Bombay blasts of 1993. Maritime security remained the exclusive preserve of the Central Government and its enforcement agencies like the Navy, the Coast Guard and the Customs (Marine). As will be analysed, almost all matters dealing with maritime affairs, including security, were either handled by the Union Government or were dominated by it.

The Seventh Schedule of the Indian Constitution makes this point very specific. While the Seventh Schedule has adequate provision for ports and related facilities under which interests of the Central Government and of the coastal states are fairly balanced, items listed relating to public order (and maritime security) as also fisheries and shipping (fishing boats included) need to be reexamined in the light of present and more so future requirement of India in the context of threats posed by terrorists. In this context, it must be underlined that creation of a viable maritime security zone in the context of coastal states as well as a more appropriate fishery management system and ship identification system are complementary in ensuring a more effective security cover over the seaward approaches to India's long coast line.

List I (Union List) of the Seventh Schedule contains several items dealing with maritime affairs that are reserved exclusively for the Union

Government. They include defence of India, (item 1), armed forces of India (item 2) piracy and crimes committed on the high seas (item 21), shipping and navigation (item 25), major ports (item 27), exploitation of non-living resources on the continental-shelf (item 63) and fishing and fisheries 'beyond territorial waters' (item 57). For the purpose of our study item 1 and 2 that deal with defence and defence forces are important. They also need to be analysed in the context of List II (State List) and its item 1 and 2 that deal with public order and police, and item 21 that deals with fisheries.

Item 1 of the Union List (List I) is as follows: *"Defence* of India and every part thereof including preparation for defence and all such acts as may be conducive in *times of war* to its prosecution and after its termination, to effective demobilisation". Item 2 is its corollary. It says that naval, military and air forces and any other armed forces of the Union will be under the control of the Central Government.

The framers of the Constitution had very clearly used the term *defence* and further related it to *'times of war'*. By implication, item 1 cannot be extended to include *'security'* of the nation in *'times of no-war'*. Hence, a literal interpretation of item 1 and extending the meaning of the term 'defence' in times of war to include security in times of no-war will be saddling the Union Government with responsibility that the makers of the Indian Constitution had not envisaged. Terrorism was not a major source of threat to the nation at that time. Hence, items 1 and 2 of the Union List (List I) need to be re-examined in the light of present and future requirements of maritime security.

These two items of the Union List also need to be examined in the context of items 1 and 2 of the State List (List II) of the Seventh Schedule. While item 1 deals with public order, item 2 deals with police. In this context, it needs to be noted that the Indian Constitution treats all states, whether coastal or hinterland, on an equal footing as far as their 'territory' is concerned. The 'territory' of the coastal state too is thus limited to its 'land' territory that may at best include the inland water. But it does not include territorial waters except for purposes of fishery. Thus, its territorial limit ends at the shore/coast. Hence, the current proposal is for the setting up of Coastal Police for these states.

Though a coastal state's powers under List II (State List) item 1 and 2 do not extend beyond the shore/coast but by default it is now allowed to exercise its criminal jurisdiction in the adjoining territorial waters. Even if the state had enjoyed that power earlier, it had only remained as 'notional' jurisdiction since the coastal state had no enforcement agency of its own that was adequately equipped to perform that function. Even now, the function of the proposed Coastal Police is seen as that of a beat constable along the shore/coast rather than extending coastal state's effective criminal jurisdiction in the territorial waters *per se*.

To the best of my knowledge there is no constitutional amendment, act of the Parliament, even presidential proclamation or even the act of state legislature that extends the coastal state's criminal jurisdiction dealing with public order upto the outer limit of the adjacent territorial waters. Thus, there exists a legal and constitutional grey area which can be used by legal experts to question the activities of the State Police in those waters. That grey area needs to be formally and legally rectified either by presidential proclamation or even constitutional amendment by including maritime security in the Concurrent List of VII Schedule of the Constitution (List III).

Even if the Coastal Police is given the mandate to exercise criminal jurisdiction upto the outer limit of the territorial waters, can that be an adequate zone for ensuring security of the coast from terrorists when even an ordinary fishing trawler can cover that distance within less than two hours; time totally inadequate to mount countermeasures with a reasonable chance of success? Thus, coastal state's maritime security zone needs to be extended further deep into the sea space. Section 5 (4a) of MZI Act, 1976 has designated the contiguous zone as India's security zone. That sea space adjacent to the coast should be the minimum logical limit to coastal states' security frontier in the context of NSA and terrorists.

As noted earlier, it does not contradict the spirit of UNCLOS-III which has no provision for state action against terrorism but which provides the state powers to act against economic offences of NSA. It will be ludicrous to argue that while UNCLOS-III permits State Parties to act against economic offenders in the contiguous zone, it denies the coastal state the right to protect its security against terrorists in the same zone. If the security zone of the coastal state is extended upto the outer limit of the contiguous zone then the Marine Police along with the Customs, coastal state's fisheries enforcement authority as also the Coast Guard can evolve a cooperative mechanism to better sanitise the adjacent sea space of the coastal states. May be it cannot be done in two or three years but it can become the basis of a long-term plan to ensure a more comprehensive security cover *vis-à-vis* criminal activities of NSA and terrorists.

Closely related to the state's criminal jurisdiction in its adjacent water space is the question of the coastal state's involvement in the context of fishery. The Constitution of India was approved in 1951 when the territorial waters limit was only three n. miles. The Union List (item 57) had given to the Central Government full right to regulate fishery beyond that three n. miles limit. State List, under item 21, only mentions one word 'fishery'. By default, as also under interpretation of item 57 of the Union List, coastal states began to demand and acquire coastal state's jurisdiction over fishery in the adjacent territorial water limit. It even passed laws regulating fishery for various types of fishing vessels and thus tried to protect interests of fishermen operating small boats and fishing near the coast. That process began in the early sixties.

The Maharashtra Fisheries Act, 1962, was enacted to provide for the protection, conservation and development of fisheries in the State of Maharashtra. Under Section (2), the Act extended to the whole of Maharashtra. It was elaborated under Section 2 (1) which said that any part of the 'open sea' constitutes waters adjoining the coast of the state within a distance of six n. miles measured from the appropriate base line according to the President's Proclamation of March 22, 1956, published by the Ministry of External Affairs. Other coastal states like Karnataka, the Union Territory of Goa, Daman and Diu, Kerala, Tamil Nadu etc. also followed suit. The limit of territorial waters was subsequently extended to 12 n. miles.

In this context, the Kerala Marine Fishing Regulation Act, 1980, introduced a new element – public order – as a part of a coastal state's jurisdiction in the coastal waters. The Act aims at protecting the interest of various sections of persons engaged in fishing and provides for proper conservation and utilisation of different spices of fish. Kerala Government issued an administrative order prohibiting fishing by mechanised boats within two miles of the sea coast and reserved that area only for country crafts. It also empowered the state to regulate, restrict or prohibit fishing in any specific area by each class of fishing vessels, as also to fix the number of fishing vessels that may be used for fishing at any specific area. Fishing was permitted only to persons licensed under the Act. No vessel other than a registered fishing vessel is entitled to a licence. The vessel needs to be registered either under Section II of the Marine Products Export Development Authority Act, 1972 or under Section 9 of the Kerala Marine Fishing Regulation Act, 1980. This part of the Act intrudes into item 25 of the Union List (List I) dealing with the Union Government's power over maritime shipping and navigation. State List (List II) or Concurrent List (List III) do not provide for the coastal state's control over shipping, even fishing vessels, in coastal waters.

Kerala Government's notification reserving coastal waters upto the limit of two miles from the coast for country crafts (non-mechanised) was challenged in the court. The Kerala High Court not only upheld that order but also ruled that the state had the power of legislation over the territorial waters or matters covered under item 1 (public order) and item 21 (fisheries) of List II (State List) of the Seventh Schedule of the Constitution. Thus, Kerala High Court extended the state's criminal jurisdiction beyond its 'land' territory to cover territorial waters also, though only in cases related to fishery. It was a land-mark in the context of empowering the coastal state to frame acts and to create appropriate agencies so as to enforce its jurisdiction in territorial waters that were considered to be the exclusive preserve of the Central Government.

What was deemed to be a victory of the coastal state in the sixties and the seventies is no longer true today. Today, fishing in the EEZ has become a near monopoly of the fisherfolk of India's coastal states. Unlike the sixties and the seventies, when mechanisation of country boats and introduction of larger trawlers had just started, today the number of mechanised fishing boats and medium trawlers has increased greatly. With more fishing harbours and fish landing sites being built, their number is bound to increase in future.

Hence, rules and regulations that were designed for the sixties and the seventies need to be revised drastically.

Government introduced a draft of Marine Fisheries (Regulation and Management Bill in 2009, Marine Fisheries Bill, 2009). It seeks to enact a common legal framework for regulation of fishing, conservation and sustainable use of fishery resources in *all* maritime zones, including territorial waters. It seeks to amend or repeal parts of MZI Act, 1976 as well as MZI (Regulation of Fishing by Foreign Vessels) Act, 1981 and related Rules, 1982. It needs to be noted that under section 7, sub-section 5 of MZI Act, 1976, Indian citizens are free to fish unrestrained in the entire EEZ of India. This bill, among other things, seeks to regulate fishing in EEZ not only by foreign but also Indian vessels. Since the proposed bill covers the entire sea space including territorial waters, it will also impinge upon the coastal states' fishery rules and regulations in their respective territorial waters. It remains to be seen how the Central Government overcomes this potential area of conflict between powers and functions of the coastal states and of the Union Government as well as the organised opposition of those involved in marine fishing. The avowed purpose of the bill is to bring all Indian fishing vessels and related interests in EEZ within the legal purview so as to meet India's obligations under UNCLOS-III and related instruments like the UN Fish Stock Agreement of 1995.

Till now, Indian fishing vessels even when fishing beyond the territorial water limit in EEZ did not require any special permission from the Central Government. Now, under the proposed bill, all vessels that confine their activities within the territorial waters will come under the jurisdiction of respective coastal state's fishery departments. Those that cross that zone into EEZ would be brought under the jurisdiction of the Central Government and will need to have a fishing permit for it. One wonders how a fisherman, without sophisticated navigational instruments like GPS, will be able to judge that he has crossed the outer limit of the territorial waters. Vessels of 20 metres or less of Indian fishermen will be given preference for fishing in Indian EEZ, though they could be brought under a coastal state's fishery department. Though the fishing permit would be granted by the Central Government it could be routed through the state government. Vessels of more than 20 metres will be granted second preference.

The bill also provides for allowing fishermen of neighbouring maritime states to fish in adjacent EEZ on a reciprocal basis. Given the vast sea space covered under India's EEZ, power of search and seizure is expected to be shared between fishermen's organisations, as also fishery departments of the State Government and the Central Government – a cumbersome process indeed! The proposed bill also provides for offences and their respective punishment. In that context, Indian and foreign fishing vessels are to be treated equally. While one can welcome this spirit of creating a legal framework for regulating fishery in India's EEZ, the passage of that bill will be an uphill task since it is likely that not only states but also the fishing community will have their objections to a bill that seeks to curb the 'freedom' that they had enjoyed. Also, can a hostile fishing community be an asset in strengthening India's coastal security?

Since the fishery industry is closely linked to the society, economy and fishery related facilities along the coast, it is logical that coastal states should be given a greater share in managing the living resources near their sea space. Their role in regulating fishery in adjacent waters, therefore, needs to be extended upto the outer limit of EEZ. This will be facilitated by making marine fishery as a new item in the Concurrent List of the Seventh Schedule through an amendment so that the Central Government and coastal states can jointly evolve a suitable policy to regulate marine fishery in future.

Such a change will not only be in tune with the needs of modern fishery activity but will also strengthen India's maritime security *vis-à-vis* NSA and terrorists. Instead of only the Coast Guard and occasionally Marine Wing of the Customs, this maritime security zone of India will be monitored individually or/and collectively by four enforcement agencies; the Coast Guard, Marine Customs, Marine Police and the enforcement wing of the fisheries department of the coastal state as also the Central Government. Also, fishermen operating in the area can prove very effective in monitoring the sea space for any suspicious activity if some framework like Marine Guard (equivalent to Home Guard) is worked out at the level of the coastal states and integrated with other maritime enforcement agencies. The Parliament, under Articles 246 (4) and 248 has also the right to legislate on the items listed in the Union List and the Concurrent List.

Maritime Security: need to fill the legal gaps

Though Government of India has passed (and repealed) laws that deal with criminal activities of NSA and terrorists, yet there are grey areas and gaps in law that need to be identified and necessary steps taken so that maritime enforcement agencies are better armed legally. Legal grey areas and loopholes, that can be taken advantage of by competent defence lawyers, need to be eliminated. Piracy is a crime and is so listed under item 21 in the Union List (List I) of Seventh Schedule of the Constitution. A Pirate is also listed as an enemy under the Navy Act, 1957. Yet India had no specific law against piracy, not even under IPC. India had intercepted *MV Alondra Rainbow* owned by a Japanese firm near its Arabian Sea coast on November 17, 1999 and brought it to Bombay for further legal action.

When the charge-sheet was filed against the culprits, in the absence of any anti-piracy section in IPC, offenders were charged under various other sections of IPC as also under Indian Arms Act, Indian Passport (Entry into India) Act and Foreigners Act besides quoting section 1 of the outmoded Admirality Offence (Colonial) Act of 1848. The legal shortcoming, according to Rear-Admiral O.P. Sharma, not only faced criticism from the High Court but also the country faced embarrassment internationally (Sharma, 2005, p. 380).

Now that there are proposals since March 2011 to update Indian criminal law on piracy, other maritime crimes like hijacking of vessels or transport of WMD related material as well as terrorism that are emerging as new maritime crimes should also be included so that enforcement agencies are authorised under Indian laws to take appropriate measures against these new crimes that are not covered either under traditional international law or the UNCLOS-III. The modified act can also prescribe, like the SUA Act, 2002, procedure for arrest, trial as also punishment for various facets of these criminal activities.

Another grey area that needs to be cleared deals with laws and enforcement mechanism to give a practical shape to Section 5, Sub-section 4 (a) of MZI Act, 1976, that defines contiguous zone as India's security zone *vis-à-vis* NSA/terrorists. Such a step will be very useful in combating maritime terrorism since it will provide maritime enforcement agencies with clear legal basis for interception (and seizure) of vessels carrying unauthorised arms, ammunition, explosive devices as also personnel (terrorists) that can target India's coast in this zone.

Section 6, Sub-section 5 (bii) of MZI Act, 1976 provides for "safety and protection" of off-shore installations on the continental-shelf. One wonders if the Government of India has enacted any law that can authorise enforcement agencies to preempt even the entry of unauthorised vessels in the 'safety and protection' zone around these installations. The act can also specify the 'safety' zone and 'protection' zone separately since their purposes are different. While UNCLOS-III prescribes 500 metres as the outer limit of safety zone, it does not mention protection zone. Therefore, lack of adequate provision in UNCLOS-III needs to be filled by an appropriate national legislation that 'protects' the high value targets within the broader framework of freedom of the high seas. For greater effectiveness, the act should complement India's SUA Act, 2002.

Laws dealing with shipping, especially indigeneous ships below 300 GRT and used for coastal/overseas trade, ferry service and fishing, need to be streamlined in view of India's security requirements so that their presence or lack of presence in concerned waters can be effectively monitored. These small vessels are increasingly being employed for anti-national activities, especially by terrorists. Hence, there is urgent need to tighten shipping laws to monitor their movement at all times and in all concerned sea space.

Though UAPA (amended) is now the basis of India's anti-terrorism law, it still has some shortcomings in the context of maritime security. Matters dealing with maritime security are largely ignored. It is still land focussed and provides more for arrest and trial rather than for preemptive action in various maritime zones. As noted, preemptive action will be the basis of maritime security.

As suggested above, India needs to enact laws to give effect to Section 5, Sub-section 4a dealing with 'security' in contiguous zone and Section 6, Sub-section 5 (bii) of MZI Act dealing with safety and protection of off-shore installations on the continental-shelf. These acts like the Customs Act will enable Indian enforcement agencies to operate legally beyond the territorial waters limit of 12 n. miles and intercept vessels and effect seizure on what constitutes high seas under UNCLOS-III. An updated maritime security act will need to take cognisance of these new demands so as to strengthen the legality and legitimacy of preemptive action especially against maritime terrorism and to intercept NSA and terrorists before they reach their intended targets.

It is time that Indian decision makers and those dealing with maritime security start making a distinction between legal norms that govern India's maritime relations with state actors and the legal norms that determine its criminal jurisdiction *vis-à-vis* NSA and terrorists. Till now, India has not crossed the legal limit set by UNCLOS-III after it ratified it in 1995. There is no need to do that even in future as far as India's relations with state actors are concerned. But, surely no one can dispute India's sovereign right to take legal steps that would empower its enforcement agencies to sanitise waters adjacent to its territory *vis-à-vis* actual or potential threats due to criminal activities of NSA and especially those of terrorists while simultaneously retaining its legal position *vis-à-vis* state actors, as defined under UNCLOS-III.

It will not be inappropriate to say that the *de jure* legal regime of today that revolved around UNCLOS-III protects terrorists by restricting state action. It is high time that state action against these crimes of terrorism, hijacking, WMD proliferation etc. be given the same status as is being given to act of piracy. If it is not possible to amend UNCLOS-III, then Indian state practice should evolve its own legal code in these matters that protects the UNCLOS-III terms *vis-à-vis* state actors and yet allows Indian enforcement agencies the tool to apprehend the criminal elements especially terrorists before they can reach their target *via* the adjacent sea space.

India's maritime laws have been passed under the sponsorship of various ministries and related departments that deal with maritime affairs. Two things have resulted from this mark of administrative autonomy. Firstly, very often there is little coordination in law making among concerned ministries. Secondly, such laws often do not take into account the security-related implications. Now, that the nation is becoming aware of the security implications of India's adjacent sea space, it is time that a review of these acts as also of acts proposed, be undertaken so as to identify the areas that need to be suitably amended to meet the new requirements.

Three steps can be initiated in that context. A committee of legal experts from concerned ministries and related departments and representatives of enforcement agencies can compile all related laws, acts, UN resolutions, international conventions etc that have a bearing on maritime security. They can be analysed by the committee which can then suggest ways and means of closing existing gaps and for removing grey areas, if any, or else suggest suitable amendments so as to lay down clear guidelines for enforcement agencies, prosecuting authorities and the judiciary for their respective roles. That might also provide for preemptive action to various maritime security zones of India so as to apprehend and successfully try the culprits and punish them under the appropriate law. The entire procedure may take some time and hence, sooner it starts better it will be for the maritime security of India.

MARITIME ENFORCEMENT AGENCIES

Defining the Strategy

Efforts to neutralise threats posed by NSA and terrorists, often termed as Maritime Low Intensity Conflict (MLIC), need to be directed simultaneously at two levels; national and international. While each state will need to initiate moves at the national level, keeping in view its national capabilities and requirements, concerned states cannot overlook the need for bilateral and multilateral cooperation that will help buttress efforts at national level. In this context, it needs to be underlined that efforts at individual state level also add up as important inputs in meeting the new challenge to the freedom of the high seas at regional and even at global level. This reciprocity cannot be overlooked.

Does combating the new threat of MLIC need a totally new strategy or can the naval strategy, that has evolved over the years in the context of state actors, be modified to neutralise the new challenge of MLIC? Conventional naval strategy revolves around a combination of three variables; sea denial, sea control and force projection. To these are added the new inputs based upon modern technological innovations that have paved the way for Revolution in Military Affairs (RMA) and Net-work Centric Warfare (NCW). It is not so much the RMA but the NCW that will prove more effective in meeting the new challenge by synergising efforts of multiple enforcement agencies that are bound to be involved in combating the new threat at national as also international level.

Though there may be a change in actors, from state actors to NSA and terrorists, the medium of confrontation remains the same – the adjacent sea space. Hence, denial of unimpeded access to that sea space to the adversary has acquired primacy in combating MLIC. Since the target is often the homeland or off-shore platforms, emphasis will have to be put on strengthening the sea denial capability in various layers or zones of adjacent sea space. Sea denial strategy is easier to formulate in the case of state actors since it is easy to identify the real or potential adversary as also the weapons of conventional warfare that are likely to be employed. Hence, it is easy to design counter-measures. That is not easy in the case of NSA and terrorists. It is difficult to pin-point them. Also, one cannot take the war to the enemy. The initiative invariably rests with the adversary who enjoys advantages like element of surprise, time, place and mode of attack. It is, therefore, possible that steps taken by a coastal state to deny sea space to them may even be challenged by other states on grounds of denial of freedom of the high seas. As noted in previous chapters, conventional legal norms based upon UNCLOS-III favour NSA and terrorists.

Sea control is difficult in the case of MLIC since one cannot really identify the exact sea space that needs to be controlled even in the case of piracy in Indian Ocean. Equally difficult is the option of force projection. US-led coalition has been following that strategy in the Horn of Africa and the Arabian Sea region to prevent movement of piracy, terrorists as also WMD-related material. The failure even to control piracy/hijacking in those regions since 2004 has put a question mark on the efficacy of that strategy. Even after the Security Council, with the consent of the 'notional' regime of Somalia, passed a resolution in 2008, authorising use of force even in the territorial waters of Somalia, none of the states operating their warships along that coast have opted to target the bases of these pirates on the shore of Somalia.

Three facets of the naval strategy in the context of MLIC; sea denial, sea control and force projection, to be really effective, depend upon bilateral, regional and international cooperation among state actors. Unlike conventional conflict that can be fought on a bilateral level, war on maritime terrorism or MLIC has global dimension. While evolving a maritime strategy in that context, a state needs to keep in mind the trans-national dimension, besides augmenting its national capability, so as to overcome the new challenge. Hence, India's enforcement agencies will need to operate in both these environments, national and international, so as to neutralise the new challenge.

Since maritime terrorism was not perceived as a threat to national security till recently, no maritime enforcement agency was created to deal specifically with that threat. However, existing maritime enforcement agencies have been entrusted with the new responsibility. Since these agencies were not created to combat maritime terrorism *per* se, their orientation, training and equipment were not geared to fulfil the new role that was being assigned to them. It is also possible that disjointed and knee-jerk responses would have led to duplication of role as also of equipment.

Maritime enforcement agencies of India that have been entrusted with the task of confronting maritime terrorism at the level of the Central Government are the Indian Navy, the Indian Coast Guard and the Customs (Marine Wing). Since 2004-2005, Marine Police is being formed in different coastal states. Seaward security of the ports in the context of maritime terrorism is negligible as was proved during the events of 26/11 in Mumbai. Though security of off-shore installations is theoretically shared by several agencies, including the Navy and the Coast Guard, one wonders if these installations have viable arrangements for their basic point security against attack by a determined band of terrorists, launching suicide-boat attack from under the platforms.

Enforcement Agencies: Central Government

The Indian Navy

The Indian Navy has its roots in the Bombay Marines created by the East India Company soon after it obtained a *firman* to establish a factory at Surat in 1613. Its major role was to offer protection to shipping against attacks by indigeneous groups along the western coast of India as well as along the coast of the Arabian Peninsula and Bab al-Mandeb by Arabs. Beside this 'anti-piracy' role, it also fought against the Maratha Navy and the Navy of the Mysore state either on its own or in cooperation with the ships of the English Navy. Thus, at best, it was conceived of as a coastal/brown water navy. Even that role was downgraded after 1858 when the British Crown took over the governance of India from the East India Company.

The nationalist pressure for the creation of an Indian Navy as also the rise of Japan in the Pacific forced the British to grudgingly lay the foundation of the Indian Navy. Though in its infancy, it played an important role during World War II. Despite Indian independence, the Indian Navy continued to remain under the tutelage of the British Admiralty and its naval chiefs continued to be British till 1957. At that time, the Navy was so designed that it could play a supportive role, within the framework of larger Commonwealth strategy, in the Indian Ocean region. The Indian Navy was designed for a role that was more appropriate for SLOC protection between Aden and Singapore. The weapons' mix comprising of one or two light aircrafts carriers, two light cruisers, a few destroyers and frigates and a few minesweepers was found to be appropriate for that role. The aircrafts carrier was neither equipped for strike role nor was India provided with a submarine even for conducting ASW exercises. Indian Navy, thus, remained hostage to the British Admiralty till the Soviet Union opened its doors. That helped India develop a more balanced and effective "blue water" capability.

It must be noted in this context that under the earlier British tutelage and then with the Soviet help, Indian Navy began to blossom as a blue water navy equipped to fight a conventional war on the high seas. Its responsibility for coastal protection, at best protection of the port/base, which anyway was limited even earlier, was further reduced, following the formation of the Indian Coast Guard in 1977-78.

Thus, though Indian Navy retained its constabulary role as one of its missions (*Arun Prakash*, 2005, p. 32), its capability was limited to maintaining a minimum presence in the sensitive Palk Straits and the Gulf of Manar and in the Andaman Sea. Even in that context, its capability was inadequate. Very often, due to paucity of vessels, fishing trawlers were hired and armed with medium machineguns for operation in the area between Rameshwaram and Nagapatnam (Hiranandani, 2003, pp. 153-54).

The Indian Navy had not geared itself for an anti-terrorist role. Suddenly, after 2004, and more so after the events of 26/11 in Mumbai, the Indian Navy, as the primary maritime enforcement agency of the Central Government, was saddled with the responsibility of protecting the coast against maritime threats posed by NSA and terrorists. How well is the Indian Navy equipped for that role?

As noted, Indian Navy had been geared up since India's independence as a part of India's comprehensive defence *vis-à-vis* other state actors. It is now tasked with simultaneously performing two totally asymmetric roles; to be ready to fight a conventional war at short notice *vis-à-vis* state actors and to be engaged in a sustained MLIC *vis-à-vis* NSA and terrorists. Both these roles demand different strategies, weapons mix, base facilities and foreign policy orientations.

Beside these roles, Indian Navy has other roles like SAR operations which are a part of international obligations. Also, Indian decision makers have unilaterally taken upon themselves a totally new international obligation that is not mentioned either in traditional international law, UN Charter, UNCLOS-III, resolution of the Security Council or SUA Convention, 1988 and WMD Convention, 2005. It is the protection of international SLOCs in its adjacent sea space. Admiral Suresh Mehta had stated that India had a "duty" (not even an obligation) in ensuring the security of SLOCs and an unhindered flow of legitimate maritime traffic in the *entire* region. He, however, qualified that duty by adding that it can be ensured through interlinked domain awareness and active maritime cooperation (Mehta, 2007, pp. 6-7).

No viable framework in that context has been put in place as yet. In its absence, this duty/obligation is likely to be criticised by others as India's desire to dominate the adjacent sea space (the high seas) in the name of SLOC protection. In diplomacy, it is always useful not to cross the limits set by international norms. However, if India does take steps to monitor water of its strategic concern even upto the outer limit of its EEZ, it will be able to offer SLOC protection to international shipping without stepping out of the bounds of international law and associated state practices.

It will be wrong to say that the Indian Navy was unaware of the threat to homeland due to criminal activities of NSA and terrorists. It was reflected in its attempt to sanitising Indian waters in the Palk Straits and the Gulf of Manar, as also off the coast of Maharashtra after the 1993 blasts in Mumbai. Also, steps were initiated to provide security to India's off-shore installations in the Bombay High. However, that role was never projected as its prime security concern. After 2004-2005, focus began to shift to coastal security against acts of maritime terrorism, for instance, events of 26/11 in Mumbai and the media focus it generated projected as if it was of prime priority.

The new focus on maritime terrorism was reflected in India's Maritime Doctrine of April 2004. Among the missions of the Indian Navy is included the task of providing security to the coastline, island territories and offshore assets. In that context, it also foresaw increasing cooperation with other navies to combat emerging international common concern such as terrorism, transportation of WMD, sea piracy and drug trafficking (*The Hindu* (Delhi), June 24, 2004). According to Vice-Admiral S.C.S. Bangara, "The Navy is constantly involved in operations aimed at prevention of maritime terrorism, contraband transfer and piracy. This surveillance and vigilance that the Navy exercises and the deterrence it provides against anti-national elements are crucial elements of our security" (Bangra, 2005, p. 76).

Indian Navy: counter MLIC capability

As noted, Indian Navy has now been entrusted with two roles; fighting a conventional war against determined state adversaries including Pakistan and China, as well as combating MLIC. A conventional war fighting capability against state actors will require a mix of sophisticated weapons like aircrafts carriers, missile-armed destroyers and frigates with anti-air, anti-surface and anti-subsurface capability, submarines both conventional and nuclear-powered, amphibious vessels, fleet replenishment vessels as also medium and long-range maritime reconnaissance and ASW aircrafts (for details see Singh, 2008, pp.58-113). Joint naval exercises that are conducted by the Indian Navy with navies of other powers reflect the interoperability of these sophisticated weapons and related strategies.

Though Indian Navy is probably the largest regional navy in the Indian Ocean yet its primary focus on anti-state capability does not really equip it to neutralise the challenges of MLIC in adjacent waters. That will require different strategy and weapons mix so as to effectively sanitise the adjacent sea space. Among other things, it will require the capability for sustained vigil and surveillance over a vast sea surface to monitor major SLOCs and offshore installations on the continental-shelf.

This vast sea space will be crowded not only with large and small vessels engaged in overseas and coastal traffic but also with thousands of large and medium-size mechanised fishing vessels and trawlers, both Indian and foreign. Criminal elements can well hide in this crowd which has legitimate reasons not only to operate in those waters but also to commute to and fro from several non-major ports, fishing harbours and fish landing sites spread all along the coast. Identifying criminal elements will indeed be difficult in the absence of reliable intelligence inputs. Also, even when identified, a quick response will be needed to intercept them either by forces operating nearby or dispatched from the coast. This will need a great deal of coordination among multiple agencies operating in various maritime zones. Where does the Indian Navy fit into this composite structure of counter-MLIC operations?

If the Indian Navy desires to play a more direct role in neutralising the threat of maritime terrorism, it will need to enhance not only its surveillance capability but also appropriate surface forces like offshore patrol vessels, inshore patrol crafts and SDB, large, medium and small patrol boats as also inshore mine counter-measure force for sanitising approaches to various ports and naval bases from threat from mines likely to be planted by the terrorists.

Indian Navy has a multi-tiered maritime reconnaissance capability comprising of UAV, deck-based helicopters, as also medium and long-range fixed-wing MR aircrafts. It will also benefit from various surveillance satellites launched by India that have a maritime spin off. It must be underlined that this capability was built over the years to enable the Navy to fight a conventional war against state actors. Yet, some of that can also be used for MLIC and anti-terrorist operations. While the Navy has designed sophisticated warships, it has yet to design a warship suitable to combat terrorists and which could be procured in large number. The requirements for the proposed *Sagar Prahari Bal* will provide some insight in that direction. Even in its anti-piracy operations around the Horn of Africa, Indian Navy is employing very sophisticated surface fleet. This operation can be performed equally well by the *Godavari-type* of vessel which was designed to operate two helicopters and can be deployed for a long duration in these waters. If such a vessel can also be modified for ASW role with long range missile /torpedo combination like ASROC, instead of being armed with anti-ship missiles, it will also strengthen India's ASW capability.

As noted, Indian Navy was, over the years, being geared to neutralise threats posed by state actors. Hence it acquired and will continue to acquire and upgrade its weapon systems designed for that role. They include aircraft carriers, submarines both conventional and nuclear-powered, large sophisticated surface vessels like destroyers and frigates armed with long-range anti-surface and anti-air missiles. Naval air-arm will include, besides aircrafts operating from aircraft carriers as also helicopters operating from destroyers and frigates, long and medium range maritime reconnaissance (MR) aircrafts and anti-submarine warfare (ASW) aircrafts. India has also large number of corvettes primarily armed with anti-ship missiles to deny adjacent sea space even to large surface vessels of the adversary. These weapons are very sophisticated and costly to be used for counter-MLIC operations and for coastal security though large surface vessels like destroyers, frigates and even corvettes can and have been used in anti-piracy operations, not only in far off waters of North-West Indian Ocean but also waters adjacent to the coast. The missile armed corvette was employed not only to compel the pirated Japanese ship, *MV Alondra Rainbow*, to veer its course towards Mumbai but also in 2011, against motherships of Somali pirates.

Requirements for sustained surveillance and rapid intervention so as to neutralise the threat posed by NSA and terrorists need different types of surface vessels and aerial platforms that are deployed in various maritime security zones of India. As noted in previous chapters, sea space around Indian landmass and island territories can be broadly divided into four maritime zones. They are, starting from the land mass/shore:

(a) internal waters, estuaries and extending upto the outer limit of territorial waters,

(b) waters covered within India's contiguous zone that extends upto a maximum distance of 24 n. miles from the coast;

(c) waters extending beyond the outer limits of the contiguous zone upto about 50 n. miles. That would also include oil and gas structure on the continental-shelf and

(d) the sea space beyond 50 n. miles from where NSA and terrorists are expected to enter into various layers of maritime security zones and finally the homeland.

In these four maritime security zones, Indian Navy will need to deploy a combination of large off-shore patrol vessels (OPV), in-shore patrol crafts (IPC) and SDB, large patrol boats, as also smaller interceptor boats and in-shore minesweepers. Beside these surface crafts, equipped with weapons appropriate for the task, Indian Navy will also require medium-range fixed wing MR aircrafts as also light and medium helicopters designed for swift intervention across some distance from the main hub (MARCOS role). It will also need UAVs and even small dirigibles for surveillance of the coastal belt and high value targets like ports and offshore installations on the continental-shelf. It will also need inshore minesweepers for sanitising approaches to the harbour and bases as well as some amphibious capability to neutralise groups of criminal elements who might succeed in occupying some islands far away from the mainland.

It must be understood that these maritime security zones are not to be seen as water-tight compartments except in the context of the limit of jurisdiction of various maritime enforcement agencies likely to operate in these zones. Marine Police's role is presently restricted to the territorial waters, that of the Customs (Marine) upto the outer limit of the contiguous zone. The Coast Guard's enforcement role, as per the preamble of the Coast Guard Act, 1978, was limited to India's maritime zones. Navy has no such restraints. Hence, Indian Navy can legally operate in water space, extending from the inland sea to the outermost limit of India's maritime security zone and even beyond it in 'international waters' over which no state exercises sovereign jurisdiction.

Indian Navy's enforcement capability in the context of neutralising threats posed by NSA and terrorists, will need to be analysed under two broad heads. The one will deal with anti-piracy operations even in far off areas as in the Horn of Africa and North Eastern Indian Ocean. The other is anti-NSA and anti-terrorist operations in sea space of India's immediate security concern.

Table: Indian Navy, Counter-MLIC Operations

Surface Fleet	Number	Displacement (tons)	Max. speed (knots)	Weapons	Helicopter
Anti piracy operations					
Destroyers					
R-class	5	(5,000)	28	SSM, SAM, guns, torpedo tubes etc.	1 medium
Delhi-class	3	6,700	32	SSM, SAM, Torpedo tubes, 100 mm gun, 30 mm gun AKS 630	1 medium
Kolkata-class	0+3(4)	7,500	32	SSM, SAM, Torpedo tubes, 100 mm gun, 2x30 mm gun AKS 630	2 medium
Frigates					
Nilgiri-class	2 (likely to be deleted soon)	(3,000)	28	Gun, torpedo tubes etc.	1 small
Godavari-class	3	4,200	28	SSM, SAM, 76 mm gun, 4x30 mm AK 630 and Torpedo tubes	2 small
Brahmaputra-class	4	4,500	27	SSM, SAM, Torpedo tubes, 76 mm gun,4x30 mm AK 630	1 medium
Talwar-class	3+3(3)	4,035	32	SSM, SAM, Torpedo tubes, 76 mm gun, 30 mm gun AK 630	1 medium

Shivalik-class	1+2(7)	5,300	(32)	SSM, SAM, Torpedo tubes, 1x3" gun, 30 mm cannon	1 medium
Corvette (large)					
Kora-class	4	1,460	25	SSM, 1x76 mm gun, and 2x30 mm AKS 630	nil
Khukri-class	4	1,423	24	SSM, SAM, 1x3" gun and 2x30 mm AKS 630	nil
Project 28 Anti-ship+ASW role	0+4(8)	na	na	na	na
Counter-MLIC Operations					
Off-shore patrol vessel (OPV)					
Sarayu-class	0+4	2,215	25	1x3" gun and 2x30 mm AK 630	1 light
Sukanya-class	6	1,890	21	2x40 mm and 4x12.7 mm MG	
Inshore patrol craft (IPC) and SDB					
Tarabai-class (SDB-MK 3)	2	210	30	2x40 mm	nil
Bangaran-class	6	260	30	1x30 mm and 2x7.62 mm MK	nil
Car-Nicobar-class (improved Bangaran-class)	4+3(3)	288	35	1x30 mm and 2x12.7 mm MK	nil
Large patrol boat Super Dvora MK2	7	60	50	2x20mm2x20mm	nil

	Number	Equipment			
Fast interceptor-boat (reportedly ordered)	(15)	na	na	na	nil
Small patrol boat for SPB	(80)	na	na	na	-
Inshore mine-counter measure ship	na		na	na	
Maritime Reconnaissance	Number	Equipment for counter MLIC role			
Fixed wing aircraft Long range					
TU-142 M	8	Search radar			
Il-38	5	"			
P-81 (on order)	(6-10)	"			
Medium range	number	Range (miles)	equipment		
Dornier	14	940	Search radar, FLIR, camera, search light		
Norman Defender likely to be replaced by new aircraft with MR/ASW role	6(+6)	1,500	Search radar		
UAV					
Heron	4	Na	Search radar, ASM		
Searcher-II	8				
(Three more on order)					

Table based on data provided in *Jane's Fighting Ships 2010-2011*. SSM, anti-ship missile: SAM, anti-air/missile missile; ASM - air-to-ship missile; FLIR forward looking infra-red system.

While anti-piracy operations will require large warships capable of operating in far off places for a longer patrol, operations against NSA and terrorists nearer the main coast and island territories will require diverse types of large, medium and small surface platforms like OPV, IPC and SDB, large and small patrol boats and small (inshore) mine counter-measure ships. While large maritime reconnaissance (MR) aircrafts will be useful for longer patrol in distant waters, medium-range MR aircrafts equipped with radar, infra-red detection system, cameras, search light etc, as well as large and medium UAVs will be more useful in keeping watch over adjacent sea space stretching from inland waters to the outer limit of India's EEZ. The Table giving details of Indian Navy's capability for counter-MLIC operations gives approximate details of the force level available for different roles today and in the near future.

For anti-piracy operations further away from the coast as in the Horn of Africa and North-Eastern Indian Ocean, Indian Navy has the option to deploy any of the eight destroyers and ten modern frigates. For operations nearer home, any of the eight large missile corvettes can be deployed. It also has 13 LRMR/ASW aircrafts that can be used to patrol these waters, if necessary. Air support in far off areas can also be provided by helicopters (often armed) carried on board destroyers and frigates.

In this context, it needs to be underlined that utilisation of high value and sophisticated destroyers and frigates for anti-piracy operations on a sustained basis will adversely affect the life of these vessels that are specifically designed for operations *vis-à-vis* state actors as adversaries. Since anti-piracy operation will remain a long-term responsibility of the Indian Navy, it will be useful to acquire warships appropriate for that role. A replacement for aging frigates like the *Nilgiri-class* and the *Godavari-class* can be designed for such a role besides giving it an ASW capability. A ship with a displacement of 2,500 to 3,000 tonnes, capable of operating two medium-lift helicopters, armed with one 3" gun, one 30 mm cannon and two 12.7 mm heavy machine gun and capable of launching two fast crafts for search and visit role will be very useful. If possible, it should also be capable of being converted for ASW role with the addition of tubes capable of launching a 25 km range missile, like the ASROC carrying ASW torpedos. ASW-specific medium-lift helicopters and long-range missile/torpedo combination will prove useful in conventional war also. The Navy's ASW capability needs to be further strengthened since India is facing an ever increasing threat from submarines operated not only by the Pakistan Navy but also by the Navy of China. It needs to be noted that China is keen on augmenting Pakistan Navy's frigate as also its submarine fleets.

For operations against NSA and terrorists in waters nearer home, Indian Navy has the option to deploy several categories of surface fleets, ranging from small patrol boats to large off-shore patrol vessels. As shown in the accompanying table, Indian Navy possesses six *Sukanya-class* OPV. Some of these ships need replacement. Indian Navy is acquiring four new *Sarayu-class* large OPVs. It is reportedly a naval version of the *Sankalpa-class* OPV of the Indian Coast Guard. In view of the expanding role of the Navy in the context of counter-MLIC operations, it is possible that the Navy might acquire more of such vessels after the first batch is inducted by 2011-12.

For operations in maritime zone between 25-50 n. miles, that also overlaps the off-shore oil and gas platforms on the continental-shelf, Indian Navy can deploy about 10 IPC/SDBs. These are medium-size vessels with adequate endurance to operate in these waters for about a week. For operations nearer the coast upto 24 n. miles (contiguous-zone limit), the Navy has seven *Super Doora Mk II* large patrol boats. Reportedly, the Navy is to acquire about 15 fast interceptor crafts to buttress its capacity to operate in these waters in the context of new requirements of coastal security. Indian Navy is also reportedly acquiring 80 small patrol boats for the newly created *Sagar Prahari Bal* (SPB). SPB is a new branch of the Indian Navy whose formation was announced in 2008. When fully operational, it will have a strength of 1,000 personnel. It will operate about 80 plus patrol boats. These are to be built by a shipyard in Sri Lanka. About 14 such crafts were to be inducted by 2010. Others were to join soon. A three-week orientation course was started from January 11, 2010 at *INS Dronacharya*, Kochi. The course reportedly includes small-arm training, navigation and operation of fast interceptor crafts.

As seen from the accompanying table, Indian Navy's capability for maritime reconnaissance comprises of large MR aircrafts like Tu-142 M and Il-38. Though they are optimised for ASW operations, yet their long endurance enables the Navy to deploy them for MR role as and when necessary, even in distant waters. Dornier medium-range MR aircrafts allows sea space nearer the main coast and island territories to be kept under observation. Indian Navy also operates Norman Defender aircrafts but they are reportedly due for replacement. New medium-range aircrafts is being recommended which can also have ASW capability and can be armed with air-to-surface anti-ship missile. Indian Navy also operates UAVs. While *Searcher-II* is useful for medium-range operations, *Heron* has a longer endurance. It is possible that more UAVs may be procured for sustained MR in sensitive areas.

If Indian Navy has to sanitise the adjacent sea space, especially sea lanes connecting the ports and bases to deeper waters, it will also need to acquire mine counter-measure vessels that can neutralise mines that can be sown in these approaches even by a medium-size fishing trawler modified for that role. The Navy alone is trained in mine counter-measure operations. Reportedly, last of the ex-Soviet inshore minesweepers was decommissioned in 2009. India has about 15 large ports and naval bases that will need that type of vessel. It is normally about 100 tonnes and equipped with mine countermeasure gears. If armed with 20 mm guns and heavy machine guns, it can also double up as a large patrol boat. One hopes that such vessels will be inducted during the second phase of the Coastal Security Perspective (2011-16) as a part of SPB, for coastal security role.

The terrorist attack on Pakistan's naval-air base in Karachi in June 2011, once again highlighted the need for securing high value bases in India as well. In that context, the Indian Navy too put forward proposals. In fact, such a proposal should have been put forward after the attack on 26/11 because the terrorists could well have targeted the naval base in Mumbai. Indian Navy plans to upgrade its existing harbour protection system that is designed to secure its naval assets from covert sub-surface attacks by trained frogmen, armed with sophisticated tools. The Sea Tigers of the LTTE had targeted vessels of Sri Lanka Navy.

The Indian Navy has already put in place, harbour protection systems like diver-detection sonar, underwater physical net etc. More sophistication is to be added to it. The Indian Navy also proposes to acquire 16 new ASW-specific vessels that can operate outside the harbour, to keep *enemy* submarines at bay. Such a sophisticated sub-surface attack can be delivered only with the active collaboration of state actors who are equipped with that capability. Such an attack will, therefore, raise the threshold of operation from state-sponsored terrorism to state-directed hostile acts. Pakistan Navy has reportedly three midget submarines suitable for such operation. The Indian Navy is conscious of that and has been building a capability, since 1980s, to neutralise that. Such operations qualify more as acts of inter-state conflict rather than acts of counter-terrorism *per se*.

The Indian Coast Guard

Unlike the Navy, which was designed to combat threats posed by state actors, the Coast Guard, the Customs (Marine) and the Marine Police were constituted primarily to neutralise threats posed by NSA and terrorists and not against state actors. Just as the Marine Wing of the Customs was the logical follow up of India's policy of containing the growing challenge of smuggling *via* the sea, the Coast Guard was the logical outcome of enforcing provisions of MZI Act, 1976 in various maritime zones as defined in that act (MoD, *A.R., 1976-77*, p. 18).

Steps leading to the formation of the Indian Coast Guard

A conference of Deputy Inspector-Generals of Police (CID), held in New Delhi, discussed the question of law and order, smuggling and coastal security. It constituted a committee which framed its report in May 1974. Among other things, it recommended setting up of a coastal security force as part of the Border Security Force (BSF), to begin with.

Probably it alarmed the Navy. Reportedly, at the initiative of the Navy, the Defence Secretary submitted a note on August 31, 1974, to the Cabinet Secretariat, spelling out the need for setting up a coast guard-type national organisation, for ensuring the safety of life and property at sea as also for law enforcement in the waters under the jurisdiction of India. The note suggested that a suitable inter-ministerial body could examine the adequacy of existing organisations and the possibility of closer coordination between their activities either by merging some or by establishing a central organisation similar to the coast guard.

A committee was appointed under the chairmanship of K.F. Rustamji to examine various facets of the problem. The Rustamji Committee, in its interiem report of 1975, examined the question of Marine Wing of the Customs. As regards the suggestion on the coast guard, its report (Part III) examined the issue, beyond smuggling, under changing maritime scenario world-wide, as a result of the new debate on the law of the sea and deliberated upon the need for the formation of a coast guard as well as upon its duties, functions and organisational structure so as to meet the government's responsibilities in the 'national' waters, that included safety of navigation, SAR, salvage, fishery protection, anti-smuggling, prevention of poaching, infiltration, pollution control etc.

It needs to be noted that at that time 'national' waters would have been restricted only to the territorial waters (12 n. miles). MZI Act was enacted only in 1976. Thus, the enforcement zone of the proposed coast guard expanded from 12 n. miles in 1974 to 200 n. miles after the MZI Act of 1976 and expanded India's jurisdiction upto the outer limit (200 n. miles) of its EEZ. There was a suggestion that the new organisation could be put under the Ministry of Home Affairs, like other para-military forces. But it was finally decided to put it under the Ministry of Defence (Singh, 1992, p. 14).

On January 17, 1977, Government of India approved the proposal of the Ministry of Defence for constituting an Interim Coast Guard Organisation under the Naval Headquarters, pending the approval of the plan for an independent Indian Coast Guard. The Interim Coast Guard was soon constituted on February 1, 1977. It was inaugurated by Admiral J.K. Cursetji, the then Chief of the Naval Staff, in Bombay. Vice-Admiral V.K. Kamath, the then Vice-Chief of the Naval Staff, who had been closely associated with the deliberations of the Rustamji Committee, was appointed officer on Special Duty (OSD) to head the newly created organisation and to prepare a detailed plan for the new force. The Interim Coast Guard retained the characteristics of the Navy since the Coast Guard Act was yet to be passed by the Parliament. Its ships flew the naval ensign and its personnel wore the Navy's uniform (Paleri, 2004, p. 49).

The Coast Guard Act, 1978

The Indian Parliament passed the Coast Guard Act in 1978. (Full text, see Manohar and Chitaley, *vol. 7*, 1988, pp. 367-400). The statement of objects and reasons for presenting the Coast Guard Bill before the Parliament, summed up the reasons for creating that Armed Force. It said, "The need for the setting up of a Coast Guard Organisation for the purpose of ensuring the safety of navigation in our waters, protection of our off-shore installations and fishing interests, organising salvage and pollution control measures and enforcement of national laws *in our maritime zones*, including assistance to customs authorities in anti-smuggling operations, has for some time been acutely felt as the development of these services has not kept pace with the substantial increase in the number of activities in our maritime zones...To meet these demands, an Interime Coast Guard, consisting of a few vessels was formed in early 1977, as part of the Indian Navy, for exclusive deployment on the above mentioned services. However, considering the nature of the force and the purposes for which it would be employed, it is now considered appropriate that the Coast Guard be constituted as a separate armed force of the Union under a Director-General and should be regulated under a separate self-contained statute which will provide for its special needs, especially the needs of efficiency and discipline (Manohar and Chitaley, *vol. 7*, 1988, pp. 369-70).

This was to function under the Central Government as per entry 2 of the Union List (List I) of the Seventh Schedule of the Indian Constitution that authorises the Central Government to operate naval, military and air force and *other armed forces*. Thus, the Coast Guard is an armed force and not a para-military force. The Coast Guard Act of 1978 also lists cognate acts and provisions. They include: MZI Act of 1976, Merchant Shipping Act of 1958, Customs Act of 1962, Foreign Exchange Regulation Act of 1973, Conservation of Foreign Exchange and Prevention of Smuggling Activities Act of 1974, Army Act of 1950, Armed Forces (Emergency Duties) Act of 1947, Air Force Act of 1950, the Navy Act of 1957 etc.

Duties and enforcement responsibilities are spelled out in Chapter II and Chapter III. As per Section 4 in Chapter II, "There shall be an armed force of the Union called the Coast Guard *"for ensuring the security of the maritime zones of India with a view to the protection of maritime and other national interests in such zones*". Though the term 'security' is used in Section 4, that term and related sub-clause were dropped in Section 14 of Chapter III, which deals with duties and functions of the Coast Guard. Section 14 (1) says, "It shall be the duty of the Coast Guard to protect, by such measures as it thinks fit, the maritime and other national interests of India in the maritime zones of India". Thus, it omits the first half of Section 4 that refers to *security* of the maritime zones of India. One wonders why.

Section 14 (2) specifies various duties of the Coast Guard. They include, among other things:

(a) Ensuring the safety and protection of artificial islands, off-shore terminals, installations and other structures and devices in any maritime zone.

(b) Providing protection to fishermen including assistance to them at sea while in distress.

(c) Taking such measures as are necessary to preserve and protect the maritime environment and to protect and control marine pollution.

(d) *Assisting* the Customs and other authorities in anti-smuggling operations.

(e) *Enforcing* the provisions of such enactments as are, for the time being, in force in the maritime zones, and,

(f) Any other matter, including measures for the safety of life and property at sea and collection of scientific data as may be prescribed.

Thus, the Coast Guard Act of 1978, did not list the 'international' roles or obligations *vis-à-vis* piracy, SLOC protection or combating threat of MLIC. These duties were added over the years.

As noted, Indian Coast Guard has been given responsibilities that were not specifically listed in the Coast Guard Act of 1978. Important among them are related to piracy, maritime terrorism and coastal security. Ordinarily, the Navy is entrusted with the task of combating piracy on the high seas. However, over the decades, two developments have taken place. The one is that the criminal jurisdiction of the coastal state has extended upto the maximum 200 miles limit of its EEZ. In the case of India, that sea space in the Bay of Bengal and the Arabian Sea overlaps major international SLOCs in the Indian Ocean. Over the years, Indian Coast Guard, that was created to enforce state's jurisdiction over these waters, developed the capability to monitor and project the state's power of enforcement in these waters against internationally defined criminal elements also. By the end of 1980s, piracy and crimes on board ships became a grave menace in waters adjacent to India, thereby adding one more maritime responsibility; combating acts of piracy in adjacent waters. The successful interception of the Japanese-owned ship, *M.V. Alondra Rainbow*, that was reportedly pirated in the waters of South-East Asia, off the western coast of India and the follow up enforcement action brought international recognition to Indian maritime enforcement agencies, like the Navy and the Coast Guard.

The Coast Guard is constantly monitoring reports from the Piracy Reporting Centre at Kuala Lumpur. Indian Coast Guard is the nodal agency in India, in the context of regional cooperation, to combat acts of piracy under the Japan-sponsored ReCAAP. Indian Coast Guard has made anti-piracy operations a part of its maritime diplomacy and is interacting closely with sister organisations in Japan, South Korea and some states of South-East Asia. Thus, with its role extended to cover piracy as well, the jurisdiction of the Coast Guard has now extended from the coastal waters/maritime zones of India to the high seas beyond the EEZ. It will, however, be important to verify if the Coast Guard has been *legally* entrusted with this new responsibility outside India's maritime zones, a limitation specified under the Coast Guard Act of 1978.

The Coast Guard, when it was initially formed, was entrusted with the task of neutralising criminal activities of NSA, like illegal fishing in Indian EEZ and smuggling, but combating acts of maritime terrorism or MLIC was not envisaged as part of its duties in 1978. However, the Coast Guard began to be entrusted with the new role since the eighties due to deteriorating peace and security in India's adjacent sea space. Waters along the coast of Tamil Nadu had become sensitive since mid-eighties, following the intensification of the movement for Tamil Elam in Sri Lanka. The Coast

Guard was directly involved in operations to contain Tamil insurgency, especially after 1987, following the induction of IPKF in Sri Lanka. The Coast Guard vessels and aircrafts in the adjacent bases, were placed under the Navy, since July 1987 for meeting operational requirements of the Indian Peace Keeping Force (IPKF) in Sri Lanka. Coast Guard station at Mandapam provided logistic support to the Army, the Navy and the Air Force personnel in the area (MoD, *A.R.*, *1987-1988*, p. 23).

The role of the Coast Guard did not end following the deinduction of the IPKF in June 1990 at the request of President Premdasa of Sri Lanka as also by the new regime in India under V.P. Singh. The truce between the Government of Sri Lanka and the LTTE, that had partly led to the deinduction of the IPKF, was short lived. Outbreak of fresh hostilities between the LTTE and the force of Sri Lanka posed new challenges. *Operation Tasha* was jointly launched by the Navy and the Coast Guard to sanitise the sea space around the Palk Straits (MoD, *A.R., 2001-2002*, pp. 49-50). In 1996, following renewed conflict in Sri Lanka, *Operation Nakabandi* was launched to contain the activities of the LTTE in those waters as also to offer protection to Indian fishermen in those waters. The Coast Guard was involved in enhanced patrol along the coast of Maharashtra after the RDX smuggled *via* the sea was used in bomb blasts, in Mumbai, in April 1993. *Operation Swan* was launched. It involved the joint team of the Navy, the Coast Guard, the Customs (Marine) and Maharashtra Police (MoD, *A.R., 1994-1995*, p. 22).

Anti-terrorism role of the Coast Guard got a boost after 2004. The Kargil Committee report had indicated the awareness among the decision makers in Delhi that India has a maritime frontier that is as vulnerable as the land frontier and that it too needs to be sanitised in the context of threats posed by terrorists to homeland *via* the adjacent sea space. Recommendations included strengthening of the Coast Guard and the Navy besides the creation of the Marine Police at the level of the coastal states. It is important to underline that the centrality of the Coast Guard's role in this context has been recognised. Intelligence is a valuable input in combating the threat posed by terrorism and MLIC. The key role that the Coast Guard can play in that context was acknowledged when it was designated on

September 22, 2003 as the Lead Intelligence Agency (LIA) for coastal and sea borders (MoD, *A.R., 2005-2006*, p. 51).

The Coast Guard and SAR

The Coast Guard Act of 1978 lists Search and Rescue (SAR) as a part of its duty. Part III, Section 14, Subsection 2, para b of the act entrusts it with providing protection to fishermen including assistance to them at sea while in distress. Under sub-para f, it is entrusted with measures for the safety of life and property at sea. That also reflected India's commitment in that context under the International Convention for Safety of Life at Sea (SOLAS-1974). The new International Convention on Maritime Search and Rescue, 1979, required signatories to create infrastructure required under that convention. India took time to ratify it. According to Rahul Roy-Choudhury, though India was willing to implement the Global Maritime Distress and Safety System (GMDSS), it was hard pressed to meet the deadline of February 1999. Also, it could not meet at that time, the cost involved in the establishment of Rescue Coordination Centres (Roy-Choudhury, 1997, p. 680). Consequently, India could ratify the 1979 convention only on May 17, 2001.

According to Prabhakaran Paleri, it was in 1987, that the impetus for a dedicated maritime SAR (M-SAR) organisation was envisaged in India when a joint working group was constituted under the Director-General Shipping. It comprised of representatives from various agencies. The group was headed by the nautical adviser to the Government of India with members from the Navy, the Air Force, the Coast Guard and the Department of Communication. It evolved modalities for establishing an effective SAR network in the context of SAR Convention of 1979. The group recommended the formation of a national board to look after activities related to M-SAR. It also identified the Coast Guard as the nodal agency for coordination.

Subsequent to India's ratification of the SAR Convention of 1979 on May 17, 2001, Government of India passed a resolution to set up a National SAR Board (NSARB) with the Director-General of the Coast Guard as its chairperson. It was set up on January 28, 2002 (Paleri, 2004, pp. 162-64). Members of NSARB include representatives from the Navy, the Indian Air Force, Ministry of Shipping, Air Port Authority of India, Customs, India's

Meteorology Department, Department of Space, Ministry of Agriculture (Fishery), shipping companies, sailing vessel operators, representatives of the fishing community and of the coastal states. The NSARB is responsible for laying down guidelines, manuals, plans and directions etc. so as to ensure cooperation among various departments and organisations for SAR system effectiveness (Donny, 2002, p. 209).

The Indian Coast Guard formulated a National Search and Rescue Contingency Plan in 2002. It established three maritime rescue coordinating centres (MRCCs) at Mumbai, Chennai and Port Blair and nine maritime rescue sub-centres (MRSC) at Porbunder, Marmagao, New Mangalore, Kochi, Visakhapatnam, Paradip, Haldia, Diglipur and Campbell Bay. The MRCCs and MRSCs coordinate SAR operations in Indian Search and Rescue Region (ISRR). SAR operations are assisted by the Global Maritime Distress Safety System (GMDSS) which became operational on February 1, 1999.

Indian Search and Rescue Region (SRR) covers a large part of Bay of Bengal as also that of the Arabian Sea as well as part of the Indian Ocean, west of the Maldives, north of the Mauritius and east of the Seychelles. This area covers six million square kilometres of sea space (Donny, 2002, p. 213). This is divided into three zones or areas. In SRR West, efforts are coordinated by MRCC Mumbai. Operations in SRR East are coordinated by MRCC Chennai, and in SRR Andaman and Nicobar islands, operations are coordinated by MRCC Port Blair. These in turn, are assisted in their respective SAR operations, by appropriate Maritime Rescue Sub-Stations (MRSS) located along the coastal belt and in islands of India.

The role of the Indian Coast Guard has become a part of global network under the Global Maritime Distress Safety System (GMDSS) operations, as required under SAR Convention of 1979. Though India had formally ratified it only in 2001, yet it had acquired the capability to respond to GMDSS even earlier. Signals requesting help are passed on to the Coast Guard by the International Maritime Coordination Centre, Bangalore. India also operates the reporting system called India Maritime Search and Rescue System (INDSAR) since February 1, 2003. This computerised ship reporting system is a voluntary and toll free ship reporting system designed to assist

MRCCs to divert the most suitable ship to the scene of distress as also to keep track of ships that are overdue or may need urgent assistance.

Ships can also send voyage message to INDSAR centre at MRCC Mumbai *via* INMARSAT (toll-free Code 43). Indian Coast Guard also operates Island (M-SAR) Ship Reporting System (ISLFREP) that enables communication with ships, closing island territories within 25 miles. It is a VMF network system and adds to the overall navigational safety while passing through the islands (Paleri, 2004, pp. 168-69 and MoD, *A.R., 2003-2004*, p. 60). SAR responsibility helps in monitoring movement of ships in sea space adjacent to Indian coasts and thus indirectly helps in monitoring the likely activities of NSA and terrorists. The Coast Guard is, thus, in a more favourable position to monitor activities of ships of 300 tonnes and above in the waters of its zone of SAR responsibility, in the context of coastal security.

Coast Guard: The Establishment

During the formative period, Indian Navy had provided personnel as also training to the newly formed Coast Guard. Recruitment of Coast Guard *navik* began in 1979. Since the Coast Guard was also entrusted with the role of checking smuggling *via* sea, the move was also initiated to merge the Coast Guard and the Marine Wing of the Customs. It was approved in principle in 1980 and a committee was formed to work out the modalities (MoD, *A.R., 1980-81*, pp. 30-31). Fortunately for both, the merger did not materialise. Their roles were complementary but not synonymous.

In the eighties, some senior naval officers like Rear-Admiral Madhvendra Singh, who subsequently retired as the Chief of the Naval Staff, in an article in *Trishul*, journal of the National Staff College, Wellington, had questioned the very need for the Indian Coast Guard as a separate organisation and had advocated its merger with the Indian Navy (Singh, 1992, pp. 13-23). May be, Admiral Singh had a better perspective when he became the Naval Chief since he did not raise the question. By that time, the Indian Coast Guard was a well-established and a fast growing arm of the Defence Ministry and had a well defined focus that was different from that of the Navy. The relevance of the Coast Guard increased further after 2004 in the light of the new thrust on coastal security.

Coast Guard's growing role and responsibilities has led to enhancement of its force level as also establishment. Thus, within a span of three decades, because of its regional headquarters, district headquarters, Coast Guard stations as also air enclaves and air stations, Indian Coast Guard has been able to establish its presence in almost all important places along the long coastline as well as in the island territories of Andaman Nicobar and the Lakshadweep.

Those who had planned the development of the Coast Guard had decided to establish three Regional Headquarters at Mumbai, Chennai and Port Blair. They covered the three almost autonomous maritime regions of India; the Arabian Sea, the Bay of Bengal and the Andaman Sea respectively. These three Regional Headquarters were established on August 19, 1978, the day after the Coast Guard Act, 1978, was passed by the Indian Parliament. A new Regional Centre was commissioned in Gandhi Nagar in December 2009, to coordinate action in view of the enhanced threat of maritime terrorism, and special attention was paid in that context to the sea space adjacent to the coast of Gujarat.

The Coast Guard also established eleven District Headquarters. These were: Porbundar (Gujarat), Mumbai (Maharashtra), Vasco (Goa), New Mangalore (Carnatic), Kochi (Kerala), Kavaratti (Lakshadweep), Chennai (Tamil Nadu), Visakhapatnam (Andhra Pradesh), Paradip (Orissa), Haldia (West Bengal), Diglipur (Andaman) and Campbell Bay (Nicobar). Besides, Coast Guard established and proposes to establish several more Coast Guard Stations to strengthen its presence in strategic locations. They include Jhakau, Wadinar and Okha in Gujarat, Dhanu and Murad Janjira in Maharashtra, Karwar in Carnatic, Beypore and Vizingam in Kerala, Minicoy in Lakshadweep, Tuticorin and Mandapam in Tamil Nadu and in Puducherry. More Coast Guard Stations are likely to be established at Vadinar, Gopalpur, Androth, Karaikal, Hutbay and Nizampatnam to strengthen its strategy of hub and spokes in the context of coastal security.

The Coast Guard has established three Pollution Response Centres at Mumbai, Chennai and Port Blair. As a part of its national role and international obligation, Coast Guard has been established in all three MRCCs at Mumbai, Chennai and Port Blair as well as MRSCs at Porbundar,

Goa, New Mangalore, Kochi, Visakhapatnam, Paradip, Haldia, Dighlipur and Campbell Bay.

In view of growing importance of an effective air wing to monitor and help take the necessary action, the Coast Guard has established several Air Stations in Porbundar, Daman, Kochi, Chennai, Kolkata and Port Blair, Air Squadrons at Mumbai, Chennai and Port Blair and Air Enclave at Goa. There is the proposal to start an Air Station at Ratnagiri. The far flung and well integrated network of Coast Guard's establishment enables it to play an important role in the context of coastal security as well.

Table: Budget of the Indian Coast Guard (Rs. mn)

Year	total	Capital expenditure	Percentage of total budget
1979-80	21.7	Nil	
1981-82	199.2	167.8	84.23
1984-85	565.4	397.2	70.25
1987-88	951.8	500.8	52.60
1992-93	2,029.6	1,398.0	58.90
1999-2000	3,437.6	1,827.5	53.17
2004-2005	6,830.0	4,000.0	68.30

(Source: Paleri, 2004, 349, and Singh, 1992, 15)

The growth of the Indian Coast Guard was also reflected in its budget allocation. As seen from the accompanying table, the Coast Guard was provided with only Rs. 21.7 mn in 1979-80. It almost touched Rs. 1,000 mn in 1987-88. The budget for 2004-2005 rose to Rs. 6,830 mn. An examination of that table will also reveal that a large percentage of that budget was earmarked for capital expenditure and, thus, for acquisition of new equipment and constructing necessary infrastructure.

Force level of the Coast Guard

The force level of the Coast Guard at any given time not only determined the optimum capability of the Coast Guard but also the pattern of its growth. It also threw light upon the way the Coast Guard was expected to function within the overall framework of India's maritime security environment as perceived at that time. Over the decades, the enforcement capability of the Indian Coast Guard has been steadily enhanced by increasing the number of its personnel as also by improving the quantity and quality of its equipment including different types of surface vessels and aircrafts. For details, see the accompanying table on the *Growth of the Indian Coast Guard* between 1980 and 2010.

Table: Growth of the Indian Coast Guard

Year	Personnel	OPV and (ASW frigate)	IPC/SDB	PC large	PC small	MR aircraft
1980	na	2	2	5	-	na
1985	400 (80 officers)	4	4 (14)	8	-	2
1990	2,496 (266 officers)	8	18	8	-	5
1995	3,600 (680 officers)	10	12 (11)	2	-	11
2000	4,400 (760 officers)	12	12 (21)	16	6 hovercraft	16
2004	na	13	22 (2)	10	6 hovercraft	16
2010	na	13(1)	21(5)	10 (13)	6 hovercraft 5 PC	16

Table based upon data provided in Jane's Fighting Ships of respective years.

When the Indian Coast Guard was established, it was offered two small *Khukri-class* ASW frigates and five *P-class* patrol boats. As will be seen, its strength and capability improved over the years. As per the data provided in *Jane's Fighting Ships, 1980-81* (p. 22), in 1980, Indian Coast Guard operated two ex-Navy *Blackwood-class* Type 14 ASW frigates to patrol offshore waters. It had two SDB Mk2 for inshore operations. About five *Poluchat* (P-class) patrol crafts (PC), were reportedly operated for the Customs duty near the coastal waters and served as fast interceptor boats.

Soon, the Coast Guard began to acquire vessels designed for its specific requirements. *Vikram-class* Off-shore Patrol Vessels (OPVs) were inducted as replacements for ex-Navy ASW frigates. The new vessel could operate a light helicopter (*Chetak*) from its deck. It was housed in a hangar on board the ship. Its fleet of IPC/SDB was improved with the induction of new *Rajhans-class* and *Jijabai-class* ships. The Coast Guard also operated *Shallow-class* patrol crafts acquired from South Korea primarily for customs duty. Ex-Navy P-6 PC were phased out. Two *F-27 Fokker-Friendship* aircrafts were acquired on lease for MR purposes and were based at Kolkata. Two *Chetak* helicopters were stationed at Goa.

The Coast Guard continued to improve its capability over the years. By 1990, its IPC fleet included *Tarabai-class* vessels that were based on a design from Singapore. By 1995, Indian Coast Guard began to acquire new *Samar-class* OPVs. These were a modified version of the *Sukanya-class* OPV of the Navy. The new ship was larger than the *Vikram-class* OPV and had a range of 7,000 miles at 15 knots. It was armed with a heavier 76 mm OTO Melara gun. It could operate from its deck either light *Chetak* or medium *Dhruv* ALH. Four ships of that class were acquired. That gave the Coast Guard the ability to operate in distant waters beyond the 200 mile outer limit of India's EEZ. The old *Shallow-class* PCs were being replaced by new large PCs based upon a design of the *Archer* PC. These were 49-tonne large PCs armed with 20 mm guns or 12.7 mm heavy machine guns. It has a top speed of 40 knots. In view of its commitment for pollution control, Coast Guard placed orders for three sophisticated dedicated pollution control vessels. These were ordered from M/S ABG Shipping, Surat in March 2004, at a cost of Rs. 424.07 crores (MoD, *A.R., 2003-2004*, p. 60).

By 2004, just before the new thrust on coastal security, the Coast Guard was operating four *Samar*-class OPVs (redesigned WPSOH) and nine *Vikram*-class OPVs. There were 22 SDBs/IPCs that included two *Raj*-class SDB Mk2, six *Tarabai*-class, seven *Jijabai*-Mod1 and seven *Priyadarshani*-class vessels. Five new *Abakka*-class IPC of 275 tonnes were on order. They are armed with one 30 mm gun, beside machine guns.

They are fitted with water jet propulsion systems that give them a top speed of 35 knots as well as greater agility.

As per details provided in *Jane's Fighting Ships, 2010-2011*, Indian Coast Guard's force level comprised of the following. Its air-wing comprised of 16 Dornier MR aircrafts and 14 helicopters that included 2 Dhruv ALH. Its off-shore patrol vessels (OPVs) fleet comprised of 7 *Vikram-class* OPVs, four *Samar-class* large OPVs, and two large OPVs of *Sankalpa-class*. One more of that class was under construction. Its fleet of IPCs and SDBs included eight *Priyadarshani-class* IPC, six *Tarabai-class* SDBs and seven *Jijabai-class* Mod 1 SDBs. Orders have then been placed for five *Abakka-class* IPCs which are an improved version of *Priyadarshani-class* IPCs. These will replace old SDBs and IPCs. Its fleet of large fast patrol crafts included one old *Swallow-class* PC and nine *Archer-type* large patrol boats. Thirteen fast interceptor crafts (FIC) are being inducted. Five more are likely to be ordered by Coast Guard. For operations near the shore, it has six hovercrafts and five small (5.5 tonnes) patrol crafts (PCs). More might be ordered.

Jane's Fighting Ships, 2010-2011, has mentioned that Indian Coast Guard was likely to order 84 *Motomarine Invador* PCs of Greek origin as well as 110 *Motomarine Hellraiser* PCs of 12 tonnes. One wonders if these boats are meant for the Coast Guard or are meant for Marine Police of coastal states that are being trained by the Coast Guard. Almost similar number of small PCs were to be acquired for the Marine Police during the first phase of Coastal Security Perspective (2006-2011).

The aviation wing of the Indian Coast Guard took some time to grow, despite the realisation that maritime reconnaissance (MR) was of primary importance while monitoring a vast sea space of EEZ that was almost two-third in size of India's land space. Coast Guard also needed light helicopters for operating from *Vikram*-class OPVs that it had ordered as also for SAR operations near the coast.

The aviation wing of the Indian Coast Guard took the first step when the first helicopter squadron was commissioned in Goa in May 1982. *Chetak* helicopter also began to be operated from *Vikram-class* OPV since February 1984. The Coast Guard also required two *F-27* aircrafts from

Indian Air Lines on dry lease in May 1983 for MR in the Bay of Bengal. They were replaced with *Dornier* MR aircrafts.

The air-wing continued to expand over the subsequent years. More and more *Dornier* MR aircrafts were acquired as also *Chetak* light helicopters. They were stationed at various air stations. The Coast Guard also began to induct *Dhruv ALH*. It also put forward the proposal for acquisition of larger MR aircrafts to supplement role of *Dornier* MR aircrafts as also for medium-lift helicopter for operations further away from the shore.

By 2008, Indian Coast Guard had developed a reasonably large and yet integrated network of air bases and air stations along the coast as also in Andaman-Nicobar Islands. The accompanying table reveals that while the air wing does cover the entire maritime zones of India, areas of major concern like northern half of the Arabian sea and the sea space along the coast of Tamil Nadu were given greater attention.

Table: Coast Guard, Air Wing (2008)

Zones	Fixed Wing aircraft (Dornier)	Helicopters (Chetak/Dhruv)
Western Coast		
Daman	CGAS-750 8 Dorniers	CGAS 842 4 Chetak
Mumbai	-	CGAS 800 3 Chetak
Goa	-	CGAS 841 4 Chetak 3 ALH (Dhruv)
Kochi	CGAS-747 2 Dorniers	-
Eastern Coas		
Chennai	CGAS-744 7 Dorniers	CGAS 848 3 Chetak
Kolkata	CGAS-700 2 Dorniers	-
Andaman and Nicobar Islands		
Port Blair	CGAS-745 2 Dorniers	(2) Chetak

(Based on data from Jane's Fighting Ships, 2008-2009).

After 2004, the Coast Guard got a boost following the new thrust upon enhancing coastal security. It was allotted Rs. 7,000 crores during the current plan period (*Hindu*, May 30, 2005). Vice-Admiral R.F. Contractor, Director-General of the Coast Guard, on the eve of the 30th anniversary of the Coast Guard, said that the Coast Guard was planning to induct 16 major ships and 33 aircrafts, including multi-mission MR aircrafts, twin-engined helicopters and UAVs in the years ahead (*The Times of India*, New Delhi, February1, 2007).

Under the XIth Plan, Coast Guard is expected to acquire 98 ships/ boats and 55 fixed-wing aircrafts and helicopters. They would include 16 Dorniers, six multi-mission MR aircrafts, three Chetak helicopters, 14 twin-engined helicopters and 16 light aircrafts. Some of these would replace those that are getting old and obsolete. As per the Annual Report of the Ministry of Defence, 2009-10, force level of the Coast Guard was 43 boats/ crafts and 23 non-commissioned crafts. Several ships/boats were under various stages of construction. Many of them would replace those that needed to be phased out. Thus, there is not going to be a very great addition to number of large vessels like OPV and IPC. However, the number of interceptor boats and small patrol boats is likely to increase rapidly due to new thrust on coastal security.

The Central Government recognised the major role that the Coast Guard could play in the context of coastal security. It was granted Rs. 56 crores under the scheme to be jointly sponsored by Ministry of Home Affairs and Ministry of Defence. It was reported in October 2009 that Government had sanctioned additional 3,000 personnel, as well as procurement of 20 fast attack crafts, 41 interceptor boats, 12 Dornier MR aircrafts and 7 OPVs besides 46 coastal radars, to provide coverage along the coast and in union territories. In view of the sensitive sea space around Gujarat and Maharashtra, the fourth Regional Headquarter was operationalised in Gandhinagar. It was commissioned in December 2009. In all, nine new Coast Guard stations were proposed to be established. Funds were promised to be released on a fast track. Since the Coast Guard was facing shortage of trained officers, Coast Guard proposes to open its own academy at Azhekkal near Kannur in Keral. Defence Minister A.K. Anthony laid the foundation stone in July 2011. Defence Minister A.K. Anthony had promised that within a span of two years the Indian Coast Guard would be among the best in the world (*The Hindu*, October 29, 2009).

The Customs (Marine)

Independent India faced the serious problem related to large-scale smuggling of foreign exchange, gold, silver, and different types of consumer goods *via* its maritime borders. Smuggling not only destabilised Indian economy but also paved the way for the emergence of the so-called 'underworld' mafia linked to anti-national elements abroad. The traditional three n. mile territorial water limit of that period offered legal advantage to the smugglers since they could not be apprehended on the 'high seas' beyond the three mile limit. Also, the Customs had yet to develop a viable maritime wing for operating in waters adjacent to the long coast line of India.

Combination of two factors led to the gradual strengthening of the Marine Wing of the Customs. The one was a rapid increase in smuggling and the other was the expanding maritime zones of enforcement of the Customs Act under presidential proclamations of March 23 and December 3, 1956. The presidential proclamation of March 23, 1956 extended the outer limit of the territorial waters to 6 n. miles. Soon after, on December 3, 1956, another presidential proclamation created a contiguous zone that extended 6 n. miles beyond the limits of the new territorial waters, thereby creating in all, a 12 n. mile zone in which the Customs could exercise its jurisdiction (Rao, 1983, p. 295).

The Customs Act, 1962 (Act 52 of 1962) updated previous Sea Customs Act of 1876 and Sea Customs Amendment Act of 1955. (For full text of the Customs Act, 1962, see, Manohar and Chitaley, vol. 19, 1988, pp. 719-39). That Act too has been periodically updated. Under Section 2, Sub-section 28, Indian Customs waters means the waters extending into the sea upto the outer limit of the contiguous zone of India under Section 5 of the MZI Act, 1976 and includes any bay, gulf, harbour, creek and tidal river. The act limits the import and export of items in areas other than the specified customs ports. Under Chapter IV, Section 11, Subsection 2, the act not only includes the prevention of smuggling and the conservation of foreign exchange but also provides for *the maintenance of security of India* (Manohar and Chitaley, vol. 19, 1988, p. 737), thus bringing it in consonance with Section

5 (4a) of the MZI Act of 1976. This provision needs to be underlined since it not only empowers but also makes it obligatory for the Customs (Marine) to act in the context of maritime security upto the outer limit of the contiguous zone.

Earlier efforts to prevent smuggling were not very fruitful. In 1962-63, the value of total seizure of smuggled goods amounted to only Rs. 4.09 crores. Of that, gold amounted for Rs. 2.77 crores. (MoF, *A. R., 1962-63*, p. 63) Government of India passed acts like the Conservation of Foreign Exchange and Prevention of Smuggling Activities (COFEPOSA) of 1974. It only allowed for preventive detention of those who were suspected of being the key figures in smuggling activities. That act was not only inadequate but was often criticised as an instrument of arbitrary arrest for political reasons. In 1987, under that Act, detention orders were passed against 936 persons. 775 persons were detained and only 207 were convicted. In 1987-88, the total seizure was valued at Rs. 25.0 crores. Of that, gold accounted for Rs. 6.54 crores (MoF, *A.R., 1987-88*, p. 76). This was in spite of the strengthening of the Customs (Marine) and the cooperation of the Coast Guard in anti-smuggling role. One reason for this was the reluctance of the Union Government to actively involve the government of the coastal states in checking smuggling. Thus, India paid the price of inadequate division of power between the Union Government and the coastal states under the Seventh Schedule of the Indian Constitution.

Customs Marine Organisation

Now that the scope of the Customs was gradually expanding seawards, it needed an organisation to shoulder the new responsibility. Also, smuggling activities were increasing. A committee was appointed under the chairmanship of Dr. B.D. Nagchaudhury to recommend measures on strengthening the Customs in that context. Deliberations led to two-fold recommendations; need to establish a separate wing to look after the sea space, and steps to improve the force level for that role.

The government approved, on August 2, 1974, the formation of a Customs Marine Organisation. It was to have its headquarters in Bombay. It was to be headed by the Director (Marine), a post that was held by a naval officer on deputation, with serving and retired personnel from the

Army and the Navy on his staff. He reported to the Director (Preventive Operations), New Delhi. The Customs Marine Organisation or Customs (Marine) had shore facilities in place by 1975. They included four marine workshops at Magdalla Port, Bombay, Ratnagiri and Baypore, as also a central store yard at Bombay and an *ad hoc* training school at Magdalla (MoF, *A.R., 1974-1975*, pp. 29-30).

The progress must have been slow. *Annual Report, 1987-1988*, of the Ministry of Finance noted that in order to streamline the Custom's marine fleet and to bring it under one umbrella, setting up of Customs Marine Organisation had been approved by the Government and 58 posts were sanctioned in Phase I. A 7-year Customs Marine Perspective Plan for modernisation of Customs Marine Fleet was also approved by the Cabinet (MoF, *A.R., 1987-1988*, p. 77).

An effort was made for a more intimate cooperation between the Customs and the coastal state's enforcement agencies following the Bombay blast of 1993. Efforts were made to further streamline and strengthen the anti-smuggling policy (MoF, *A.R., 1993-1994*, p. 52). It came as a surprise that while Annual Report of the Finance Ministry mentioned that subject, the Annual Report of the Ministry of Home Affairs of that year was silent on it. No breakthrough was, however, possible in building this cooperation largely due to the constitutional constraint mentioned above. One hopes that the new initiative of involving the coastal states in maritime security and the formation of Marine Police will create a better opportunity for synergy between the Customs (Marine) and the Marine Police at the state level.

Customs (Marine): Enforcement Capability

As long as the Customs was working within the narrow confines of three n. mile territorial water limit, it did not need sophisticated and sea worthy interceptor boats. But, as its zone of operation began to expand upto 12 n. miles in 1956 and to 24 n. miles in 1976, need was felt for strengthening its capability to operate further away from the coast. Ministry of Finance had taken the decision in 1962 itself to augment the fleet of launches by acquiring 26 new launches over the next four years. Orders for the same were placed with the Director-General of Supplies and Disposal. According to Prabhakar

Paleri, the Indian Navy was operating six Italian-built SDBs (*INS Sarayu, INS Subhadra, INS Sharda, INS Savitri* and *INS Sukanya*) on behalf of the Customs. Four of them were placed at Mumbai and two at Madras (Chennai). According to him, they were relatively slow and grossly inadequate to deter sea-borne smugglers who operated fast moving crafts (Paleri, 2004, p. 35).

Efforts were made to enhance the capability to intercept boats of smugglers further away from the shores. A committee was constituted under the chairmanship of Dr. B.D. Nag Chaudhury on January 23, 1970. Other members included Air Marshal O.P. Mehra and Admiral R.D. Katari (Retired). The committee was tasked to recommend among other things, the number and type of crafts required, their source of supply and availability, as also suitability of hovercrafts, helicopters and fixed-wing aircrafts for the Customs. The committee presented its report in August 1971.

The committee recommended a three-tier system for intercepting smugglers. It also suggested the need not only for early acquisition of surface vessels but also the need for indigeneous construction. It supported the need to acquire hovercrafts as also surveillance aircrafts under a phased programme. It emphasised upon the need for creating a separate and properly equipped force for conducting sea-borne anti-smuggling operations.

Subsequent to the presentation of the Nag Chaudhury report, a meeting was held under the Chairmanship of V.C. Shukla, Minister for Defence Production, to expedite the process for acquisition of suitable boats for the Customs. It initially recommended two types of vessels. The one was a large patrol boat with 1,000 mile range and maximum speed of 30 knots. It was to carry light armament and was to be manned by a crew of 16. The other was a smaller crafts with a higher speed and a crew of 12. It was also to be lightly armed. This recommendation was not implemented. In a subsequent meeting on November 22, 1973 with the Ministry of Defence Production, the Customs indicated a requirement for 20 modified seaward defence boats (SDB) for the Department (Paleri, 2004, pp. 36-7).

In September 1974, Committee of Secretaries, under the chairmanship of the Cabinet Secretary, appointed a committee to examine the shortcomings of anti-smuggling and other maritime activities, as also the creation of the Coast Guard. That committee was chaired by K.F. Rustamji, the then Special Secretary, Ministry of Home Affairs. This committee, in effect, carried forward the work undertaken by the Nag Chaudhury committee on the question of revamping and strengthening the marine wing of the Customs.

The Rustamji Committee examined the terms of reference in three parts. These were submitted separately in its report. Part I dealt with intelligence and allied aspects of the problem of smuggling. Part II dealt with operational matters related to anti-smuggling. Only Part-III dealt with the Coast Guard. Thus, Rustamji Committee discussed the question of Customs (Marine) as also that of the Coast Guard. It also recommended that the Coast Guard, when formed, should cooperate with the Customs in anti-smuggling operations.

One result of these recommendations was the growth in surface capability of the fleet of Customs (Marine). As noted, in the sixties it had only a few SDBs that were operated by the Indian Navy and were acquired from Italy. They were found to be unequal to the task. The marine fleet of the Customs was augmented by the induction of new boats from Norway. These *Saab Scania SS-40* boats were classified as Customs Patrol Crafts (CPC) and were expected to replace the Italian SDBs. About 19 of these new boats were to be acquired. Ten of them had reached India by March-April 1975 while the remaining boats were to join shortly thereafter. These CPCs were armed with light machine guns. They also had echo-sounders to detect goods dumped in the sea during the chase as well as radars and night vision devices. These boats were initially staffed by Indian Navy personnel on deputation, and subsequently by retired personnel from the Navy and other armed forces recruited into the Customs Marine Organisation (Kamath, 1979, p. 232). The Customs also operated at that time about 50 confiscated and subsequently appropriated *dhows* that were classified as Customs Auxiliary crafts (CAC). Two water jet crafts were also added. (Paleri, 2004, p. 417).

The fleet of Norwegian boats (*Scania SS-40*) was further augmented by the addition of new and more sophisticated *Swallow-class* interceptor boats acquired from South Korea (MoF, *A.R., 1980-81*, p. 214). Probably financial constraints restricted their numbers. As per the report of Ministry of Finance, 1987-1988, under the 7-year Customs Marine Perspective Plan for modernisation of Customs Marine Fleet, phased action was being taken to acquire 45-feet and 54-feet Customs Patrol Launches (CPL). As a beginning, 10 CPLs of 45 feet were ordered. An order for import of four rubberised boats from UK had also been placed. The gap in the force level was met through improvisation. Three confiscated vessels were appropriated. Also, 17 plastic boats and 38 outboard motors were distributed to Marine Collectorates for anti-smuggling operations (MoF, *A.R., 1987-88*, p. 77).

The force level of the Customs (Marine) remained not only inadequate but also outmoded. Data in the *A.R., 1993-1994* of the Ministry of Finance provided insight in the gross neglect of a major component of India's maritime security. As per that report, four wooden hulled *dhows* of 80 feet with a top speed of 13.6 knots (only) were being built by M/s. N.M. Wadia & Co., Billimore and were likely to be inducted in July 1994. 12 crafts were being retrofitted at M/s Bristol Boat, Aroor, Kochi. Proposal was also to retrofit 3 CPCs. The Department had a total of 18 CPCs. It also said that order was placed for ten 60-feet CPLs with M/s Bristol Boat, Aroor, Kochi. Its maximum speed was to be 20 knots. The first vessel was to be delivered by July 1994 and the rest at the interval of two months. Proposals for acquiring 20 fast interceptor boats were under consideration. Also efforts were afoot to acquire 80 CPCs of 80 feet. For surveillance, the Department had acquired 15 Furuno Marine Radars, Model 1940, from m/s Ultra Marine Air Aids (P) Ltd., New Delhi in 1993-94. They were to be retrofitted to CPCs. Several might-vision binoculors (almost 400) were already required in 1992-1994 (MoF, *A.R., 1993-1994*, pp. 52-3).

The Marine wing of the Customs, after a good start, had lost the momentum and remained a neglected wing of India's maritime enforcement agencies. There are several reasons for it. The Customs Marine Organisation remained a part of a larger organisation and thus was subjected to inevitable intra-departmental constraints. Its policy of depending upon Navy and retired personnel from the armed forces meant that it could not develop, unlike the Coast Guard, a dedicated base and cadre for itself. The Coast Guard, though created after the formation of Customs Marine

Organisation (CMO), soon acquired its independent organisational status. Its overlapping role of anti-smuggling also tended to overshadow the role of the Customs (Marine) since the Coast Guard began to acquire a more suitable force level for the task.

According to Madvendra Singh, when the Coast Guard was established, a decision was taken by the Government that the finances for the Coast Guard would be provided by the Department of Revenue (Customs) (Singh, 1992, p. 15). It was even suggested that the CMO be disbanded and units of CMO be turned over to the Coast Guard so that the Coast Guard could take on the maritime jurisdiction from the land outwards (Carneiro, 1991, p. 514). The end result of these debates was that the Marine wing of the Customs remained fossilised during the eighties and the nineties. Yet, despite several setbacks, Marine wing of the Customs has survived and remains functional even now.

It was unfortunate that Customs (Marine) was seen only as an instrument to check smuggling of consumer items *via* the sea. No one highlighted the links likely to be developed between smugglers, the so-called underworld mafia and the terrorists. Bombay blasts of 1993, for which the RDX was smuggled *via* the sea, could have been an eye opener. But, the decision makers seem to have their own perception of maritime terrorism. It is an irony that while the *A.R.* of the Ministry of Finance, while dealing with the Customs, mentioned the need to strengthen and upgrade anti-smuggling operations (MoF, *A.R., 1993-1994*, p. 52), the Annual Report of the Ministry of Home Affairs had not even mentioned it. That reveals the narrow 'continental' mindset of 'security analyst' in the corridors of power at the Central Government those days. Units of the Customs did participate along with the Navy, the Coast Guard and the Maharashtra Government police in patrolling the coast of Maharashtra after 1993 but one had to wait for a decade before the Home Ministry became actively involved in neutralising the threat of maritime terrorism. The events of November 26, 2008 (26/11) gave yet another jolt. But, while decisions were taken to upgrade and strengthen the Coast Guard, create *Sagar Prahari Bal* for the Navy and set up new Marine Police at the level of coastal states, there was no comparable reference about a role for the Customs Marine Organisation, a force dedicated for maritime security under the Customs Act of 1962.

As noted earlier, the Customs Act, in Chapter IV, Section 11, Sub-section 2, para a, mentions "maintenance of security of India" as one of its purposes. Also, the MZI Act, 1976, under Section 5, Sub-section 4, para a, dealing with contiguous zone, mentions that the Central Government may exercise such powers and take such measures in or in relation to the contiguous zone as it may consider necessary with respect to the *security* of India. Thus, the Customs Act and the MZI Act, read together, confer added responsibilities upon the Customs (Marine) in the context of meeting new threats from maritime terrorism in the water space at least upto the outer limit of the contiguous zone, which is the zone of operation of Customs (Marine).

As noted, after the Bombay blasts of 1993, the Customs was involved along with the Navy and the Coast Guard, in strengthening the surveillance of the coastal waters of Maharashtra. That role will be more crucial in the context of the new policy being evolved since 2004-2005 of further strengthening of maritime security in the coastal waters of India. The Customs (Marine), along with the Coast Guard and the Marine Police, can play a more constructive role in that respect. It is, therefore, important that it be suitably modernised and equipped so that it is able to play the desired role on behalf of the Central Government in further strengthening maritime security in the decades to come.

There were reports that the Ministry of Finance was seeking to revive and re-equip the Customs (Marine). A study group was constituted by the Central Board of Excise and Customs (CBEC) in 1988. It had allegedly recommended the revival of CMO by inducting modern vessels capable of patrolling the Customs waters. Prabhakar Paleri, Director-General of the Coast Guard, in his book commented, "Modernisation of the Customs Marine is a welcome sign and will be effective for maritime monitoring in close coordination with the Coast Guard" (Paleri, 2004, p. 321, footnote 29). It is high time that Customs (Marine) be suitably strengthened and inducted as an active component of India's maritime security structure.

Security of ports and off-shore platforms, role for CISF (Marine)

Marine security of these high value targets need to be examined from two interrelated angles; area security and basic point security. While area security can be entrusted to maritime enforcement agencies like the Navy and the Coast Guard that are well equipped for that role in the adjacent sea space, basic point security of these high value targets need a specialised and a dedicated force. When experts talk of port security they normally refer to efforts made to 'secure' port from the landward side or at best of Container Security Imitative. Very often the question of seaward side of the port, harbour and the anchorage is neglected even though International Maritime Organisation (IMO) has almost equated criminal activities directed against ships near these areas with piracy on the high seas. In India, the events of 26/11, when foreign terrorists came to Bombay *via* sea, revealed not only the total absence of any security mechanism but also the absence of any authority that could really be blamed for that lapse. The real lapse was in the perception of the threat itself. Even after 26/11, nothing much seems to have been done to secure these areas in a structured manner.

The casualness with which the matter was being perceived was revealed by a photograph published in the Annual Report of the Ministry of Home Affairs for the year 2005-2006. While dealing with the Central Industrial Security Force (CISF), the Annual Report carried a photograph of a few CISF *jawans* armed with assault rifles on board a slow moving tug-like vessel. The caption mentioned that they were patrolling the waters of the Jawaharlal Nehru Port Trust (JNPT) area (MHA, *A.R., 2005-2006*, p. 77). Even a layman could question their competence to prevent and/or neutralise the threat from dedicated terrorists who wish to target ships or other value targets in that sea space or to use that sea space to attack other targets on shore.

No one questions the competence of the CISF to ensure security of high value installations on land. But, it is time that CISF's role in meeting the new challenge of maritime security in the adjacent sea space be assessed and if found suitable, its capability be suitably upgraded so that it can offer basic point security not only to the landward side of the installation but also to the adjacent waters and sea lanes of traffic in those waters as also to off-shore installations.

The sheltered waters of the port, the harbour and anchorage as well as overland communication facilities near the port encourage setting up of installations like oil/CNG terminals, refineries, fishing harbour, ferry services, hotels etc. in close proximity to the port. Vessels going there are allowed access *via* the main traffic lanes of the port/harbour. It is, therefore, logical that any framework of maritime security of waters adjacent to the port should take into account the multiple traffic in that sea space and evolve appropriate mechanism to monitor and enforce traffic rules and, if need be, to foil attempts by criminal elements including the terrorists.

Either an appropriate organisation is raised and trained for the task or the CISF, like the BSF, be provided with its own marine wing that is suitably equipped with vessels, weapons and surveillance system so that it can offer effective security in its designated zone of operation. In this connection, it may even be suggested that the basic point security of high value installations on the continental-shelf can also be entrusted to the proposed Marine Wing of the CISF. Its personnel can man the platform and even patrol its immediate vicinity to sanitise the surrounding sea space. While UNCLOS-III allows for a 500 metre "safety" zone around these installations, MZI Act, 1976, Section 6, Subsection 5 b (ii) provides for the *safety and protection* zone. Government can identify its own appropriate "surveillance" zone around them for *protection*. Thus, while the Navy and the Coast Guard can provide for area security, CISF's Marine Wing, if and when created, can offer "basic point security" to these installations. Thus, the Marine Wing of the CISF can be a part of the wider network of maritime security and synergise its role with those of other maritime enforcement agencies operating or likely to operate in that zone like the Navy, the Coast Guard, the Customs, Fisheries Department and the Marine Police.

India is opening up its economy to private sector. Private sector participation in maritime affairs like port/harbour, shipping, refineries, off-shore oil and gas installations on the continental-shelf etc is going to increase in the years to come. They too would need a security cover. The CISF Act was amended to enable it to provide consultancy service in the field of industrial security to the private sector industries on cost recovery basis (MHA, *A.R., 2001-2002*, p. 83). CISF has been awarded the role of providing security cover to the headquarters of the Infosys Technology Ltd., Bangalore since August 2009. It was reported that under the deal, CISF would depute 100 personnel to assist the 300-members security team of the Infosys to provide security cover for the establishment. CISF was to charge rupees one lakh per day for that service (*The Hindu*, August 1, 2009). Thus, CISF can offer maritime security to private sector as well under a mutually agreed formula. Such a policy will also mean that the private sector not only benefits from policy of economic liberalisation but also contributes to the security of its establishments from threats emanating *via* the sea space.

In the context of maritime security of private sector undertakings, attention needs to be drawn at the Private Security Agency (Regulation) Act, 2005, passed by the Government of India. It was notified in the Gazette of India on June 23, 2005 and brought into force on March 15, 2006. Under that Act, state governments have been given the power to appoint a controlling authority for the purpose of granting licence to these agencies. Holding of that licence will be mandatory for carrying on the business of security agencies and other related matters. The Central Government has framed the Private Security Agency's Central Model Rules, 2006. That was notified by the Government on April 26, 2006. It was forwarded to all state governments to enable them to frame their own rules in conformity with the Central Model Rules (MHA, *A.R., 2006-2007*, p. 61). Thus, the state government can also sanction private security agencies in maritime affairs. Jurisdiction of the Private Security Agency (Regulation) Act of 2005 extends upto the outer limit of the territorial waters. If such agencies have to operate beyond that on the high seas, the act will need to be suitably amended. Some mechanism needs to be evolved so that their activities can be coordinated/synergised with those of other agencies like the Marine Police, Customs and the Coast Guard for a more effective operation at the level of coastal states.

There are moves to privatise maritime security in some parts of South-East Asia. This can include options ranging from private police force, protection service on board sea going vessels, armed/unarmed ship escorting vessels etc. The demand seems to have increased during the past few years. There are major constraints on using arms on board non-military vessels since it could limit the right of innocent passage. Peter Lehr, however, mentions that there are some agencies that offer protection to ships in the Straits of Malacca. These agencies are Singapore based and licensed. They offer armed escorts to propective customers. The legal implication of their use of force in the territorial waters of other states, however, remains a matter of legal debate (Lehri, 2008, p. 196 and Pon, 2008, pp. 377-79). Reportedly, there are moves to legalise such armed guards in India as well.

While the question of port security was not debated earlier, the question of security of off-shore installations was first discussed by the Rustamji Committee in 1974, long before India even began to exploit its off-shore oil and gas resources. Vice-Admiral V.A. Kamath, who was a member of the committee, had argued that the security of these offshore installations be entrusted to the Navy. He had argued that the Navy was better equipped for that role than the proposed Coast Guard. He also requested the Government to provide necessary tools to the Navy to perform that new role. The committee, however, did not accept that suggestion. Instead it made the following recommendations:

(a) CISF be responsible for security of shore installations under the Ministry of Petroleum and Chemicals.

(b) Off-shore security to be entrusted to the Coast Guard. The committee reasoned that the Navy, although better equipped, was a defence force and it would not be appropriate to divert its energies to a limited task of such a nature.

(c) The responsibility of onboard security(basic point security) would be with the facilities that may seek such assistance from the Navy or the Coast Guard if things were beyond its own capabilities (Paleri, 2004, pp. 43-4).

By the time the committee finalised its report, the issue of off-shore security of these platforms rested primarily with the Indian Coast Guard as the leading maritime agency during situations other than war and as a support agency during the war (Paleri, 2004, pp. 244-45). The Coast Guard Act, 1976, specified, under Chapter III, Section 14, Subsection 2 para g that the Coast Guard would ensure the safety and protection of artificial islands, off-shore terminals, installations and other structures and devices in *any* maritime zone.

Though the Coast Guard was designated as the prime agency entrusted with the security of off-shore installations, it was the Navy that continued to play a major role in that context, in the eighties. According to Commodore J.P. Carneiro, protection of the off-shore installations was with the Navy but was transferred to the Coast Guard. In the sharing of duty, the Coast Guard was required to prevent entry of unauthorised ships, including fishing vessels, and minimise risk of collusion by passing ships and to regulate sea traffic (Carneiro, 1991, p. 514).

During the eighties, the maritime threat to these platforms was felt, especially from Pakistan's sub-surface capability and from aircrafts armed with Exocet missiles. Maritime terrorism was till then not perceived as a major threat. Hence, it was natural that the security of these off-shore platforms be perceived by the Navy in the context of threat from state actors or state-sponsored NSA. Pakistan Navy was strengthening its fleet of conventional submarines by acquiring *Agosta-class* submarines from France. It was also building midget submarines designed for covert action. According to Vice-Admiral G.M. Hiranandani, Indian Navy acquired 'chariots' (a mini-submarine) in 1975, to defend Bombay and off-shore oil and gas rigs and platforms from attack by similar crafts. *INS Abhimanyu* was commissioned in Bombay as Interiem Chariot Complex. Proposal to form Indian Marine Special Force (IMSF) as Marine Commandos (MARCOS) was put forward in 1983. Three *Sea King MK 42 C* medium-lift helicopters were ear-marked in 1985 for IMSF. These were to be used to defend Bombay High against clandestine attacks, including eviction of terrorists who could have taken control of the rig or the platform (Hiranandani, 2003, p. 186). The Navy also acquired *Sukanya-class* offshore patrol vessels. One of the tasks of these vessels was the security of Bombay High. These vessels, however, had no ASW capability.

As the capability of the Coast Guard expanded in terms of manpower and equipment, it began to be entrusted with roles that were being handled by the Navy. It was made responsible for the security of off-shore installations as also of SBM (off-shore) like the SBM of IOC in the Gulf of Cutch under a MoU signed in 1981. Since the Bombay High straddles the customary sea lanes to Bombay harbour, a traffic regulatory scheme was promulgated in 1985. It required vessels destined for or departing from

Bombay to follow recommended routes. Since those routes were recommendatory they were not always followed A mandatory traffic separation scheme was under consideration (Hiranandani, 2003, p. 196).

Though the Coast Guard was entrusted with the security of off-shore installations, it was realised that cooperation of other concerned agencies was also required to give effect to that obligation. The Ministry of Petroleum, Chemicals and Fertilizers had constituted an Off-shore Security Coordination Committee (OSCC) on May 30, 1978. It was entrusted with the task of identifying threats to off-shore oil facilities at all times and to find ways and means to protect them from identified threats. Terrorists were not an identified threat at that time. Terms of reference of the committee were formally approved only in 1981. They were revised in 1984.

In the meanwhile, an Off-shore Defence Advisory Group was also constituted in July 1983. It was headed by an officer of the rank of Rear-Admiral (FODAG) and was tasked to plan and advise the Navy and the ONGC on the security and defence of the Bombay High. Keeping in view the growing threat from NSA, approval was given in 1985, for added resources required for 'peace time threats' (Hiranandani, 2003, p. 196).

Threat to security of off-shore installations from covert activities sponsored by state actors as also by terrorists was recognised since mid-eighties. The terms of reference of OSCC included identification and neutralisation of threats in situations other than war, like internal sabotage, hijacking, accidents, threats from frogmen etc. The OSCC instituted a sub-committee to periodically evaluate these threats. It was constituted on December 15, 2000. Its members included, apart from the Director-General of the Coast Guard as the head of the OSCC, representatives from the Navy, the Air Force, Intelligence Bureau, ONGC, Oil India Limited and Director-General of Hydrocarbon. The sub-committee recognised the peculiar characteristic of the job, increased vulnerability and complicated security and defence arrangements. Not only are the off-shore installations dispersed over a wide sea space but are also located in rich fishing grounds. That makes access control and monitoring, a difficult task.

The sub-committee recommended emphatically the pivotal role of the Coast Guard and the need for strengthening it with appropriate force level and professional competence. It also made recommendations regarding traffic rules around the off-shore areas, monitoring of fixed platforms by Vessel and Air traffic management system (VATMS). These recommendations span agencies other than the Coast Guard like the Navy, the CISF, Director-General of Shipping and oil facilities operators both in public and private sectors (Paleri, 2004, pp. 251-54).

A very sophisticated Vessel and Air Traffic Management System (VATMS) for surveillance of western off-shore oil and gas installations was reportedly installed by the ONGC in 2007. As per the company release, the state of art surveillance system was suggested by the ONGC on the recommendation of the Naval Headquarters and Off-shore Defence Advisory Group (*The Times of India*, New Delhi, September 14, 2007). The ONGC was operating, in 2006-2007, 12 complex processes and more than 130 well-head platforms located in the western off-shore area. It was reported in March 2009 that the Off-shore Development Area Vessel and Air-Traffic Management System has been put in place for all off-shore development area (*Hindu,* March 1, 2009).

These are very important and sophisticated inputs but in view of the density and diversity of traffic, including large numbers of fishing boats from adjoining coastal states like Gujarat and Maharashtra, the time for response to neutralise a dedicated, even suicidal attack against these high value targets by using fishing boats laden with high explosives will be very limited. Even if the movement of such a fishing boat is detected at the distance of one kilometre from the intended target, the reaction time, given the speed of the fishing boat even at 8 knots per hour, will be about five minutes. If the boat is allowed to approach to a distance of 500 metres, the reaction time will be about two minutes; too little for an effective response from the Navy or the Coast Guard unless their vessels are in close proximity to the intended target.

Hence, there is the need for installing basic point security system for at least important high value oil and gas platforms. Who can be entrusted with that role? Since it will need use of weapons like heavy machine guns and even missiles like anti-tank rockets to neutralise the vessel before it can reach the intended target, only a highly trained team belonging to the armed forces or para military forces can be entrusted with that role. The feasibility of equipping the CISF with such a role has been discussed earlier while dealing with port security.

Initially, security of off-shore installations involved only public-sector undertakings like the ONGC. Of late, private sector is also entering into this field. Not only is the private sector building large ports and SBM away from the coast but is involved in oil and gas exploration/exploitation in India's continental-shelf. Keeping in view the new development, Chairman OSCC had constituted a sub-committee, under the Flag Officer Defence Advisory Group (FODAG) on October 15, 1997, to examine issues related to problems associated with joint ventures off-shore security arrangement (Palleri, 2004, p. 253). One doubts if the private sector would be so easily roped in even if it is a question of their heavy investment. It would rather put the onus on the maritime enforcement agencies like the Navy and the Coast Guard.

India will witness a quantum jump in the number of oil and gas installations in its continental-shelf along its western as also eastern sea space. ONGC as also private sector undertakings like the Reliance and Ruia are expected to expand their presence in these waters. Will the Central Government offer the private sector undertakings similar security cover as is being provided to public sector undertakings? Will the private sector be satisfied with it or will it prefer to upgrade its security cover? Can the private sector be allowed to establish its own security cover? Even after the private sector is allowed that, the question will still remain about coordinating its policies and enforcement measures with those of the Central Government forces like the Navy, the Coast Guard, the Air Force, Director-General of Shipping etc. Hence, India needs to look afresh at the entire question of security of off-shore installations, especially in the context of threats posed by terrorists.

Maritime Enforcement: State Level

For long, decision makers had compartmentalised threats as land oriented and sea oriented. In the past, emphasis was given to threat, across the land border. In that context, India's air-land battle capability was strengthened. Also, new para-military forces like the Border Security Force and Indo-Tibetan Border Force were formed. These were placed under the Ministry of Home Affairs. Maritime security was treated separately. The Navy and subsequently the Coast Guard were made responsible for it. They were placed under the Ministry of Defence. Efforts were made to check smuggling *via* sea by creating the Marine wing of the Customs. It operated under yet another ministry. All these different agencies worked under the Central Government. India has a long coast line. However, under the Indian Constitution, coastal states are not assigned any significant role in the context of neutralising threats posed by NSA and terrorists *via* the adjacent sea space, despite the fact that it is the coastal belt that sufferes most due to this ill-conceived emphasis upon the supremacy of the Union Government over the state governments. Fortunately, this mindset is now slowly changing after 2004.

The formation of the Marine Police and its support by the Ministry of Home Affairs is a major step in recognising the crucial role that the coastal states and union territories (UTs) are destined to play in combating maritime threat posed by NSA and terrorists. One will witness further strengthening of maritime enforcement agencies at the level of the Central Government as well as state governments. Unless their roles are synergised, it will complicate matters further.

India has a long coast line of about 7,516 km. Several coastal states have long and vulnerable coastlines: Gujarat 1,600 km, Tamil Nadu 992 km, Andhra Pradesh 960 km, Maharashtra 720 km, Kerala 575 km, Orissa 430 km, Carnatic 287 km etc. These coastal states account for almost 50 percent of the total population of India. According to Manoj Gupta, the coastal belt alone accounts for 25 percent of total population (Gupta, 2002, p. 393). Its major urban/industrial centres include Kolkata, with a population of about 13.2 mn, Greater Mumbai with 16.43 mn, Chennai with 6.56 mn etc.

Thus, a large part of Indian territory, population, and industrial centres are subjected to threats emanating *via* the sea. Till now, that threat was evaluated primarily in the context of state actors. While those threats have not diminished, new dimensions of maritime threat like terrorism have been added. Also, the more India develops its maritime/coastal assets, more targets will be available to these criminal elements. Since these threats affect the coastal states directly, it is logical that they be intimately involved in maritime security measures.

India had started facing since mid-eighties, the threat of maritime terrorism that had support base across the seas. It highlighted the need for active cooperation of the enforcement agencies of coastal states. Tamil Nadu police had to be more actively involved in meeting the fallout of Tamil militancy in Sri Lanka which had support base in Tamil Nadu as well. Support of the Tamil Nadu police was, however, restricted to operations on land only. Threat of terrorism drawing support from across the Arabian Sea became evident during the series of bomb blasts in Bombay in 1993. That led to joint patrol along the western coast, particularly of Maharashtra coast, by the Navy, the Coast Guard, the Customs (all under the Union Government) and the state police. But that also did not lead to any concrete step that would enable the coastal state to play an active and autonomous role in combating that threat posed *via* its adjacent waters.

There were no moves to establish specific Marine Police at state level to monitor and counter activities related to maritime terrorism. This author had suggested, as early as September 1993, the need to establish the Marine Police under the authority of the coastal states. It was argued that counter-measures needed to be planned in a more systematic manner than the knee-jerk response that had been displayed till then. Such measures would revolve around three main variables; reconnaissance, identification and interception. For more effective countermeasures, these three steps needed to be coordinated between the forces operating on the sea as also on the land, with a special force linking the two. The author had suggested that the crucial gap between the land forces i.e. the state police and maritime forces of the Central Government like Navy, the Coast Guard and the Customs can be filled by establishing a specialised wing; Marine Police under the authority of the coastal states (Singh, 1993, p. 6).

Participation of coastal states in maritime security raises constitutional as well as practical constraints. As noted, the Constitution had conferred all powers related to maritime security upon the Central Government. As analysed in Chapter IV, item 1 of the Union List (List I) of the VIIth Schedule of the Constitution allocates *defence* of India to the Union Government. It was, therefore, appropriate that defence forces be under the Central Government. But, as analysed earlier, there is a difference between 'defence' *vis-à-vis* state actors and 'security' *vis-à-vis* NSA and terrorists. Union List does not provide for that. Hence, by default, coastal states can claim, if they so decide, jurisdiction in such cases under item 1 of List II (State List) dealing with state's power under 'public order'. Item 2 of List II notes only 'police'. Normally, that was equated only with 'land' police though the Constitution does not expressly forbid raising of Marine Police by the coastal state. All states have their special police force. Hence, coastal states can have Marine Police as well since *Constitution does not expressly prohibit it*. It only prohibits a state from employing military (defence) forces of the Union Government.

A point can also be raised about the extent of criminal jurisdiction of the coastal state in its adjacent waters. In the case of fisheries, coastal states have managed to acquire jurisdiction upto the outer limit of the territorial waters. Such a jurisdiction can also be extended to matters dealing with criminal law: CrPC, IPC, UAPA and other related Union acts. One can argue that item 1, 2 and 3 of the Concurrent List (List III), that refer to criminal law, criminal procedure and preventive detention, can be stretched to provide the necessary constitutional legitimacy for such a jurisdiction for the state's police as well. If necessary, the Concurrent List can be amended to include maritime security as an independent item in that list.

One can also raise the pertinent question whether the territorial waters limit is the appropriate limit for coastal state's criminal jurisdiction in the context of maritime security, or can the 24 n. miles of the contiguous zone be considered as a more appropriate outer limit of coastal state's criminal jurisdiction. MZI Act, 1976, under Section 5, Sub-section 4a, however, authorises only the Central Government "to exercise such powers and take such measures in or in relation to the contiguous zone as it may consider necessary with respect to the *security* of India." MZI Act, 1976, however, does not expressly prohibit the Union Government from either delegating that responsibility or sharing it with the coastal state's maritime enforcement agencies. It needs to be highlighted that the 24-n. mile distance can also be covered even by a fishing trawler in less than three hours; a bare minimum time for assessing and responding positively to the threat.

In the context of maritime security, one factor needs to be underlined. That is the extent of coastal state's responsibility in that context, and its share in the overall national effort towards ensuring maritime security. Not all coastal states are rich and hence cannot afford the extra financial burden of coastal security on their own. Today, the Central Government, especially the Ministry of Home Affairs and the Ministry of Defence, are contributing towards that. But it is necessary to work out a long term burden sharing arrangement between each of the coastal states and the Union Government. May be this point will be taken up more seriously during Phase II (2011-16) of Coastal Security Scheme.

Marine Police

The Ministry of Home Affairs, at the level of the Central Government, initiated steps to strengthen coastal security and in that process to authorise and subsidise the formation of Marine Police and the acquisition of related equipment including patrol boats. For the first time in India, coastal states were not only authorised but also assisted financially as well as technologically by the Central Government to strengthen their maritime enforcement capability as well as to integrate that new organisation in the over-all framework of coastal security. Its role is, however, seen as a supplement rather than as a complement to the overall coastal security framework.

A more formal shape was given to the concept of coastal security by 2004. Annual Report of the Ministry of Home Affairs, 2004-2005, said that keeping in view the vulnerability of the coast to exploitation by anti-national elements and criminals, a Coastal Security Scheme had been formulated to provide assistance to coastal states to establish coastal police stations (MHA, *A.R., 2004-2005*, pp. 7-8). The next year's Annual Report mentioned that the newly proposed scheme would have a component of Marine Police personnel trained in maritime functions (MHA, *A.R., 2005-2006*, p.40).

Annual Report of 2006-2007 further elaborated upon that scheme. It said, "A Coastal Security Scheme has been formulated for *strengthening* (as if it existed) infrastructure for patrolling and surveillance of country's coastal area (*particularly the shallow areas close to the coast*) to check and counter illegal *cross border* (?) activities and criminal activities using coast or sea"(MHA, *A.R., 2006-2007*, p. 38). The Annual Report, 2008-

2009, of the Ministry of Home Affairs said, "A *supplemental scheme* called Coastal Security Scheme is under implementation in nine coastal states and four coastal UTs since 2005, for strengthening infrastructure for coastal patrolling and surveillance".

Under the scheme that was implemented in all the nine coastal states and four union territories of India, assistance was provided totalling Rs. 551 crores for a period of five years. Of that amount, Rs. 400 crores was to be spent on non-recurring expenditure and Rs. 151 crores on recurring expenditure. (MHA, *A.R., 2008-2009*, pp.33-5). Under that scheme, assistance was to be provided to set up 73 police stations, 97 check posts, 58 outposts and 30 operational barracks, along the coast. These were to be provided with 204 boats, 149 jeeps and 318 motor cycles for *mobility along the coast and close coastal waters.*

This allotment by the Central Government as given in Annual Report, 2006-2007, was slightly more than what was initially provided for in the Annual Report of 2005-2006 in which there was provision for only 68 police stations, 194 boats, 124 jeeps and 279 motor cycles (MHA, *A.R., 2005-2006*, p.40). Under the scheme, a lump-sum assistance of Rs. 10 lakhs per police station was to be given for acquisition of equipment, computer, furniture etc. Assistance was to be provided to the coastal states and union territories to meet the cost of fuel, maintenance and repair of boats for five years. Thus, under the new scheme, Marine Police is designed to have the role of "beat constable" along the shore instead of a role in the adjacent coastal waters in which enforcement action was retained with the enforcement agencies of the Central Government.

As noted, the Central Government finally agreed to provide 204 small patrol boats to the Marine Police of the coastal states and union territories. Of these, 120 are of 12 tonnes and 84 of 5 tonnes displacement. Ten of the 12-tonne boats, with higher qualifications, were to be built at the Garden Reach Shipbuilders and Engineers Limited for Andaman-Nicobar (MHA, *A.R., 2010-2011, p. 48)*. These boats were to be acquired through public sector undertakings only. Goa Shipyards Ltd. built 62 boats of 12 tonnes and 54 boats of 5 tonnes each. The Garden Reach Shipbuilders and Engineers Ltd. in Kolkata built 58 boats of 12 tonnes and 30 boats of 5 tonnes each. These were expected to cost Rs. 329 crores. Each 5-tonne boat was to cost Rs. 105 lakhs and 12 tonne boat, around Rs. 215 lakhs. By 2010-2011, 101 boats of 120 tonnes and 82 boats of 5-tonnes (a total of 183 out of the 204 ordered) were constructed and distributed to different states and UTs (MHA, *A.R., 2010-2011*, p. 194).

Table: Marine Police: Patrol Boats

States/UT	12 tonne boats		5-tonne boats		Total	
	Promised	Delivered	Promised	Delivered	Promised	Delivered
Gujarat	20	19	10	9	30	28
Maharashtra	6	6	22	22	28	28
Goa	6	3	3	9	2	5
Karnataka	10	10	5	5	15	15
Kerala	16	16	8	8	24	24
Lakshadweep	2	2	4	4	6	6
Daman/Diu	2	2	2	2	4	4
Tamil Nadu	12	12	12	12	24	24
Andhra Pradesh	12	7	6	6	18	13
Orissa	10	6	5	5	15	11
West Bangal	12	8	6	6	18	14
Pondicherry	2	2	1	1	3	3
Total	110	101	94	82	204	183

(MHA, *Annual Report, 2010-2011*, p. 49).

While the Central Government has agreed to supply patrol boats to coastal states and union territories, some states are reportedly acquiring so-called sophisticated and hence expensive equipment in the name of ensuring coastal security. There were reports that Maharashtra Government has acquired six *Sealeg* amphibious vessels from Switzerland. It is a relatively small vessel capable of carrying 3-4 persons. It has a top speed of 30-35 knots in water and 10 kph on land. Its wheels retreat when floating. These vessels were expected to cost Rs. 3.5 crores each. Total cost was estimated to be Rs. 21 crores. These were to be deployed along the coast of Mumbai and were expected to help in securing about 124-mile long coast line of Mumbai (*Hindustan Times*, New Delhi, September 21, 2009).

Probably such a vessel was useful in monitoring the "international" lakes of Switzerland to prevent inter-state smuggling but one wonders how such a vessel will be able to operate effectively in open seas even in moderately rough sea conditions. Moreover, one wonders if it has the necessary range to enable the police team to patrol even waters along the shore of that city. The *Sealeg* that is equipped with radar, echo-sounder, GPS and wireless communication system is probably more appropriate for Customs duty near the coast rather than for the state Police trying to combat maritime terrorism.

The Coast Guard has been assigned the task of imparting training to the police personnel of the coastal states. The training is being given at various District Headquarters of the Coast Guard. The Coast Guard will be paid for the training. It was paid Rs. 1.52 crores till 2009-10 (MHA, *A.R., 2009-2010*, Annexure VI). The Coast Guard has also evolved the 'hub and spoke' strategy for coordinating action with the Marine Police; the Coast Guard providing the hub and the Marine Police the spokes. One wonders how this pattern dovetails with the linear nature of their deployment along the coast. Also, how will such bilateral pattern dovetail with the overall framework of synergy among various other agencies like the Navy and the Customs (Marine) in the context of the wider concept of coastal security?

With the creation of the Marine Police wing in various coastal states, it is expected that the overall legal and judicial framework of coastal security would improve with the creation of a new dedicated enforcement wing that can tackle both enforcement and prosecution. Hitherto the Coast Guard, though empowered to arrest offenders, was required to handover the arrested persons, with the evidence, to the police. It often resulted in failed prosecution, both due to lack of efficient working arrangement and also due to the shortage of personnel on both sides (Vasan, 2006, pp. 153-54).

Though steps have been initiated towards the setting up of the Marine Police, its role, enforcement powers as also zone of operation still remain clouded. Unless some common denominators are arrived at, it is possible that some of the coastal states might formulate their own policies though they would continue to depend upon the Central Government's agencies for financial aid and training as also for broader area security of their coast. It might even lead to Centre *vs* state controversy. This would prove counterproductive.

The Marine Police is still in the process of being created. This is the most critical phase because the shape that is envisaged for it now will shape its profile for the coming decade. Hence, the following things need to be taken into consideration while doing long term planning for the Marine Police. The first consideration is that coastal states and union territories should be increasingly geared for taking greater responsibility for maintaining order in their adjacent sea space. The nature of this responsibility, over the coming years, will have to be negotiated between the coastal states and the Central Government. In that context, necessary legal and constitutional groundwork needs to be laid down even if it means amending certain sections of the Constitution, especially of the Concurrent List (List III) of the VIIth Schedule. The coastal states can be better empowered to play the desired role if items like 'maritime security' and 'maritime fishery' are added as new items in List III.

As analysed in this chapter, India has multiple maritime agencies entrusted with enforcement operations in India's adjacent sea space in the context of MLIC. The analysis reveals that none of them is capable, on its own, to fulfil the assigned task. Hence, it is imperative that they need to synergise their operations so that their individual capability can be best utilised in the context of coastal security. How best can it be done? Will India pursue the model based upon hierarchy with command/leadership role flowing from the top to the bottom? Or, will it follow the model based upon net-work centric organisation as well as net-work centric operation? In this model, each agency is given equal respect so as to create an environment of mutual cooperation. This is especially essential since many of the agencies involved belong to different departments and ministries and might even object to taking orders from another department or accept the policy or follow the leader. The next chapter will discuss the need for synergy as also other issues related to the new framework of coastal security as is evolving since 2004-2005.

COASTAL SECURITY AND SEA GOVERNANCE

6

From enforcement to sea governance

Phase I of Coastal Security Perspective (2005-2011) witnessed two different responses to coastal security. The one, following the Kargil Committee Report, was directed towards strengthening enforcement mechanism by further strengthening the Indian Coast Guard as also by directly involving the coastal states and union territories (UTs) through the formation of the Marine Police wing. The inadequacy of that response was revealed during 26/11.

Post-26/11 responses prompted the decision makers to find ways and means of strengthening the fabric of sea governance. That change in the mindset will have long term implications since it will help to ushur in long overdue reforms in sea governance. Attempt to synergise policies of various ministries and departments dealing with maritime affairs is only one step in that direction. Other long overdue steps on which action is now being initiated include a centralised monitoring mechanism to identify and communicate with vessels operating in sea space around India, centralised registration of all types of Indian vessels, including even small fishing vessels and fitting them with equipment that will facilitate their identification and monitoring, need for a more comprehensive fishery policy including maritime fishery laws and associated enforcement agencies etc.

While these steps are been initiated in the context of maritime security, they will also help strengthen mechanism for sea governance. Much more remains to be done. One hopes that some of the crucial gaps can be filled during Phase II (2011-2016) of the Coastal Security Scheme. These will include formulating a comprehensive legal norm dealing with various maritime crimes so as to enable enforcement agencies to apprehend the criminals in multiple maritime zones away from the shore as also for the judiciary to pass speedy judgement. While the government has constituted a National Committee for Strengthening Maritime and Coastal Security under the Chairmanship of the Cabinet Secretary, one needs an autonomous body to handle matters not only of security concern but also of sea governance. Another aspect that has been given a low priority is the need to evolve mechanism for regional cooperation at multilateral level so as to strengthen maritime security. Two such maritime regions can be identified; the Andaman Sea and South Arabian Sea. India has instituted some steps in that context, at bilateral level but time has come to raise that level of maritime cooperation from the bilateral to the regional.

Coastal Security: Post-Kargil approach

Ever growing challenge of terrorism, actively supported by forces from across the border, forced the Government of India to review the question of border security, including the security of its 'maritime borders'. It will not be wrong to say that a relook at the entire border security, following the Kargil conflict, opened a new chapter in the context of role of coastal states in enhancing maritime security of India's homeland in times of 'no war – no peace'.

The Government of India had instituted a committee to examine the events leading to the Kargil conflict. The Kargil Committee Report, among other things, underlined the need for a more strict approach to border management. Though its major recommendations were land border oriented, it had also recommended a review of the entire issue. "The Committee is, therefore, of the view that the entire issue needs detailed study in order to evolve force structures and procedures that ensure improved border management and a reduction, if not elimination, in the flow of narcotics, illegal migrants, terrorists and arms" (*Report of the Kargil Review Committee*, 2000, pp. 38-9).

Task Force on Border Management was set up as a follow up of these recommendations. George Fernandes, the then Defence Minister, commenting on the question of maritime security, wrote that the Task Force came up with the shocking revelation that the 7,500 km long maritime border of the country *had not figured in the thinking of nation's leadership*, not once in more than 50 years of freedom and that maritime borders had practically been left unguarded. According to the Report of the Task Force, roles of the Navy and the Coast Guard did not tantamount to protection of nation's coast-line. He wrote that smuggling, poaching, terrorism, unguarded border have provided an open invitation to subvert India's security. The Andaman Islands, for instance, have been an open house to force inimical to India (Fernandes, 2000, pp. 53-4).

One wonders if that sweeping condemnation was really justified in the context of demonstrative steps that were taken in the past to check activities of NSA and terrorists by the Customs (Marine), the Coast Guard and the Navy. The question was (and is) not the inadequacy of the maritime enforcement agencies of the Central Government but of the fact that they were the only forces that were entrusted with the task of ensuring multiple facets of maritime security. There was no realisation of the need to induct coastal states in combating anti-national activities of NSA and terrorists along their adjacent waters.

Despite the concern shown by the Task Force, it took some time for the Group of Ministers (GoM) to recommend a policy in that context. Even the subsequent measures, as will be analysed, were half-hearted, as if the Central Government was afraid that the coastal states might usurp its prerogative of managing India's 'national' security. The old mindset that preserving the security of India was the prerogative of the Union Government alone had yet to be altered though steps in that direction were being initiated.

That change was very briefly reflected in the Annual Report, 2002-2003, of the Ministry of Home Affairs. The 'land' border still remained the focus of attention. The creeks of Gujarat were seen in that context, with the BSF being equipped with boats to meet the new challenge. Also, airwing of the BSF was to be augmented. Concept of 'floating border posts' with speed boats that would check infiltration and smuggling *via* river boundaries was introduced (MHA, *A.R., 2003-2004*, pp. 3, 52).

Yet, in that report, probably for the first time, Ministry of Home Affairs mentioned the term 'coastal security'. It mentioned that the Report on

Reforms of National Security System observed that little had been done over the years to understand or take action to create the infrastructure for the protection of India's vast coastal area against poaching, infiltration of illegal migrants, smuggling, narco-traffic, clandestine cross-border transit and landing of the contraband like arms and ammunition, explosives etc. Was such a sweeping comment justified? Surely, Ministry of Home Affairs had not taken steps in that context but the Customs (Marine) as a part of the Ministry of Finance and the Coast Guard under the Ministry of Defence were already entrusted with that task.

In that context, coastal states were asked to establish matching security system, formulate perspective plans for action and strengthen coastal security and surveillance, keeping in view the following indicative parameters:

(i) Strengthening the existing infrastructure for policing and patrolling the coastal area.

(ii) Identifying the sensitive stretches of coasts in terms of their actual vulnerability and to establish police stations/outposts in those stretches as also to acquire suitable equipment, vehicles, boats, communication equipment and weapons.

(iii) Create a Marine Police cell/wing in the coastal police station by developing teams with sea/water faring skills.

(iv) Create separate intelligence capabilities in the coast and police stations for gathering intelligence on coastal security like smuggling, landing of contraband, illegal migration, entry of unidentified vessels/ persons, subversive activities etc. A tall order indeed!

The Coast Guard was requested to prepare a Model on Coastal Security to standardise the specification of boats and equipment suitable for coastal patrolling by state governments, keeping in view their jurisdiction in the coastal waters (term coastal waters left undefined) (MHA, *A.R., 2002-2003*, pp. 51-2).

The new initiative was warmly received by the administration of the coastal state. A.K. Anthony, the then Chief Minister of Kerala, made a statement as early as May 23, 2003 that the proposed Coastal Police to monitor and curb operations of criminals and anti-national elements in the coastal area, would start functioning by that year itself (*The Hindu*, May 24, 2003). Director-General and Inspector-General of Police, Karnataka, Bhupendra Singh Siel, said in November 2005 that a Coastal Security Force for the state would be operational soon (*The Hindu*, November 9, 2005).

Department of Border Management was created in 2004 under the Ministry of Home Affairs, to pay focussed attention to management of borders (that included maritime border/frontier as well). Though the perception that coastal states need to be more closely engaged in meeting maritime threats from NSA and terrorists, was beginning to reshape the approach to homeland security, yet the old mindset was difficult to be totally discarded. This was revealed in the miniscule sum of Rs. 551 crores that was earmarked for five years, beginning 2005, to be spent on strengthening the enforcement measures of all the nine coastal states and four union territories (UTs).

Coastal Security Perspective Phase I

Under the Perspective Plan (Phase I), a sum of Rs.551 crores was earmarked for a five year period for all the nine coastal states and four union territories. Of that, Rs. 400 crores were earmarked for non-recurring expenditure and Rs. 151 crores for recurring expenditure. Of the non-recurring expenditure, Rs. 329 crores were for acquisition of patrol boats for Marine Police. The first phase was extended upto 31.3.2011 and an additional sum of Rs. 95 crores was earmarked for that extra period (MHA, *AR, 2010-11*, p. 47). Details of type of assistance provided to individual coastal states and UTs under Phase I are given in the table on the next page.

Table: Progress of Coastal Security Scheme

State/UT	Coastal Police Stations					
	Sanctioned	Nos.	Made Oper-ational	Constru-ction complete	Constru-ction in progress	Construct-ion not yet started
Gujarat	Coastal PS	10	10	10	-	-
	Check-posts	25	25	25	-	-
	Out-Posts	46	44	44	2	-
Maharashtra	Coastal PS	12	12	2	2	8
	Check-posts	32	32	19	-	13
	Barracks	24	24	18	-	6
Goa		3	3	-	2	1
Karnataka		5	5	5	-	-
Kerala		8	6	6	2	-
Tamil Nadu	Coastal PS	12	12	12	-	-
	Check-posts	40	35	31	9	-
	Out-Posts	12	10	10	-	2
Andhra Pradesh		6	6	6	-	-
Orissa		5	5	2	1	2
West Bengal	Coastal PS	6	6	3	1	2
	Barracks	6	4	4	-	2
Puducherry		1	1	-	1	-
Lakshadweep		4	4	1	2	1
Daman & Diu		1	1	1	-	-
A&N Islands		-	-	-	-	-
	Coastal PS	73	71	48	11	14

Total	Check-posts	97	92	75	9	13
	Out-Posts	58	54	54	2	2
	Barracks	30	28	22	-	8

Source: MHA, AR, 2010-11, Annexure VII, p. 291.

The progress in the implementation of the scheme was slow during the initial period. As per the Status Paper on Internal Security produced by the Ministry of Home Affairs, of the total allocation of Rs. 551 crores, only Rs. 13.04 crores were released in 2005-2006 and Rs. 11.65 crores in 2006-2007. The scheme soon picked up steam. Rs. 99.15 crores were earmarked for 2007-2008. Of the 73 coastal police stations, only 41 were commissioned by March 31, 2007 (MHA, *Status Paper on Internal Security*, June, 30, 2007, pp. 6-7). By 2010-11, 71 of the 73 police stations were operational. Details are as follows: Gujarat (10), Maharashtra (12), Goa (3), Karnataka (5), Kerala (6), Tamil Nadu (12), Andhra Pradesh (6), Orissa (5), West Bengal (6), Puducherry (1), Lakshadweep (4) and Daman and Diu (1). By 31.12.2010, a total of 183 boats (101 of 12 tonnes and 82 of 5 tonnes) were delivered by the vendors to various coastal states and UTs (MHA, *AR, 2010-11*, pp. 48-49). Utilisation of the financial outlay sanction for the scheme, as seen from the accompanying table, is also satisfactory.

The Annual Report of the Ministry of Home Affairs for 2010-11 reiterated the need for according priority to the coastal waters of Gujarat and Maharashtra. As after 1993-94, when those waters had drawn attention after the Mumbai blasts of 1993, this time also it was decided to organise joint coastal patrolling off the close coastal waters of these states by a joint contingent of the Navy, the state police and the Customs. One wonders why the role of the Coast Guard in this joint patrolling is not mentioned. The report, however, mentions that, more infrastructure facilities were to be provided to the Coast Guard to enable it to undertake joint coastal patrolling in Coast Guard vessels. For that purpose, three new Coast Guard stations were to be established at Veraval in Gujarat and Dhanu and Murad Janjira in

Table: Coastal Security Scheme

Sl. No.	Name of State/UT	Approved Outlay	Financial Progress		
			Approved estimated Boat component	Approved component for construction cost of coastal PSs, sum assistance for office equipment & furniture etc.	Total release of funds
1	Gujarat	5,842.60	5,000.00	842.60	842.600
2	Maharashtra	4,092.60	3,400.00	692.60	692.600
3	Goa	1,653.50	1,500.00	153.50	153.500
4	Karnataka	2,711.90	2,500.00	211.90	211.900
5	Kerala	4,356.00	4,000.00	356.00	356.000
6	Tamil Nadu	4,408.00	3,600.00	808.00	808.000
7	Andhra Pradesh	3,267.00	3,000.00	267.00	267.000
8	Orissa	2,765.75	2,500.00	265.75	265.750
9	West Bengal	3,353.40	3,000.00	353.40	353.400
10	Puducherry	544.60	500.00	44.50	44.500
11	Lakshadweep	936.80	800.00	136.80	136.800
12	Daman & Diu	668.35	600.00	68.35	68.350
13	Andaman & Nicobar	2,603.90	2,500.00	103.90	103.900
14	Sub-total (States/UTs)			4,304.30	4,304.300
15	Sub-total (payment for Boats) Sub-total (payment for Boats)		32,900.00		25,818.7-864
16	Sub-total (Non-recurring)	37,204.30			30,123.0-84

17	Training charges to Coast Guard	-			173.786
18	Advance POL charges				1,121.000
19	Sub-total (Recurring)	15,100.00			1294.786
20	**GRAND TOTAL**	52,304.30	32,900.00	4,304.30	31,417.970

Source: (MHA, *AR, 2010-11,* Annexure VII, p. 292)

Maharashtra. One more station has been established in Mundra in Gujarat. Contracts for 15 more interceptor boats suitable for operation in these waters by the Coast Guard were signed. The scheme was jointly implemented by the Ministry of Home Affairs and the Ministry of Defence (MHA, *AR, 2010-11*, P. 52).

The performance index of coastal security during Phase I was evaluated and the Coast Guard as also coastal states and UTs were asked to submit the proposals for the Phase II (2011-16) of Coastal Security Scheme. Based on these inputs, the Coastal Security Scheme (Phase II) was formulated and approved of by the Government for implementation from 2011-12.

While certain gaps will be plugged, what is more important is to define the future role of the coastal states in the context of maritime security. Will the role of the Marine Police remain confined to the current role of a beat constable along the shore or will it be better equipped to take on the responsibility of maritime security at least upto the outer limit of territorial waters adjacent to the shore of each of the coastal states and UTs. In that case, it will be necessary to work out a permanent arrangement for burden sharing between the Central Government and each coastal state. It will also be necessary to give the present *ad hoc* arrangement a constitutional legitimacy for that role, if necessary by amending the Constitution. The Concurrent List (List III) of the VIIth Schedule can be amended so as to include maritime security as one of the items listed under it. In that case, maritime security will be a common objective to be shared between the

Central Government and coastal states. It will also constitutionally empower the Marine Police of various states not only to operate in the adjacent sea space, without limiting its zone of operation to territorial sea, but also to cooperate with maritime enforcement agencies of the Central Government under a constitutionally approved framework.

Post 26/11 developments

As is usual, the first response following the events of 26/11 was apportioning of blame on others. Admiral Suresh Mehta, while speaking on the occasion of the Navy Day, said that the entry of terrorists into Mumbai by using a trawler appeared to indicate a systems failure by the law enforcement agencies (*The Hindu*, December 3, 2008). The Naval Chief seems to have forgotten that the Navy and the Coast Guard, besides the Customs, were the only maritime enforcement agencies in Mumbai at that time and that not only were the bases of the Indian Navy and the Indian Coast Guard adjacent to the targets of terrorist attack near the Gate Way of India but their boats must have passed by these bases. The Joint Intelligence Task Force, formed on the behest of the then National Security Advisor, M.K. Narayanan, among other things, wanted the state police to be accountable for the responsibility of preventing terrorist attacks (*Defence Watch*, 2010, p.5).

Terrorists attack in Mumbai in November 2008, not only had a populist impact thanks to live TV coverage but also revealed how easy it was to reach India's coast *via* the adjoining sea space. It led to a public outcry against the failure of the government. Heads rolled; mostly of the people who were not really guilty of allowing those terrorists to reach the coast. There was the usual hue and cry and it became yet one more incident of terrorism. The significance of its maritime dimension was however soon understood and assurances were given to further strengthen maritime security of India.

The Navy, along with the Coast Guard, had been conducting Defence of Gujarat Exercise (DGX) at least since 2006, if not earlier. Its objective was to protect offshore assets, shipping, ports and deep water channels leading to these ports. DGX-08 was conducted between November 10-22, 2008 (MOD, *AR*, 2008-2009, p. 32).

Despite the new awareness since 2004, about threats from terrorists, these exercises were possibly directed against threats from state actors. That underlined the shortcomings of such exercises in the context of confronting maritime threats posed by terrorists since 26/11, took place within a week of the DGX–08. Also the fact that the terrorists had passed by the bases of the Navy and the Coast Guard in Mumbai before landing must have come as a shock to concerned authorities. Fortunately, the press went after the politicians and ignored this aspect of the shortcoming of maritime security agencies despite the new focus after 2004. Probably, the concept of *Sagar Prahari Bal* (SPB) can be traced to the Navy's anxiety to secure its base facilities against possible terrorist attacks in future, besides strengthening coastal security.

Changing the mindset

There is a new realisation that India is going to face an increasing threat to its homeland security *via* the adjacent sea space. Hence, there is the need to chalk out a long term strategic response to meet the new challenge. The present approach to what is officially designated as coastal security is not only conceptually inappropriate but also inadequate to meet the new threat. This approach, as per details given in the Annual Reports of the Ministry of Home Affairs, was based upon two variables. One revolved around the mistaken notion that responsibility for national security is by and large entrusted to the Central Government alone under the Constitution. Consequently, the Government at the Centre is obliging the governments of the states along the coast of India by allowing them to share it with the Central Government. This is true even of the so-called coastal security.

It is often forgotten that the coast is secure only when the adjacent water space, together with the adjacent land space, are secure. Very often the fact is ignored that 'coast' has no accepted legal definition. It can mean the sea shore *per se*, the sea near it or the large sea space extending further away from the shore into the adjacent sea. At best it can have a geographical definition. Hence, as far as security is concerned, coastal zone ought to encompass the land space as well as the adjacent sea space. The depth of these two spaces, land and sea, will depend upon the terrain as well as the national requirements. This gives a new legal and administrative dimension to the question of coastal security.

Since the coast is under threat, it is not Delhi but coastal states that are the primary target of activities of NSA and terrorists approaching *via* the adjacent sea space. Hence, these states too need to play their appropriate role in the context of coastal security. Concept of coastal security is more than mere patrolling the coastline or even adjacent coastal waters. These waters are crowded with thousands of fishing boats and trawlers operating from hundreds of fish landing sites and fishery harbours all along the coastal belt of India. Different types of ships use major and non-major ports. The coastal belt will also have hundreds of high value industrial units and related installation like nuclear and thermal power plants, refineries, CNG terminals and shipyards. Thus, one cannot look at maritime security in isolation of development along the coast.

Only a strong coastal state that has a stake in maritime development and is empowered to do so will develop the incentive and generate the capability to provide for security against maritime threats posed by NSA and terrorists. The Union Government alone cannot do so. It is, therefore, imperative that coastal states be made equal partners, while formulating a long term mechanism for maritime security. One wonders if this concept has been realised not only at the level of the Union Government but also of the coastal states and union territories.

Indians have often been accused of having so-called continental mindset. It got reflected in their perception of border/frontier which was primarily land oriented. That was essentially the legacy of the British colonial rule that did not want Indians to look beyond their land border. That colonial ethos was inherited by Indian constitution makers and was reflected in the pattern of sharing of powers and functions between the Central Government and the governments of the coastal states under VIIth Schedule of the Indian Constitution. In the division of responsibility, maritime affairs was the responsibility of the Central Government while the coastal states played only a minimum role in a subject that concerned them the most.

That traditional ethos got reflected in the functioning of various ministries like the defence, the shipping and even the agriculture. It affected the functioning of the Ministry of Home Affairs also, whose focus remained on land border rather than maritime frontier. The Department of Border Management, created in the Ministry of Home Affairs after the Kargil cries, in the initial years, focussed more on land borders though the report on National Security System presented by the Group of Ministers had made recommendations on the management of land and coastal border. Annual Report of 2001-2002 of the Ministry of Home Affairs uses the term 'coastal border' thereby reflecting the approach of a fixed border. Sea has frontiers not border. The newly created department continued to focus on borders with Bangladesh, Bhutan, Nepal, Myanmar and Pakistan. There was no mention of any maritime border. At best, a new focus was given to India's coastal border in the Kutch *vis-à-vis* Pakistan and riverien border *vis-a-vis* Bangladesh (MHA *AR,* 2001-2002 pp. 6, 13-47). It was only after 2004 that the Union Government rather grudgingly conceded to the coastal states, the right to police a narrow margin of sea space, beyond its shoreline.

As yet there is no legally valid provision, an amendment to the Constitution, a presidential proclamation or even a state legislation, as is on coastal fishery, that clearly defines the extent of the coastal state's criminal jurisdiction *vis-a-vis* NSA and terrorists in the adjacent sea space. Some experts claim that it extends upto the outer limit of the territorial waters. Even if it were so, is that narrow 12 n.mile maritime zone a viable maritime security frontier? Also, can the maritime security frontiers of the coastal states and the Union Government be different? Can that be so where the security as also good governance on the land and the adjacent the sea space are intertwined?

Sea Governance and Maritime Security

More significant was a new look at maritime security and its links with sea governance. Concerted attempts were initiated after 2008-2009, to synergise activities of various ministries and departments related to maritime affairs so as to help evolve a coordinated approach to meet the new challenge. Maritime affairs in India are distributed among multiple agencies and ministries like Shipping, Finance (Customs), Agriculture (fisheries), ONGC, Port Authorities etc. beside Ministry of Home Affairs, Ministry of External Affairs and Ministry of Defence. It was not realised till then that maritime security is the end product of coordinated management by multiple agencies that deal with various facets of maritime affairs.

Till recently, each of these agencies was an island in itself. Though the concept of coastal security, as propounded in 2004-2005, did underline the need for coordination among these multiple agencies, the focus of coordination was largely between the Ministry of Home Affairs, Ministry of Defence and the police of the coastal states and union territories. It was deemed to be adequate enough to ensure coastal security. The broader issue of structured and coordinated coastal water management had been, by and large, ignored.

The events of 26/11 gave a jolt to that narrow concept of coastal security. Decision makers were forced to realise that coastal security cannot be achieved without a mechanism for management of adjacent sea space. It, therefore, needed effective coordination among various agencies that are involved in it, both at the central level as also at the level of the coastal states and the union territories. That awareness kickstarted the new process of coordination among multiple agencies, dealing with maritime affairs at national and regional levels.

The fact that India had largely ignored the concept of sea governance reflected its so-called continental mindset as also the administrative and decision making structure inherited from the colonial past. Under the traditional approach to the government's formulation of policy, as also its implementation, one sees that it is often restricted to the concerned ministry and the related department. This approach is not only inadequate but also counter-productive in the context of sea governance and associated issue of maritime security *vis-à-vis* NSA and terrorists. Sea governance demands coordination and synergy of action among multiple ministries/departments that deal with maritime affairs like shipping, ports, maritime fishery, besides Ministry of Home Affairs, Ministry of Defence and Ministry of External Affairs at the level of the Central Government and related ministries and departments at the level of coastal states and UTs.

The main reason for lack of sea governance in India is that India does not have a single ministry or department that can take decisions related to sea governance as also implement them. Given the diversity of issues involved, such a centralised framework for decision making and implementation cannot even be recommended. Multiple stakeholders would like to hold on to their autonomy and might be far from cooperative if they are forced to follow the decision of other agencies. This will be true both in the field of policy making as well as implementation. Hence, there is the need for a new approach that would facilitate the creation of a framework that will ensure willing cooperation and synergy of operation among multiple agencies that are involved in sea governance as also in maritime security both at the level of the Central Government as also that of the coastal states and UTs.

In 2004-2005, when the issue of coastal security was being debated, little attention was paid to the question of sea governance. The focus was on strengthening enforcement. Its responsibility was to be shared primarily between the Navy, the Coast Guard and the proposed Marine Police. One noticed a shift in approach after 26/11 and greater attention was paid to involve/coordinate activities of all the major stakeholders in the field of ports, shipping, fishery, enforcement agencies at the level of the Central Government, coastal states and UTs etc.

The shift in focus was on the need to streamline and strengthen the overall framework of sea governance. Several meetings involving these government agencies have been held since 26/11 to coordinate policies at national level. For example, the Shipping Ministry took a decision to set up a broad based committee comprising of various agencies for sharing information on traffic, port and issues related to ship security. The decision was taken at a meeting of the Maritime States Development Council, that was presided over by the Shipping Minister G.K. Vasan. The committee comprised of representatives of the Ministry of Shipping, the Navy, the Coast Guard, State Police, Customs, Members of State Maritime Boards and the concerned maritime states (Balchand, 2009). One hopes that the committee does function as desired.

According to Annual Reports of the Ministry of Home Affairs, several meetings were held since 2008, involving representatives of the Ministry of Home Affairs and other concerned ministries, to address the question of coastal security and related matters. The Union Home Secretary undertook detailed review meetings on December 5, 2008, December 18, 2008, January 21, 2009 and June 10, 2009. Secretary, Border Management, Ministry of Home Affairs, convened a meeting on December 29, 2008. Ministry of Shipping, Road Transport and Highways also convened a meeting on December 22, 2008.

A meeting was held on February 28, 2009 during which the Cabinet Secretary discussed and reviewed issues related to coastal/maritime security as also the follow up actions taken on the decisions arrived at in several meetings held at different levels, following 26/11. The meeting was attended by the Union Home Secretary, Deputy National Security Adviser, Defence Secretary, Secretary Shipping, Secretary Fisheries, Secretary Border Management, Secretary (West) Ministry of External Affairs, D.G. NIC, Deputy Chief of the Naval Staff, Registrar General of India, DDG Coast Guard and other senior functionaries of Government of India. Home Secretaries and Secretary Fisheries or their representatives of nine coastal states and four union territories also participated in the meeting. The meeting focussed on the implementation aspects and progress *vis-à-vis* the entire range of issues relating to maritime/coastal security which, *inter-alia*, included the coastal security scheme and uniform system of registration for ships. (MHA, *A.R., 2008-2009*, pp. 33-5).

During these meetings, especially those held in 2009-10, several decisions were taken. They included the formulation of Coastal Security Scheme (Phase II) keeping in view additional requirements for coastal police stations, interceptor boats and other related infrastructure facilities. Details of these requirements were to be provided by coastal states and UTs after carrying out vulnerability gap analysis in consultation with the Coast Guard. That would help to decide upon additional requirements needed for the formulation of Phase II of Coastal Security Scheme. The Coast Guard had, on its own, recommended for the establishment of an additional 131 coastal police stations. That requirement includes the upgrading of the existing 21 police stations in Andaman and Nicobar. The new proposals are under consideration for necessary approval. (MHA, *A.R., 2009-2010*, p. 37).

An important step was taken in August 2009 when a National Committee for Strengthening Maritime and Coastal Security Against Threat From the Sea was constituted under the Chairmanship of the Cabinet Secretary. It comprises of representatives of all the concerned ministries/ departments/organisations in the Government of India as well as Chief Secretaries/ Administrators of the coastal states and UTs. The National Committee, in its meetings, held on September 4, 2009, January 22, 2010, May 12, 2010 and November 23, 2010 reviewed the progress of implementation of all the major decisions with respect to coastal security. (MHA, *A.R., 2010-2011*, p. 52). Various decisions taken are being followed up by the concerned agencies as well as by the National Committee for Strengthening Maritime and Coastal Secretary against Threats From the Sea.

While analysing the overall question of coastal security one notices that the Customs (Marine) under the Finance Ministry, even though empowered for maritime enforcement role under the Customs Act, 1962 and MZI Act, 1976 upto the outer limit of the contiguous zone (Customs Water) of India, is being given less role than it deserves. Is it deliberate or is it an oversight? If an oversight, it needs to be corrected since the role of the Customs (Marine) can never be ignored in the context of curbing criminal activities of NSA who have close nexus with terrorists.

Maritime Security and Intelligence

Since India's security concerns were land-centric even in the context of terrorism, its intelligence network had focussed on that aspect. Over the decades, Indian intelligence agencies have multiplied. The senior most among them is the Intelligence Bureau (IB) whose origin can be traced to 1887. The Research and Analysis Wing (RAW) was founded in 1968. All the three armed forces (Army, Navy and Air Force) as well as the Coast Guard and para-military forces like the BSF, CRPF, ITBP etc. have their own means of acquiring intelligence. There are also state-level intelligence units, Special Branch of CBI and local intelligence units.

After the Kargil crisis, efforts made towards revamping and streamlining intelligence remained land-centric. In 2002, National Security Council (NSC) was created as a decision-making body headed by the

National Security Adviser. NSC has Joint Intelligence Agency which is responsible for analysing inputs from the IB, RAW and units of the Armed Forces. National Technical Research Organisation (NTRO) is responsible for gathering technical intelligence. It operates in close collaboration with RAW and IB (Jasbir Singh, 2008, p. 33)

In the post-Kargil period, various ministries and agencies had recommended modifications in the system of intelligence gathering and assessment. A Joint Intelligence Task Force was formed to examine the related issue and make suitable recommendations. Its report was presented to the government in November 2009. One of the recommendations was for the creation of multi-agency centres in all states. They would keep the DGPs of the respective states informed so that states could be made accountable for the responsibility of preventing terrorist attacks (*Defence Watch*, January 2010, p. 5).

Thus, new bodies are being created, beside the existing agencies, like the Joint Intelligence Committee (J.I.C.), the National Security Council Secretariat (NSCS), the National Security Advisory Board (NSAB) as also the National Counter-Terrorism Centre (NCTC) created in the Ministry of Home Affairs. It would work under the supervision of the Director, National Intelligence (Raman, 2010, pp. 27-30). P. Chidambaram, Home Minister, said that the NCTC was likely to be in operation by the end of 2011, if final decision was arrived at, by the end of 2011 (*The Hindu* December 1, 2010). One does not know how all these agencies are being related to the question of maritime terrorism.

Since these are classified as intelligence agencies, are they authorised/ expected to freely share even their 'information' with other concerned agencies? Is it permitted under their rules and practices? Are these agencies expected to focus/specialise on matters concerning maritime security? In view of these questions, it has become all the more important now that those who are concerned with maritime terrorism seek to evolve some dedicated mechanism for pooling information and for sharing intelligence with concerned agencies.

Sharing of information/intelligence assumes great significance in the context of maritime security especially when multiple agencies not directly related to intelligence *per se* are involved and the data (whatever is made available) generated by them is pooled and classified by agencies that are entrusted with analysing them and for recommending appropriate action. While 'information' *per se* should be shared as widely as possible, 'intelligences' that flow from it and other classified sources, need to be shared only among those that are entitled to it under the given circumstances. That includes 'actionable intelligence' as opposed to vague information or speculation and so-called 'recommendation' made on that basis.

Even though coastal security was seen as an emerging threat even in 2004, specific agencies that could focus on generating and analysing maritime dimension of intelligence were not put in place at that time. Of course the Navy and the Coast Guard had their own intelligence wings but much more was needed to be done. Events of 26/11 and the need for robust-system of sea governance, of which maritime intelligence is an intrinsic part, compelled the government agencies to address that question more seriously.

Since 26/11, a proposal was mooted for creating an intelligence network to detect, share and neutralise threats swiftly. Towards that end, the Indian Navy submitted an exhaustive technical blue print on an integrated National Maritime Domain Awareness (NMDA) project. The proposal was submitted to all concerned Union Ministries as also to all the coastal states and union territories. The NMDA proposal also includes creation of monitoring centres in coastal states/UTs to act as part of the NMDA network as also upgradation of the four existing Joint Operation Centres at Mumbai, Kochi, Visakhapatnam and Port Blair besides creation of a shipping hub and fisheries monitoring centre. There is also the need to set up vessel traffic management system (VTMS) at 65 non-major ports that handle international traffic. Only Port Blair, a non-major port, has that system. Thirteen large ports of India have or will soon have that system. The project also recommends that a VTMS be set up for the eastern off-shore development areas like the one set up for the western ones. (Pandit, 2010).

The Naval Chief, Admiral Nirmal Verma, told the press that the project on NMDA, which was cleared in principle, in November 2010, by the National Committee for Strengthening Maritime and Coastal Security was to be placed before the Union Cabinet in January 2011 (*The Times of India,* December 6, 2010).

The Navy has also put forward another proposal - National Command, Control, Communication and Intelligence (NC³IN). It is being set up as the main backbone for the proposed NMDA project. The central hub for the NC³IN is being created in Gurgaon near Delhi. The Navy claimed that an additional Rs. 500 crores will be required to implement the entire NMDA project.

The objective of the scheme is to generate a common operational picture of all ongoing activities at sea through an institutionalised mechanism for collecting, fusing and analysing information from technical and other sources like coastal surveillance network radars, space-based automatic identification systems, vessel traffic management system, fishing vessel registration and fishermen biometric identification databases.

There is no doubt that the NC³IN system proposed by the Navy will be able to coordinate data from multiple sources, analyse them and suggest actionable proposals. However, its success depends upon close and sustained cooperation of multiple maritime agencies. Also, these agencies will first need to upgrade their own information systems before they can communicate the data to the NC³IN of the Navy.

While the NC³IN can be the ultimate goal, it will be more practical to initiate the project at micro and regional levels *viz* at the level of the newly formed Joint Operation Centres at Mumbai, Kochi, Visakhapatnam and Port Blair as also by gradually widening the network not only of the participating agencies but also improving coordination among these four centres at the level of a central organisation. This step by step process will also provide various agencies time to upgrade their systems as also to familiarise themselves with the nature of cooperation that is sought. The gradual process will also enable the concerned agencies to modify the program for more effective results.

Securing adjacent sea space: Role of Surveillance

The most important aspect of maritime security is the need to secure the adjacent sea space since those who wish to target the coast would be reaching there *via* these waters. These criminal elements will be using surface vessels. Hence, surveillance of the sea surface and accounting for the movement of all vessels will be crucial factors in strengthening maritime security. Indian Navy's proposal on NC³IN is based upon these inputs. While developed states of the North seek to sanitise their sea space in the context of large vessels, tankers and containers, the primary threat for a country like India will come from terrorists using relatively small cargo vessels and fishing crafts of different types. The cargo vessel can be used to transfer men and material on the high seas while fishing boats can land them along the coast. Misuse of fishing crafts for that purpose as also for smuggling of consumer goods and drugs is common in India, be it in the context of the LTTE of Sri Lanka, landing of RDX for Mumbai blast of 1993 or of the terrorists in 26/11. Thus, issues that need to be analysed in this context include; collection of information/intelligence about movement of all types of vessels in the concerned sea space by using technology as also human intelligence.

Several modes of surveillance as also of accounting for surface vessels in the area of concern are suggested. They include space-based satellite system, fixed wing MR aircrafts and UAV, coastal radar network as also human intelligence. Local fishermen who habitually operate in a given sea space are better capable of observing and reporting in a structured manner, if a suitable scheme is proposed, something that they find unusual. Information provided by them can be directly fed at the level of evaluation/decision making and implementation in the concerned maritime sub-zone.

As mentioned, several sophisticated means for monitoring of the sea space are now available, that enable the coastal authorities to monitor traffic along its sea space. In that context, role of aero-space based monitoring and communication systems are becoming increasingly relevant in the context of maritime security. Various types of satellites help in ocean surveillance, weather forecasting, directing fishermen to better sites for fishing, assist in disaster management, including locating oil spills and in SAR operations as also help surveillance of the EEZ so as to prevent poaching by unauthorised vessels.

Many of these devices are used to monitor movement of commercial vessels. Space-based technology is employed in Long-Range Identification and Tracking (LRIT) system that is used for monitoring of a ship's passage. Another device, Ship-Loc, beams a ship's position fifteen times a day. It allows the shipping company to use personal computers with internet access facilities to monitor the exact location of the vessel. The IMB recommends its use as an anti-piracy/hijacking measure. A UK-based company, Recal-TRACS, has offered Time Division Multiple Access (TDMA) and SAT/C. They provide a radio-data and satellite-based tracking network. The system can even be covertly installed on the ship. It is, however, more expensive than the Ship-Loc system (*Jane's Naval Intelligence*, May 29, 2002, p. 16).

Space-based technology is of vital assistance in SAR missions. The core of the global SAR network is the satellite communication system called Global Maritime Disaster and Safety System (GMDSS). It is provided by International Navigation Marine Satellite (INMARSAT) under the aegis of IMO. The system became operational since February 1992. Videsh Sanchar Nigam of India is a signatory to INMARSAT and provides a gateway *via* its earth station near Pune (Roy, *2002*, p. 412). India has taken this international obligation seriously. The Ship Reporting System for SAR in India's SAR Region came into effect since February 1, 2003 for participation of foreign flag vessels of more than 300 GRT operating/transiting in India's SAR Region.

India has its own INDSAR. It depicts position of all ships that enter Indian zone. It is helpful in locating the vessel if it activises its International Safety Net (ISN). It is voluntary for foreign flag vessels. It was reported that the scheme was to be made mandatory for all Indian flag vessels, including fishing vessels, for a better monitoring of their position on the adjacent sea space. The scheme is to be operated and maintained by the Indian Coast Guard through the Maritime Rescue Coordinating Centre at Mumbai. Participation in INDSAR is voluntary and ships do not incur any charge. All the charges are borne by the Indian Coast Guard.

The Indian Space Research Organisation's satellite in the INSAT series, INSAT-3A, took over the satellite-aided SAR services that were being provided earlier by INSAT-2B that was launched in 1993. INSAT-3A, a Geo-stationary Orbit Satellite-Aided Search and Rescue (GEOSAR) service, covers a large area between Europe and Australia in the Indian Ocean. US satellites cover the remaining area. This device is provided under the international COSPAS-SARSAT system that provides location information of the distress signals transmitted by beacons mounted on board ship and aircrafts. The GEOSAR transponder on INSAT-3A complements the Low Earth Orbit COSPAS-SARSAT in receiving the distress signal transmission and its detection. The ISRO Telemetry, Tracking and Command Network (ISTRAC) operates two ground stations to receive and process the distress signals detected by Low Earth Orbit COSPAS-SARSAT spacecrafts, besides a ground station capable of receiving and processing distress signals detected by the GEOSAR transponder on INSAT spacecrafts in geostationary orbit. Mission control centre is located at Bangalore. The location and other details of the beacon, transmitting the distress signals, are determined instantaneously and rescue coordination centre are informed for carrying out SAR operation of the affected ships, aircrafts or individuals (*The Hindu*, June 4, 2003).

There are other means for monitoring movement of vessels. Some of them are recommended by the IMO under the new ISPS code. They are satellite-based Long Range Identification and Tracking (LRIT) systems noted before as well as the VHF-range Automatic Identification System (AIS). This new system is an improvement over the Vessel Traffic Management and Information Service (VTMIS) that is based upon radar stations along the coastline. It cannot cover the entire coastline or the chain of islands in the EEZ. The AIS provides a better option.

AIS consists of a transponder on the vessel which is linked to the GPS nodule. It constantly transmits basic vessel information like the name, call signal, IMO number, DWT as also traffic relevant information like course, speed etc. AIS transponders are now mandatory for all vessels above 300 DWT, carrying commercial cargo. Though introduced earlier, it has become mandatory for all commercial vessels since 2004 under the new ISPS Code. It was reported as early as 2006 that India would implement satellite-based 'national' Automatic Identification System (AIS) that would require ships to automatically transmit information periodically so as to enable India to monitor shipping up to a distance of about 50 n. miles from the coast (Dixit, 2006).

With AIS in place, control, management and dispatch of vessel traffic is expected to become easier. By means of a network of AIS receivers ashore, a more comprehensive VTMIS can be set up quite easily which will provide more accurate and comprehensive information than what was possible with only the radar network. It is possible that in the long run, AIS will supercede the coastal radar stations as the prime means of managing and directing vessel traffic (Joergensen, 2008, p. 369).

All types of boats are to be fitted/provided with navigational and communication equipments to facilitate their identification and tracking. The Department of Shipping is the nodal department. The Director-General Shipping has issued two circulars to ensure that all types of vessels, including fishing vessels, other than fishing vessels of less than 20 metres categories, are to be installed with AIS type B transponder for the purpose of identification and tracking. Annual Report, 2010-2011, of Ministry of Home Affairs mentioned that a group under the Chairmanship of Nautical Adviser has worked out the specifications of the AIS transponder required for installation on fishing vessels and has submitted the same to Department of Shipping for further action (MHA, *AR, 2010-2011*, P. 50).

Facilities required in the context of SAR can prove to be useful tools to monitor the activities of these fishing vessels. The Union Agricultural Ministry had issued an order as early as November 1, 2002, under which all trawlers larger than 20 metres had to report their position to the Coast Guard control at Chennai at 8 AM every day. The reason given for that order was to guide them away from the marine sanctuaries and also to facilitate quicker response in an emergency. That order was to come into effect since February 1, 2003 (*The Hindu*, February 2, 2003). Can such a practice be made compulsory for all?

Prabhakar Paleri, who retired as Director-General, Indian Coast Guard, had advocated that *all* vessels should carry appropriate continuous synopsis record (CSR) showing details of the past sailing of that vessel. He had also advocated that ship identification number (SIN) be allocated to fishing vessels so that they could be monitored by the Coast Guard. Reportedly, that is being implemented after 26/11. He had also advocated that Ship-Loc system be introduced for all deep sea fishing vessels so that their movement can be easily tracked electronically (Paleri, 2004, pp. 219-20).

India had set to improve monitoring its sea space at least in two sensitive areas. The one is the Bombay High where the ONGC had taken the initiative, supported by other maritime agencies, to prepare a plan to monitor the sea space and the off-shore installations therein. The other was a Coastal Vessel Traffic Regulation System in the Gulf of Cutch. It took about four years to be ready and cost Rupees 117 crores (*The Hindu*, January 2, 2006). Reportedly, VTMIS is being finalised for the Arabian Sea coast of India; a priority area for India's maritime security.

Besides space-based systems, other systems are also employed to monitor traffic of vessels in adjacent sea-space. They can be based on inputs provided by platforms like the fixed-wing aircrafts; helicopters, UAVs and dirigibles, both manned and unmanned. These can be very useful in getting real time information of the desired sea space, especially when it is coordinated with inputs obtained from space-based platforms. As noted in the previous chapter dealing with enforcement agencies, India uses several types of fixed-wing aircrafts for maritime reconnaissance.

Increasingly, reliance is being placed upon UAVs for monitoring of the sea space near the coast/base. UAVs are cost effective and provide real time data that is comparable to that provided by manned aircrafts. Type of UAV to be used will be determined by variables like range/loiter time, type of power plant, speed, sensors installed and weapons if they are to be armed. Indian Navy operates UAVs that were acquired from Israel. While the *Searcher* has longer range/endurance, *Heron* is a medium range machine. They carry optical, radar, electronic warfare payloads etc. Indian Coast Guard was seeking to induct Indian *Nishant* UAV and had given its own specifications for the UAV (*Jane's Defence Weekly*, October 12, 2005, p. 15). Reportedly that program is on hold.

Inflated derigibles, manned or unmanned, fixed or powered, equipped for monitoring the sea space, especially upto the outer limit of the contiguous zone, or of areas around off-shore installations and other high value targets, port/harbour as also sensitive areas along the coast line and island territories will also prove cost effective and supplement the role of more expensive MR aircrafts and UAVs.

Radars along the coast and on islands are also used to monitor movement of vessels. There were reports after the event of 26/11 that more sensitive coastal areas would be brought under greater radar coverage. Since radars are fixed on land they are less expensive to operate than those operated from fixed wing MR aircrafts. Normally, their range is limited though adequate to cover the significant sea space upto the outer limit of the territorial waters. Such short range radars will be useful for monitoring coastal waters in the context of Marine Police, Customs/ Excise, Fisheries, Port authorities and the Coast Guard. There are reports that more radars are being installed along the coast and islands at a cost of Rs. 300 crores. (*Hindu*, November 13, 2009). Surveillance of the sea space from the coast will also improve when facilities of the light houses situated along the coast and on islands are integrated with other regional inputs.

Monitoring smaller vessels

While ISPS Code provides the mechanism for monitoring commercial vessels above 300 DWT, smaller vessels used for overseas and coastal traffic, for ferry services as also for fishing also need to be identified and their movement monitored. That will need domestic measures.

Many India-flagged *dhows* of less than 300 DWT are employed in coastal as also overseas trade. Reportedly, some of them get themselves upgraded abroad so as to enable them to operate between the Gulf and the Horn of Africa. Many of them fall victim to piracy in those waters. A proper monitoring by systems like AIS and more stringent laws about their operation will be timely even in the case of anti-piracy operations. Since these vessels operate for coastal shipping, they can also be used by terrorists to approach Indian coasts, especially minor ports all along the Indian coast line.

The Times of India reported on December 17, 2008, a few days after 26/11, that on December 3, the Coast Guard had found that 14 of the 19 fishing boats intercepted by it near the Bombay High did not have any documents like licence and identity cards. A senior official of the Maharashtra Government was quoted as saying, "We can't understand how the Coast Guard could let off these boats six days after the Mumbai attacks, when everyone knew that the terrorists came from the sea". He should have asked that question to the Fishery Department of Maharashtra and the concerned departments of the Central Government that have the power to register fishing boats. Also, is the Coast Guard authorised to take action in such cases?

It is of utmost importance to monitor movement of medium and large fishing boats that operate in thousands in waters along India's coastline and in the EEZ of its island territories. They also approach relatively less guarded fishing harbours and fish landing sites all along the coast. Since fishery is also state subject, different states have different enforcement norms. There is need to bring a degree of uniformity since the fishing boats of various coastal states operate in waters opposite other coastal states also which makes it difficult to monitor their movements.

Special attention is being paid to the necessity of registering all fishing and non-fishing vessels plying in Indian waters under a uniform system. In this case also the Department of Shipping is the nodal agency. It has issued two notifications. The one is for amending the MS/Registration of Fishing Vessels rules along with revised format for registration. The other is for notifying the list of registrars who would register these boats. They have been issued by the Ministry of Shipping in consultation with Ministry of Law in June 2009. Coastal states and UTs are reportedly taking follow up actions in this regard (MHA, *A.R., 2010-2011*, p. 50). A system of approved registration system will also help local fishermen to identify more easily a fishing boat that acted suspiciously, and to report the matter to concerned authorities.

Such a task is not easy since it involves the fishery department of coastal states, Ministry of Agriculture (Fishing), the Shipping Ministry (for guidance on registration), the Home Ministry, the Defence Ministry (for enforcement) and the newly created Marine Police. For identifying fishing vessels of less than 20 metre length, a committee had been constituted under the Director-General, Coast Guard, to suggest the type of transponders suitable for such vessels. The committee held trials of different systems in that context. These are satellite based, AIS/VHF based and VHF/GPS based. The report of the trials is under evaluation (MHA, *A.R., 2010-*

2011, p. 50). As per G.K. Vasan, the then Minister of Shipping, registration would be done by a single agency under the provisions of the Merchant Shipping Act, 1958. For that purpose,127 registrars had been appointed in various coastal states (*The Hindu*, July 2, 2009).

Associated with the identification of fishing vessels was the recommendation for providing fishermen with I.D. cards as also multi-purpose national identity cards for coastal population. These would be relatable to a single centralised database. Department of Animal Husbandry, Dairying and Fisheries, as the nodal agency, is taking necessary action in that regard in consultation with all concerned departments. The uniform formate for data collection for ID cards has been finalised and sent to all the coastal states and UTs with a request to commence the data collection process. Associated with this is the proposal to give priority to issuance of Multipurpose National Identity Cards (MNICs) to the population in the coastal villages. This step was part of the project of creating a National Population Register in the coastal states/UTs ahead of 2011 census (MHA, *A.R., 2009-2010*, p. 38)

Apart from providing a more efficient system of registration of fishing vessels, there are also proposals to equip them with microchips and Emergency Position Indicating Radio Beacon (EPIRB). This followed the 26/11 incident in which a fishing trawler from Gujarat was hijacked by terrorists to reach Mumbai without anyone taking notice. According to Mohamed Nazeer, while the rescue and law enforcement agencies can trace the micro-chip implanted vessel, the EPIRB system will ensure transmission of distress signal to rescue and law enforcement agencies *via* a satellite. He wrote that a collaborative project of the ISRO and Keltron for providing radio beacon systems to fishing vessels in the state of Kerala was in the pipeline. Its trial run was conducted by the Fisheries Department. The radio beacon is automatically activated immediately after it falls into water and sends signals to the ISRO satellite. The distress signal will be transmitted by ISRO to the Coast Guard or the Navy which can then start rescue operations within ten minutes (Nazeer, *The Hindu*, December 1, 2008). The system can also be modified to alert enforcement agencies if the vessel is being attacked or hijacked by NSA or terrorists so that enforcement agencies are forewarned on time and initiate appropriate countermeasures.

Since fishery in territorial waters comes under the jurisdiction of coastal states/UTs, there is the need to evolve a mechanism under which activities of fishing boats from other coastal states/UTs can be monitored by the respective agencies in each state in the context of fishery protection as also coastal security. P.I. Sheik Pareeth, Fisheries Director of Kerala, had told Ignatius Perreira that Kerala would make it mandatory for fishermen from other states entering the 'Kerala water', to take permit. That would be issued by the Fisheries Department for a specific period. Those seeking such permits should have local sponsors from the fishing community, preferably with E-card identity. These identity cards, to be issued to each sea going fisherman of Kerala would contain all the details about the card holder and would cost Rs. 40/-(Pereira, *The Hindu*, January 10, 2009). One hopes that similar administrative decisions are also taken by all coastal states and UTs so as to bring about uniformity.

It was also reported that Kerala had proposed fixing tamper-proof number plates on all sea going vessels, chiefly fishing boats, registered in Kerala. That decision was prompted because of two reasons. Intelligence agencies had warned at that time that the LTTE was sourcing small sea going vessels from Kerala for possible use as light gunboats. Also, the Indian Coast Guard had reported that unregistered fishing boats and those displaying fake registration number, often just scrawled in paint on the hull, were being used for criminal activities. Reportedly, the proposed security-hologram-imposed high security registration plates (HSRP) were to be uniform in pattern and would be fixed on boats only on premises notified by the Fisheries Department and the registering authority. The Government would subsidise the cost of the new HSRP.

Shri G. Anand, quoting Sajan Ambadiyil, who was heading the project, reported that the HSRPs were designed to be protected against counterfeiting and contained hidden security features (similar to those found on currency notes), which could be verified by law enforcers even at night. They would be fixed in two easily viewable places on the hull. The C. DIT will set up a computerised database containing the details of all registered boats. The law enforcers will be able to access the data base easily through their mobile phones by sending a text message conveying the registration number of any boat they want to find more about. A computer will message back the particulars including the engine and hull number and owner's name. Currently, the government had little record of deep-sea capable fishing boats operating from Kerala (Anand, *The Hindu*, December 1, 2008).

Coordination among Enforcement Agencies

While arrangements were being made for coordination of action at the level of top decision makers of various ministries/departments, mechanism for similar coordination was also being evolved at the level of various maritime enforcement agencies at national level as well as at regional level.

To ensure effective cooperation and some form of sharing of responsibilities among multiple agencies, it is important to respect the autonomy of each such unit so involved instead of following the usual pattern of hierarchy of command. While that might work in a single organisation, it is likely to be counter-productive in cases where different agencies working under different departments, are involved. Even one ministry, Ministry of Defence, is finding it difficult to see that the Navy and the Coast Guard, that function under it, do not feel discriminated against.

As per the Annual Report, 2009-2010, of the Ministry of Defence, the Navy has been designated as the *authority responsible for overall maritime security which includes coastal security*. And, for that purpose it will be *assisted* by the Coast Guard, Marine Police and other central and state agencies responsible for the coastal defences of the nation (MOD, *A.R., 2009-2010*, P. 34). Presumably they include the Customs (Marine), port authorities etc. One wonders how one ministry can order departments under other ministries to work under it.

The same report also mentions that the Director-General, Coast Guard, has been designated as *Commander Coastal Command* and made *responsible for overall coordination between the central and state agencies in all matters relating to coastal security* (MOD, *A.R., 2009-2010*, P. 49). The Coast Guard had already been designated since September 2003 as the Lead Intelligence Agency for Coastal and Sea Border. Surely some other method would have been evolved to assuage the ego of two premier maritime security agencies while defining their respective roles in coastal security.

Cooperation among agencies that are equally involved in similar operation is not best assured by asserting the supremacy of one over others. No one will question the fact that the Navy is the primary agency for the *maritime defence* of India *vis-à-vis* state actors, but, as has been analysed, it has neither the infrastructure nor the experience to be the premier agency in the context of *coastal security*. One hopes that the experience during joint operations of officers, at middle and junior level, will help to mitigate the inevitable ill feeling between members belonging to senior/junior services and would help generate mutual respect and good will among members of various agencies. Only such an environment can ensure smooth and effective coordination among these agencies in the context of maritime security.

Cooperation at zonal level

Structure for cooperation among various agencies was spelled out by Defence Minister, Shri A.K. Anthony, in Kochi on August 9, 2009. He said that Joint Operation Centres (JOC) would be established at Mumbai, Visakhapatnam, Port Blair and Kochi under the charge of respective naval Commanders-in-Chief, who would be designated as the C-in-C Coastal Defence. That would be an added designation to their formal (Naval) designation as Chief of the Naval Command of that region.

Like similar centres elsewhere, a Joint Operation Centre (JOC) has been established at Kochi as the nerve centre for all operations pertaining to coastal defence of that maritime zone. Navy, Coast Guard, State Police, Port Trust, Fisheries Department, Light House Authorities and Customs Department are part of the JOC. It will coordinate activities of all these agencies during coastal security operations so as to attain synergy and uniformity of purpose. The JOC has a central operation-cum-briefing room from where communication is possible with all agencies. JOC will receive real time feed from surveillance assets of the Navy, the Coast Guard and the Vessel Traffic Management System of the Cochin Port as well as the around-the-clock monitoring by the Navy and the Coast Guard (*The Hindu*, August 10, 2009). It was not clear as to who would monitor hundreds of small and medium fishing vessel that operate in this vast zone. It is a gap that needs to be filled.

The Table of anticipated force level of various maritime enforcement agencies, operating in different maritime security zones, highlights two aspects of maritime enforcement. The one is that each of these agencies will require appropriate platforms like small Patrol Boats (PBs), hovercrafts, large patrol boats, SDB and IPCs, as well as large OPCs for operating in different maritime security zones. Each agency can have only a limited number of such platforms. Hence, the table also reveals that if these agencies pool their resources and workout a framework of cooperation and synergy of operations, they can be more effective in the overall famework of strengthening India's maritime security. For that purpose, India's adjacent sea space is divided into four zones.

Zones:

Zone A: shore to outer limit of the territorial waters,

Zone B: upto the outer limit of the contiguous zone,

Zone C: from 24 to 50 n. miles especially covering the sea space around off-shore platforms, and

Zone D: Beyond 50 n. miles.

Table: Maritime Enforcement Agencies, Anticipated Force Level in Different Zones (by 2012-13) (number in bracket denotes proposed acquisition).

Force Level: Surface Vessels

Zone A :

Navy :   (80) PB for SPB

Coast Guard :   6 hovercraft
                       4 PB, 5.5 tonnes - more to be acquired.
                       (84)   PB, 5 tonnes
                       (110) PB, 12 tonnes   (194)*

Marine Police :   (204) (5 and 12 tonnes)

Customs (Marine):   (80) CPL. Will spillover in Zone B as well.

Total :   (374)

* *Jane's Fighting Ships 2010-2011*, list these boats from Motomarine of Greece under Coast Guard, probably by mistake. Similar boats are also to be acquired for the Marine Police. Hence these are included under Marine Police.

Zone B (large patrol boats)

Navy :	7 (15)
Coast Guard:	22 (20)
Customs :	See Zone A
Total:	29 (35) + Customs (Marine) CPL

Zone C (SDB and IPC)

Navy :	12 (6)
Coast Guard :	24 (3)
Total:	36 (9)

Zone D (OPV)

Navy :	6 (4) OPV plus 8 large missile corvettes 12 small missile corvettes 4 small ASW corvettes
Coast Guard:	16 (3) OPV
Total:	46 (7) including 24 corvettes

Air Wing Maritime Reconnaissance Fixed Wing

Navy :	14 Dorniers, 6 Norman Defenders (likely to be replaced soon)
Coast Guard:	16 Dorniers
Total:	30

UAV

Navy :	4 Heron (large)
	8 Searcher

Coast Guard:	(Likely to acquire some)
Total:	12 (3 more to be acquired by the Navy)
Helicopters	
Navy:	( ) Sea King, Dhruv, Alouette III
Coast Guard:	2 Dhruv (12) Alouette. III (more to be acquired)

Different maritime zones, i.e. waters stretching from the shore to the outer limit of maritime security in the high seas, will need different type of platforms under different agencies. While the Marine Police will be concerned mostly with security of waters near the shore, the Coast Guard, the Customs (Marine) and the Navy will also be playing major role in these waters. Navy's capability to monitor and secure waters near the shore, especially in high value areas like the naval bases and major ports is being created after 26/11 with the raising of *Sagar Prahari Bal* (SPB). While the Navy has been provided with small and medium patrol boats as seen from the table, it lacks adequate number of surface vessels like large patrol boats and Inshore Patrol Crafts (IPC) to effectively monitor and secure waters all along the coast upto the outer limit of the contiguous zone.

Navy's capacity for operating in off-shore waters is also limited, given the small number of IPC/SDB and OPV under its command. By contrast, as seen from the table, the Coast Guard is better placed in that context. Yet, even the combined strength of the Navy and the Coast Guard of about 26 OPVs, 36 IPCs and 29 large patrol crafts will still be less than adequate to secure the vast sea space beyond the 12 n. mile limit of the territorial waters. Hence, a synergy of operations between the Navy and the Coast Guard will be absolutely essential to optimise the operational capability in waters further away from the shore.

Before the events of 26/11, different agencies were given specific zones for their operation. According to Commodore Vasan, clarifications issued by the government had indicated that the Marine Police would be tasked to cover areas upto five nautical miles from the shore, the Coast Guard would be in charge of area upto another twenty-five nautical miles.

The Navy would exercise operations in areas beyond that (Vasan, 2006, pp. 153-54). It should be underlined that this division of responsibilities predated change of perception after 26/11. The Navy was provided with the SPB and thus was tasked to operate along the coast. Also, this division did not provide any role for the Customs (Marine), an agency of the Central Government tasked with anti-smuggling operations in the contiguous zone.

Operation of various maritime enforcement agencies along adjacent waters will require an agreed framework of cooperation between them. Since their zones of operation overlap, compartmentalising their activities in respective zones will not be possible. Even if it is done, it will not only be operationally difficult but will also tend to promote the blame game and game of passing the buck. It will be more appropriate if their roles are synergised under a more logical framework not only for data collection and dissemination but also for actual operation. In other words, there will have to be a mix of centralisation wherever necessary and autonomy of operation when essential so that limited available resources can be best utilised.

While monitoring of sea space beyond 24 n. miles is important to preempt terrorists from approaching the coast, as also for the security of off-shore structures on the continental-shelf, waters along the coast need to be closely monitored as also secured for several reasons. These include the density of traffic, especially of small and medium-sized mechanised and non-mechanised fishing boats operating from multiple fish landing sites and beaches along the shore and estuaries. Besides, there are value targets like ports, oil refineries, centres of tourism etc. along the coast.

This sea space stretches about 7,600 kms along the coast. Though on paper, the number of Coast Guard Stations, Customs (Marine) offices attached to major and minor ports and coastal police stations seem to be large, in effect there are bound to be long gaps of about 50-60 km between them. Also, for reasons of infra-structure facilities they would need to be grouped in bunches along the coast.

There are three main reasons why their operation needs to be synergised. The first is the legal and constitutional constraints on the limits of activities of some of these agencies. While the zone of operation of the Marine Police is limited at the moment to the territorial waters, that of the

Customs (Marine) is limited to the contiguous zones. The Navy and the Coast Guard can operate in all zones.

Synergy at the level of operation along the coast is also necessary in view of two constraints. The one is the limited capability that each of these agencies can reasonably be expected to deploy at any given time and at a given point along the long coast line on a long term basis. For example, even in a major centre like Cochi or a smaller one like Beypore, each of these agencies can be expected to deploy only four and two vessels respectively. Thus, individually they are not able to fulfil on their own, the role of coastal security that they are expected to perform. But, if they synergise their operations they can greatly enhance their overall capability. A major centre like Cochi can have a total of 8-10 vessels while other centres like Baypore can mobilise 4-6 vessels. Thus, even small stations can detail two patrol boats on routine jobs while keeping some in reserve in case of emergency.

The second constraint that will compel these agencies to synergise their operations is that all of them will need reasonably well equipped base facilities for their operations. Thus, they are most likely to be bunched in suitable places like fishing harbours and major/minor ports along the coast or in islands. This demand on sharing of infrastructure will tend to bring these agencies in close proximity and thus, indirectly prompt them towards evolving some form of synergy of operation.

To be effective, this synergy will have to be based upon network centric operation. It will enhance their total capability many times more than the sum total of capability of each constituent unit. In actual operation, the task can be entrusted to one that is best situated to perform it at the given time and place, irrespective of the agency concerned. The follow up support can be offered by others if required.

Such a network centric synergy, however, requires prior administrative approval of the concerned departments under which these agencies operate. Thus, a major policy decision needs to be taken at the top level in all concerned ministries and department at the level of the Central Government as also of the coastal states and UTs. It is expected that decision makers will take this into account while formulating their policies for Phase II of the Coastal Security Scheme.

7 | LOOKING AHEAD

Coastal Security, Sea Governance and Maritime Development

The first phase of Coastal Security Scheme (2005-2011) posed multiple challenges that were not faced earlier in policy formulation as well as implementation. Valuable lessons learnt during that phase helped to prepare the broad outline for Phase II (2011-2016) of Coastal Security Scheme. Phase I can be divided into two main parts. The first part of 2004-2008 focussed primarily upon strengthening enforcement mechanism, especially of the Coast Guard and to establish Marine Police that signified, for the first time, an active role for coastal states and union territories (UTs) in matters of maritime security.

During the second part of Phase I, period following 26/11, the scope was widened to include some aspects of sea governance as well as to create a framework, though *ad-hoc*, for synergy and cooperation among multiple ministries and departments at the level of the Central Government as also coastal states and UTs that are related to the issues of maritime security. What is needed during Phase II of Coastal Security Scheme is to convert the *ad hoc* arrangements into more appropriate institutions at national level, that not only provide for synergy and cooperation at the level of policy formulation and implementation but also provide a firm base for evolving India's maritime strategy in the context of security as also development.

Another point that needs to be highlighted in the context of maritime security and sea governance is the need for creating better environment for encouraging maritime development. That aspect had suffered in the past largely because of lack of appropriate mechanism or institution for synergising maritime development at national level. That was largely due to the inherited administrative structure that rested upon the concept of autonomy of policy making and implementation for individual ministries and even departments. Hopefully, the new approach towards sea governance will create an awareness that will highlight the need to create similar structures for maritime development.

Thus, there is the need for realising the close linkage between security, governance and development. These three facets demand a close cooperation between the Central Government, coastal states and UTs. While the Central Government can provide coordination and guidance at national level, the role of coastal states and UTs in these three facets of maritime policy can no longer be ignored. This calls for a relook at India's overall maritime policy and if necessary a structuring of administrative mechanism to strengthen all the three inter-related facets, maritime security, sea governance and maritime development.

As noted, the need for coastal security provided the impetus for evolving a better security environment in the adjacent sea space. Yet, in that process it was also realised that maritime security is dependent upon better sea governance as also some specified structure of cooperation among multiple ministries/departments that deal with maritime affairs so as to streamline their involvement in matters of maritime security.

Sea governance has emerged as a new concept since 1970s when states began to acquire varying degrees of exclusive jurisdiction over adjacent sea space, especially over the living and non-living resources upto the outer limits of their EEZ and continental-shelf. They also acquired criminal jurisdiction over smuggling and related offences in the contiguous zone. The outer limit of territorial waters also extended to 12 n. miles. India too benefited.

While ministries/departments that deal primarily with land-centric affairs can enjoy a great deal of autonomy in decision making and their implementation, by contrast, in the case of sea governance greater coordination will be necessary among multiple stake holders both in decision making as also in operation; as in the case of ports (major, minor and fishery), shipping (overseas, coastal and fishing), SLOCs both overseas and coastal, marine fishery both in territorial waters and in the high seas (EEZ and beyond), security *vis-à-vis* NSA and terrorists etc. This coordination is needed not only between the ministries/department at the level of the Central Government but also between them and those of the coastal states and UTs. These activities are interrelated and hence cannot be seen in isolation.

A few examples will illustrate the inevitable result of compartmentalisation of decision making as also implementation. Ministry of Shipping is tasked with navigational safety while navigational charts are prepared and provided by the Chief Hydrographer of the Government of India. Nodal agency for the maritime legal regime is the office of the Director-General of Shipping. Merchant vessel inspection and documentation is the duty of the Mercantile Marine Department. Power to inspect foreign ships vests with the Director-General of Shipping. When *M.V. Isabel III* of Taiwan was damaged in July 2002 on the reef of one of the islands of the Lakshadweep, two senior officers from the Director-General of Shipping had to be sent there to assess the damage.

This compartmentalisation is true even at the level of coastal states. It can act as constraints in the functioning even of other departments. In 1998, the Fisheries Department of Kerala had acquired five high-speed patrol boats. The Mercantile Department graded those boats as Class-12. That required them to be commanded by an officer of the grade of Master and maintained by a First Grade Engineer. Since the pay of the Master and the Engineer was above that of the Assistant Director of Fisheries, who was the custodian of the boats, the Fisheries Department downgraded the posts to that of Skipper and Second Grade Engineer. Boats that had cost Rs. 1.56 crores were rarely operated and fell into a state of disrepair thereby forcing the Marine Enforcement and Vigilance Wing of Kerala to hire fishing boats for operation (*The Hindu*, December 3, 2008).

Similarly, the Fisheries Department of Tamil Nadu had acquired five patrol boats at a cost of Rs. 4.5 crores. They were financed by the Central Government. These boats were built by a Pondicherry-based firm. They were delivered in February-March 2000. Due to dearth of inhouse staff to handle the boats, services of the firm in Pondicherry that had built the boat was requisitioned for a period of three months. Proposal to get the department staff trained at the Central Institute of Fisheries, Nautical Engineering and Technology, Kochi, was dropped following a decision to run the boats with private assistance. Needless to say the whole exercise had proved to be a failure. The boats left anchored for months had depreciated and suffered damages (Shankar, *The Hindu*, January 14, 2001). Under such circumstances, it would have been preferable to handover the patrol boats to the Coast Guard with provision for joint patrol with state's enforcement personnel also on board. Now that the coastal states were going to have their own Marine Police, mechanism for such operations between the Fishery Department and the Marine Police would prove to be beneficial for both. The new approach to maritime security would need to overcome such bureaucratic hurdles through a viable mechanism of interdepartmental cooperation and synergy. Even with the best of good will it will take time to break decades-old inertia and "time honoured" procedures.

Carrying forward from Phase I

National Commission for Sea-space Management (NCSM)

The need for synergising efforts of multiple ministries and departments towards policy making and implementation in the context of better management of adjacent sea space will need a separate organisation. India did not have a mechanism to coordinate policies on maritime affairs. Consequently, different ministries and departments had been dealing with different facets of India's maritime affairs.

An attempt was made in July 1981 in that direction when the Government decided to set up the Department of Ocean Development. It was to be charged with the responsibility of determining policies regarding ocean development, framing of appropriate laws and regulations, overseeing technological developments, collaborations concerning living and non-living resources etc. To ally the fear among concerned ministries and departments, the Cabinet Secretariat of the Government of India, in Allocation of Business Rules, emphasised that the new department would not takeover any of their functions but would act as a think tank for various ocean-related activities and to assist the ministries and departments in more effectively carrying out their functional responsibilities (Sharma, 2005, p. 378).

Denied any role in the affairs of existing bureaucratic organisations, the main thrust of the Department of Ocean Development (DoD) got diverted to deep sea mining, expeditions to Antarctica etc. Thus, DoD made practically no impact on other ministries and departments or on sea governance. Consequently their efforts remained fragmented and often uncoordinated.

Voices have been raised to find ways and means to coordinate these activities at national level after 2004. E.K. Nambiar, the then Deputy National Security Adviser, National Security Council, New Delhi, while speaking at a seminar organised by the University of Calicut and the Indian Navy on September 5, 2005, while dealing with maritime security, advocated for enhanced coordination of the economic, military, political, diplomatic and other dimensions of maritime affairs and for the development of a comprehensive, coherent and proactive maritime strategy for the country through the establishment of a Maritime Commission (Nambiar, 2006, p. 29).

The new thrust on coastal security in the context of maritime terrorism also evoked responses but of a more limited and practical nature. Admiral Suresh Mehta had suggested on August 9, 2008, even before 26/11, that it was time that the Government established an apex body to deal with maritime security issues. He said that a *single-window federal agency* could tackle security challenges faced by all ministries handling sea-based activities such as shipping, fisheries, ports, Navy and Coast Guard. Such an apex body can bring about uniformity and coordination among different ministries on all matters of safety and security of maritime assets. It will assure quick decision-making and rapid response. He added that there was the need for an organisational structure in which representatives of these ministries sit together to *take action required whenever there is an emergency*. Such an agency could also initiate means to net the upcoming private ports into the security framework by which naval representatives would be part of the governing bodies of the ports (*The Times of India*, August 10, 2008).

As noted in Chapter VI, steps were initiated in that direction when in August 2009, a National Committee for Strengthening Maritime and Coastal Security Against Threats from the Sea was constituted under the Chairmanship of the Cabinet Secretary. It was tasked with responsibility for coordinating activities of various concerned agencies at the level of

Central Government, State governments and UTs in matters related to strengthening maritime security as also framework of sea governance (MHA, *A.R., 2009-2010*, P. 39).

This National Committee, at best an *ad hoc* arrangement, needs to be given a permanent shape by substituting it with a National Commission for Sea-space Management (NCSM). It will not duplicate the functioning of any department but will coordinate functions of various agencies in furtherance of more effective sea governance thereby strengthening the framework of maritime security.

To be effective NCSM will

- ➤ Function under the Cabinet Secretariat
- ➤ Will have representatives of stakeholders at the level of Central Government, state governments and private sectors especially those involved in fisheries, port sector (minor ports) and off-shore oil and gas industry.
- ➤ It will hold periodic meetings; bi-annual in the initial period and annual subsequently (besides emergency meetings if needed).
- ➤ It will be tasked with:

    (i) Coordination in evolving broad policy of sea governance and role of individual stakeholders and recommend in that context:

    (ii) Means of coordination/synergy of operations among immediately concerned stakeholders

    (iii) To constitute, if necessary, committees for facilitating cooperation among concerned stakeholders.

    (iv) Revamping/updating of policies and implementation procedures of various departments.

    (v) Formation of a small Secretariat under Cabinet Secretariat, with permanent staff to:

        (a) synchronise the work of committees and the NCSM and.

        (b) prepare the agenda for the NCSM and for follow-up action.

(vi) Nominate Chairman/Deputy Chairman of NCSM to chair the main session as also various committees and to supervise the functioning of the Secretariat.

(vii) NCSM to report periodically (quarterly if possible) to Cabinet Secretary on its functioning. The report can also be distributed to stakeholders for information.

(viii) Navy-sponsored programs of National Maritime Domain Awareness (NMDA) system as also National Command, Control, Communication and Intelligence **(NC₃IN)** network can be linked to NCSM since a large percentage of data that goes into them can be generated only through active cooperation of stakeholders of NCSM.

Strengthening Enforcement Measures

As seen in Chapter VI, steps have been initiated towards creation of National Maritime Domain Awareness (NMDA) system as well as creation of National Command, Control, Communication and Intelligence (NC^3IN) network under the Navy. These will help strengthen the capability for sea space management as well as maritime security. The Navy will have a new dedicated *Sagar Prahari Bal*. The Navy, the Coast Guard and the Marine Police are going to be suitably equipped for the new responsibility.

However, one dimension of coastal security seems to have been overlooked. As analysed earlier, India's mine-countermeasure capability in approaches even of major ports and bases still remains unattended. Since sea mines are easily available and can be sown in these waters even by a medium-sized fishing trawler, it is essential that the Navy, that alone has the capability to operate vessels suitable for mine-countermeasure operations, be suitably equipped with inshore minesweepers on an emergency basis. That can even be a part of the *Sagar Prahari Bal* for operations near major ports and bases.

Customs (Marine)

While the Navy, the Coast Guard and Marine Police have been suitably strengthened, one important maritime enforcement agency, the Customs

(Marine), seems to have been neglected in the context of strengthening coastal security. As noted in previous chapters, Customs (Marine) is entrusted under Section 14, Sub-section 2 of the Customs Act, as well as under Section 5, Sub-section 4 (a) of MZI Act, 1976, with the task of security in the contiguous zone of India. Thus, it is legally empowered to conduct enforcement action in matters of maritime security also in the strategically important sea space that encompasses waters upto a distance of 24 n. miles from Indian shore. Though formally the Customs (Marine) is included in the deliberation on maritime security, there is as yet no sign that the agency's enforcement capability is being enhanced in the context of coastal security. One hopes that this crucial gap will be filled during Phase II of the Coastal Security Scheme so that Customs (Marine) is able to play its rightful role in meeting the new challenge posed not only by NSA but also by the terrorists.

CISF (Marine)

Another serious gap in maritime security that was highlighted in previous chapters dealt with the inadequacy of basic point security of ports and bases along the coast and high value installations on the continental-shelf. Though the Navy, the Coast Guard and the Marine Police are being strengthened for area security, one feels that there is a gap in basic point security of these high value targets. As was suggested in Chapter VI, the Marine Wing of the CISF should be established for that role during Phase II of the Coastal Security Scheme (2011-2016).

Since it will have to coordinate activities with the Navy, the Coast Guard, the Customs and the Marine Police, it is suggested that these agencies be also involved while framing the outlines of the new agency. It will be comparatively easier to establish the Marine Wing of the CISF since the CISF is a well-established para-military organisation under the Ministry of Home Affairs. As in the ease of the BSF, which also has a marine/riveriene wing, the Ministry of Home Affairs can decide on its own on that issue. Initial steps on an experimental basis can be taken during Phase II and, if found suitable, can be expanded in the subsequent years.

Role of Seafarers: The Sea Guard

Despite lip service being paid to the role of the coastal people, especially the fisher-folk, in the context of coastal security, any institution in that context is yet to be formally established. While one cannot ignore the collection and analysis of information from various sophisticated sources that would probably go into the NMDA and NC³IN, one should not sideline the role of human intelligence that can be provided by the daily users of adjacent sea space. Their number runs into thousands and they operate large and small fishing crafts that operate in these waters.

It is easy for them to note and identify something 'unusual'. That becomes a source of information, provided means are found to channelise that information quickly into the larger grid at sub-zonal and zonal levels. Since many of these fisherfolk operate nearer to the shore and usually carry a mobile phone, minimum that can be done is to provide them with a toll free telephone number for contacting the appropriate authority along the coast, preferably the Marine Police. The Marine Police can then initiate the necessary follow up action.

A more structured way of popular participation will be through the formation of the Sea Guards or Home Guards (Marine). This will be a trained workforce that will operate in sea space further away from the shore. Already, a force of the Home Guards is being raised in border states to support BSF's operation on land border. The concept can be extended to cover the sea border/frontier as well. The other mechanism will be more formal and will be supportive of enforcement measures of the state governments. There is provision for raising formation of Home Guards at state level. There is also the precedent of Home Guard (Border) that operate in cooperation with BSF along land border. That concept can be extended to create a marine wing of the Home Guard or the *Sea Guard*.

Its members can be recruited from among the fishing community. Those with their own fishing vessels can be given preference. Those selected can be given basic training in the use of GPS, for determining exact locations on the sea, night vision devices and appropriate communication system for keeping in touch with the coordinating agency, like the Marine Police or the Coast Guard. Like the Home Guard, they too can be provided with suitable remuneration with additional incentives for the use of their vessels.

Establishing Sea Guard from among the members of the fishing community from adjacent shore will have several advantages. They are already trained seamen and know the sea space in which they have been operating for years. They will, however, have to be trained in the use of GPS so that they can locate their exact location, as well as in the use of long-range radio communication system. Night vision device will enhance their surveillance capability. Since they own their vessels, no extra cost will be incurred in procuring patrol boats except some way of offering financial support for operation of these vessels even while on normal role as local fishing boats.

Since these vessels will be fishing boats, they will be operating as such in the designated sea space as a part of their normal routine. Thus, at least one third of the total number can be expected to be 'on duty' at any given time. Even if the first battalion comprises of 300 Sea Guards, approximately 100 trained sea men will be deployed in the adjacent sea space at any given time. No one can ignore their contribution in the collection and immediate contribution of information to designated agencies, so that timely action can be initiated by them. Initially, during Phase II, each coastal state, in consultation with Ministry of Home Affairs, can raise one battalion of Sea Guard (Home Guard-Marine). If their role is found to be contributive to maritime security, suitable decisions can be taken after the end of Phase-II.

It will be useful to appoint a committee comprising of representatives from the Ministry of Home Affairs, coastal states and UTs, the Indian Navy, the Coast Guard and the Customs to examine the viability and feasibility of the concept and to suggest ways and means as to how it can be introduced on an experimental basis during Phase II of the Coastal Security Scheme. If nothing else, these two measures will give the coastal state and the population along the coast, a feeling of participation in combating the new threat directed against them *via* the adjacent sea space.

National Committee on Marine Security (NCMS)

Steps have been taken to synergise policies and actions of multiple agencies that are involved in strengthening maritime security. Joint Operation Centres have been established at Mumbai, Kochi, Visakhapatnam and Port Blair in that context. However, there is the need for an apex body at the national level that can concentrate upon the larger issues of maritime security and suggest ways and means of further enhancing it. Such a step can be initiated during Phase II of the Coastal Security Scheme, by the formation of National Committee on Maritime Security (NCMS).

The NCMS will concentrate upon broad policy on maritime security and coordination among various enforcement agencies. The NCMS will comprise of representatives of the Navy, the Coast Guard, the Customs (Marine) and the Marine Police to begin with. Other agencies like the CISF (Marine) and of the fishery departments can be included if and when formed.

NCMS will be tasked with:

(i) Formulating policy on framework of cooperation among various maritime enforcement agencies at national level.

(ii) Holding periodic meetings, bi-annual to begin with and annual subsequently, to initiate policies as also to review their implementation.

(iii) NCMS will have a Chairman to preside over the sessions/meetings and to supervise the functioning of the Secretariat.

(iv) It will have a small Secretariat.

(v) NCMS will help organise seminars/workshops on related topics in cooperation with organisations like the USI, IDSA, NMF etc.

For that purpose, funds can be provided by Ministry of Defence, Ministry of Home Affairs as also by concerned departments like shipping, port authorities, energy etc. A working committee for the seminar/workshop can be constituted comprising of representatives of the stakeholders, funding agency and the organisation that is entrusted with that program. The working committee will prepare the agenda, list of participants and working papers. It will also prepare the summary of deliberations along with the recommendations. It will assist the organisation in preparing the compadium/book of the entire proceeding for wider distribution.

Managing India's marine fisheries

India's marine fishery policy is yet another illustration of India's inherited continental mindset and inability to move forward with the fast moving changes in international maritime environment. Till now Indian fishery is a prisoner of the division of power between the Central Government and the state governments (and UTs). Under the VII th Schedule of the Indian Constitution, as per item 51 of List I, marine fishery is the sole preserve of the Central Government. While the coastal states, as seen in Chapter IV, have been able to assert their right to regulate fishing in territorial waters adjacent to their respective shores, the Central Government still retains the exclusive power to regulate fishery in sea space beyond the territorial waters.

One would still not have objected to that if the Central Government would have enacted suitable laws to regulate marine fishery as also created an appropriate agency to enforce these laws. The only law that was passed was the MZI (Regulation of Foreign Vessels) Act, 1981, that regulated fishing by non-Indian ships in Indian EEZ. The Coast Guard is tasked to enforce that law and to take action against foreign fishing vessels that violate provisions of that act. The Central Government had passed no laws to regulate fishing in these waters by Indian fishermen. Since there was no law, there was no enforcement agency dealing with marine fishery. It needs to be underlined that almost all the fishermen who operate in these waters belong to the coastal states and UTs.

Since there is no constitutional provision that provides for synergy in this aspect between the Central Government and coastal states (and UTs) and in the absence of any law regulating marine fishery by Indians at the level of the Central Government, there was near anarchy in the sea space that constituted almost two-thirds of India's land space. An attempt to regulate marine fishery was made under the Marine Fishery Bill of 2009. But it was not only inadequate but also had provisions that were not conducive to India's maritime security. Since marine fishery, that includes, fishing, fishing boats, fishery harbour/landing sites as also suitable enforcement agencies, is closely related to the larger issue of maritime security, it is essential to fill this gap as early as possible. It is, therefore, a fit subject to be dealt with during Phase II of the Maritime Security Scheme.

In that context, it is necessary to frame a comprehensive legal framework for regulating fishery by Indians in the entire sea space from the inland sea to the outer limit of the EEZ and even beyond that, as also to suggest a mechanism for its enforcement by appropriate agencies of the Central Government as well as of the coastal states and UTs.

To update and streamline management of marine fishery it is recommended that a *Fisheries Commission* be constituted. It will comprise of representatives of:

➤ Departments dealing with marine fishery at the level of the Central Government, state governments and UTs.

➤ Department of Shipping entrusted with registration of fishing boats of different types.

➤ Fishing ports and landing sites

➤ Maritime enforcement agencies like the Navy, the Coast Guard and the Marine Police.

➤ Fisherfolk

➤ Industrial sectors related to marine fishery (ship building, processing units etc)

The Commission be tasked to propose recommendations on:

(a) a comprehensive Marine Fishery Bill (Like Fisheries Bill, 2009) that will consider marine fishery in the entire sea space from the inland sea to the outer limit of EEZ (and even beyond it). The bill should respect rights of coastal states to regulate fishery in their territorial waters.

(b) Ways and means for registration and accounting for *all* types of fishing fleet.

(c) Recommend suitable monitoring and enforcement agencies at the level of Central Government as also state governments and UTs. A law that cannot be enforced is only a law on paper.

Fishery enforcement agencies with their own ships can play an important role in keeping an eye on the activities of fishing vessels and the fisherfolk and thereby supplement information inputs for the Marine Police, the Customs, the Coast Guard and the Navy. Marine fishing management, therefore, needs to be seen in the broader perspective of maritime security.

Strengthening legal norms

As examined in Chapter III and IV dealing with international and national legal norms, it was obvious that India lacks a comprehensive legal framework to handle cases related to various facets of maritime security. After 2010-11, when Indian Navy began its proactive anti-piracy operations in the Indian Ocean, particularly in the sea space near India's western coast and islands of the Lakshadweep, need was felt to try a large number of pirates that were arrested. India has no anti-piracy law.

India is reportedly framing a new law to provide legitimacy to actions of India's maritime law enforcement agencies and to streamline the subsequent judicial processes. It is also reported that the proposed law will be in tune with piracy-related provisions of UNCLOS-III (Article 100-107). Such a restricted piracy-specific law will be totally inadequate to meet new challenges posed by NSA and terrorists, to freedom of the high seas as well as to the security of India's adjacent coastal waters.

UNCLOS-III of 1982 reflected the out-dated concept of piracy. Even the IMO had to modify the definition of piracy by adding armed robbery to it. But, piracy is only one of the several challenges to freedom of navigation on the high seas, posed by NSA and terrorists. SUA Convention of 1988 was a step towards filling the legal gap in that context. UN, especially the Security Council, has also passed resolutions after 2001 that target terrorism. State practices like the Regional Maritime Security Initiative and stationing of warships on the high seas to counter activities of the terrorists have added a new dimension to *de facto* international law. Indian law makers can well avail of these provisions to enable domestic laws to acquire international legitimacy.

Besides various international norms, the new law can also draw upon various Indian legal and constitutional sources as also state practices. Indian Constitution, under Item 21, List I, of VIIth Schedule, gives the Central

Government and its enforcement agencies, the power to take action not only against piracy but also against other crimes committed on the high seas (offences against the law of nations on the high seas). Indian Parliament has enacted several laws that give legal effect to various international conventions dealing with terrorism and hostage taking.

The SUA Act of 2002 legalised provisions of the SUA Convention of 1988. There are several provisions of the SUA Act that can become the basis for the new act. Section 3 of that act not only lists various criminal acts but also prescribes punishment for them. Piracy and hostage taking can be added to that list. Section 5 of that act provides for special courts to try the offenders. Section 13 provides for presumption of guilt under certain circumstances. Section 14 protects members of the enforcement agency from being tried for wrongful seizure on the high seas under articles 106 and 110 (3) of UNCLOS-III.

The proposed comprehensive act on maritime security can be termed: **Act to Ensure Freedom of the High Seas and Security of Homeland from Threats Posed by NSA and Terrorists.** Towards that end, one can initiate a series of steps. A committee needs to be constituted comprising of legal experts, representatives of concerned ministries/departments as also from various enforcement agencies at the level of the Central Government, state governments and UTs. It will be entrusted with the following tasks:

(i) Compile all relevant laws that have a bearing, direct or indirect, upon maritime security,

(ii) Examine if there are gaps or grey areas and suggest means to rectify them through new notifications, enactments or amendments.

(iii) The new package should have provision for preemptive action in various maritime security zones.

(iv) These acts should have provision, like section 14 (1) of the SUA Act, 2002, that protect enforcement agency personnel *vis-à-vis* articles 106 and 110 (3) of UNCLOS-III.

(v) Areas that need early legal redress deal with:

(a) Piracy and hijacking on the high seas

(b) Amendment to List III of VIIth Schedule of the Constitution by adding maritime security and marine fishery to that list.

(c) Reaffirm the provision, along with suitable follow up action, of Section 5 (4a) of MZI Act, 1976 dealing with *security* in the contiguous zone so as to reaffirm it as a maritime security zone of India.

(d) Remove the grey area in Section 6, Sub-section 5 b iii of MZI Act, 1976, dealing with *safety and protection* of off-shore installations on the continental-shelf so as to clearly bring sea space around them under maritime security zone.

Maritime security and regional cooperation

Indian sea space can be divided into three main regions with their respective maritime extensions. The one is the North Arabian Sea and its extension towards the Persian Gulf and the Horn of Africa. It is strategically very important not only in the context of international SLOCs but also national maritime security. This is the region in which India has failed to evolve structures of maritime cooperation for various well-known reasons except on a bilateral basis with a few littoral states like Oman. It will not be wrong to say that it is a hostile maritime neighbourhood for India and is likely to remain so for some time to come.

The second region is around the Andaman Sea and its maritime extension towards the Malacca Straits and beyond. It dominates a major international SLOC that connects the Pacific with the Indian Ocean *via* the Malacca Straits and the Bay of Bengal. The region is also important since it touches upon the shores of Indonesia, Thailand, Myanmar and Bangladesh. India has been developing close relations with these states mostly on a bilateral level. They include coordinated patrol of the maritime borders by the navies of India and Thailand and India and Indonesia in the Andaman Sea. Integrated regional framework of maritime cooperation is still a dream. But, unlike the North Arabian Sea region, India's relations with these states are cordial and hence one can hope that intra-regional maritime cooperation might be possible in the near future at least in the field of information sharing, if not joint action as well as in the field of fisheries, disaster management etc.

The third region is the South Arabian Sea with its extension towards Mauritius and the Seychelles. Major SLOCs of Indian Ocean traverse this region. Also, this relatively compact maritime region can provide avenues for economic cooperation like fishery, shipping, ports etc. besides cooperation to enhance regional security. This region will comprise of EEZs along the western coast of Sri Lanka, the adjacent EEZ of the Maldives and EEZ opposite the Arabian Sea coast of Tamil Nadu, Kerala and Union Territories of Mahe and Lakshadweep. Unlike other regions, the three maritime neighbours of this region have strong bilateral ties. What is needed is to create a framework that can lay the foundation of a strong trilateral regional maritime cooperation not only in the context of security but also development.

Three states of South Arabian Sea region; the Maldives, Sri Lanka and India (MASLIND) have over the years developed very intimate cooperation in political, economic and even security related fields. But, bilateral cooperation among these states could not be taken to its logical conclusion – trilateral cooperation – because of domestic constraints in these states that were casting their dark shadow even upon their bilateral relations. Now that some of those constraints have been overcome, it is possible to initiate steps towards trilateral cooperation.

Future relations among the three states of this region are going to be affected by their internal socio-economic and political compulsions as also by what shape their policies take in matters dealing with regional cooperation not only in the realm of security but also maritime development. All the three states are being affected by problems of socio-political nature largely conditioned by socio-ethnic divide as also rapid politicisation of religion. These will have their security related spin-offs.

Events of the past few years have brought about major changes in Sri Lanka and the Maldives. Military defeat of the LTTE, willingness of Sri Lanka Government to evolve a viable devolution package and India's willingness to render humanitarian aid for rehabilitating the displaced Tamil minority in the north and the north-east of Sri Lanka will hopefully usher in a positive environment which will enable India and Sri Lanka to further cement their bilateral relations.

However, there are still several hurdles in the path. The opposition of the JVP and Buddhist monks to a package that will fully accommodate the socio-political aspirations of Tamils can make the task of reconciliation difficult. The rehabilitation package will take time to generate the goodwill among Tamils that is essential for lasting peace and stability in that war-torn region. Tamil diaspora, that had played an important part in sustaining Tamil opposition, has still to respond whole heartedly to a lasting resolution of ethnic dispute despite the military defeat of the LTTE. Any spark can reignite the dormant violence. The question of fishermen seized by the Navy and the Coast Guard on both sides still remains unresolved.

Maldives will have to face the political uncertainty of coalition politics in a multiparty democracy. That as well as rising public expectations and the growing influence of radical Islamic forces have already cast their shadows over the future of peace and security of the Maldives.

Almost all the Maldivian population is Muslim. President Gayoom had used his credentials as a scholar from the Islamic University of Al-Azhar in Cairo as a political card. Maldives was not isolated from the new wave of radical Islam which was being fanned by foreign elements. Radical Islam got associated with terrorism around 2001, when *Jamaat-tul-Muslimeen* was allegedly involved in acquisition of weapons and explosives for terrorist-related activities in the Maldives. The *Tsunami* provided an opportunity to *Idara Khidmat-e-Khalq*, a front of *Lashkar-e-Toiba* of Bangladesh, to spread its activities in the Maldives.

Islamic radicals in the Maldives were also reportedly seeking to develop links with Kerala. Ibrahim Asif, a Maldivian national, was deported by Kerala Police, in May 2005, allegedly for terrorist-related activities. He was reportedly linked to *Jamaat-tul-Muslimeen*. It was reported in 2006 that Faisal Haroon, Dhaka-based activist of *Lashkar-e-Toiba* was seeking to develop links with the Maldives and to establish a logistic base there. In September 2007, the Sultan Park in Male was the target of bombing in which 12 tourists were injured. Ten suspects, held in that connection, allegedly escaped to Pakistan. Ameen Faisal, Maldivian Minister of Defence and

National Security, told journalists in April 2009 that nine Maldivian jihadists were held in the Waziristan Province of Pakistan. One of them allegedly was linked to the bombing at the Sultan Park in Male, in September 2007.

It is possible that Islamic militant groups in the Maldives may be used by anti-India elements to pose a new source of maritime threat to India's homeland security, especially in south India. The proximity of the islands of the Maldives and the Lakshadweep and the traditional links with the adjacent Arabian Sea coast of India and Sri Lanka may favour island hopping by insurgents based in these places, thereby creating security-related problems not only in India but also in Sri Lanka and the Maldives. It is significant that Indian Home Minister met his Maldivian counterpart in Delhi on February 4, 2010. Reportedly, anti-terrorist cooperation and information sharing were part of the discussion.

Time has come for the three neighbouring states to move from bilateral relations to evolving a regional approach to their maritime cooperation. This is important not only in the context of security-related issues but also in the context of regional cooperation in issues like fisheries, shipping, ports, intra-regional trade, tourism etc. It must not be forgotten that this region had close maritime linkages since ancient times.

Fisheries can become an important instrument in promoting regional cooperation. Though UNCLOS-III has given exclusive rights of exploitation of living resources to the coastal and island states, each state is trying to control the respective EEZ on its own. Since the capability to monitor the vast sea space under EEZ is limited even for India, these waters have become a favourite fishing ground for foreign trawlers and fishing boats that operate even without proper licence. If the three countries decide to cooperate and pool their information, such a poaching can be prevented or at least substantially reduced.

If these states decide to evolve a mechanism that can enable regional fishermen to fish, under a mutually agreed formula, in the EEZ of the neighbouring states, it will avoid the present awkward situation when each state is trying to arrest the foreign fishermen that are found in these waters. A trilateral agreement on fishery cooperation in their EEZs will not only bring optimum benefit for all but will also, by regulating fishery, help to conserve the fast dwindling fish stock in the region. That will also help keep foreign fishermen out because regional fishermen who are so authorised will also report the presence of these poachers.

It will also strengthen steps taken to enhance coastal security from threats posed by Non-State Actors (NSA) and terrorists using that sea space to target not only India but also Sri Lanka and the Maldives. It should not be forgotten that Tamil mercenaries, transported in fishing vessels, had tried to overthrow the legitimate government on the Maldives in 1988. The nexus between sections of fishermen from Tamil Nadu and LTTE needs no elaboration. Also, fishing boats were used to smuggle explosives used in Mumbai blasts of 1993 and for transporting terrorists to Mumbai in November 2008. Thus regional cooperation in fishery management in respective EEZs can also go a long way in creating a better security environment in this region.

Other avenues of regional cooperation are inter-regional shipping, port facilities, ship-building and repair, tourism, education, health care etc. India will have no option but to improve its coastal shipping and related infrastructure to take care of the fast growing domestic traffic that the over-saturated, land-based systems, like railway and roads will find difficult to handle. This large volume coastal traffic will also pave the way for overseas trade. A framework of intra-regional cooperation in these sectors will benefit all the concerned parties.

Regional maritime cooperation in South Arabian Sea will force the participating states to involve their littoral administration because the structure of cooperation cannot be effective without active involvement of the Arabian Sea littoral of Tamil Nadu, Kerala, Union Territories of Mahe and Lakshadweep Islands. Even under Indian Constitution, coastal states have rights in matters related to fishing (in territorial waters), non-major ports and related infrastructure and security. The new developments in the context of coastal security have allowed the coastal states to create their own Marine Police that will coordinate its actions with the Navy, the Coast Guard and the Customs etc. They can interact with their counterparts along the Arabian Sea littoral of Sri Lanka and of the Maldives. It will, therefore, be practical that these agencies, at the level of Indian littoral, be closely associated with their counterparts in other states so as to strengthen the structure of regional cooperation that may be proposed for South Arabian Sea region.

It is time that the three states, the Maldives, Sri Lanka and India (MASLIND), initiate a process for raising their present level of cooperation above bilateral level. The framework of regional cooperation for greater synergy among various participating agencies, should also suggest a space for participation of the official machinery at the level of littoral so that information sharing becomes easier and time for action taken is reduced. Such a framework of regional maritime cooperation will mark a departure from the traditional norms under which the Centre took all decisions even on matters that concerned the coastal states. The proposed structure of regional maritime cooperation in South Arabian Sea will hopefully bring about the realisation that maritime policy cannot remain the preserve of the Centre alone but must take the interests and the aspirations of the coastal states and island territories of India – the real maritime India.

As of now, an impression is being created that India's maritime security strategy is compartmentalised; international efforts that entail cooperation at regional and international level and national efforts that are primarily inward looking. One possible reason for it can be that these two aspects of maritime security are being handled at two different sets of ministries; at international level by Ministry of External Affairs and Ministry of Defence, while homeland security (coastal security) is handled primarily by the Ministry of Home Affairs and the state governments, in which the Navy and the Coast Guard are also assigned a role but within the framework that is primarily inward looking.

It is acknowledged that there exists a nexus between domestic and foreign NSA and terrorists that target the homeland *via* adjacent sea space. It is, therefore, illogical to compartmentalise the response to meet the new challenge at domestic and international levels. It is also essential to synergise the response at the level of India's coastal regions and other regional states with which Indian coastal states and union territories share immediate sea space, at least upto the extent of their respective EEZ, so that a truly 'regional' response can be formulated while respecting the sanctity of sovereignty of regional state actors.

Maritime development

Steps that will be taken during Phase II of the Coastal Security Scheme will hopefully strengthen the nexus between maritime security and sea governance. These steps will, however, be incomplete unless they are also linked to issues of maritime development like shipping, ship building and repairs, ports, coastal traffic, exploitation of sub-soil resources in the continental-shelf as also of the living resources at least upto the outer limits of India's EEZ. That will need greater initiative on the part of public sectors both at the level of the Central Government, coastal states and UTs, as also of the private sector that is being galvanized for that role.

Maritime development is the basis of sea governance and, hence, of maritime security. It is hoped that the process initiated since 2004 will ultimately lead to the growth of India as a strong maritime state capable of playing its due role not only in the Indian Ocean region, but also at the global level.

Bibliography

Abhyankar (2000), Jayant, "Piracy Today: An Overview", (*JIOS*) *Journal of Indian Ocean Studies*, 7 (2-3), March 2000.

Acharya and Withana (2008), Acharya, Arbinda and Withana, Nandeeki Prashadani, "Groups with maritime terrorist capabilities in the Indian Ocean region", in Raghvan, V.R. and Prabhakar, W. Lawrence S., eds., *Maritime Security in the Indian Ocean Region: Critical Issues of Debate*, Tata McGraw-Hill Pub. Co. Ltd., New Delhi.

Ahmedulla (2009), Mohammed, "War on terror becomes India's priority", *Military Technology*, no. 2, 2009.

Anand (2008), G., "High security number plates for sea-going vessels", *The Hindu*, December 1, 2008.

Anand (2008), G., "Police to get high speed boats", *The Hindu*, December 3, 2008.

"GAO Report calls for revamped PSI", *Arms Control Today* (2008), reproduced in *Strategic Digest*, 39 (3), March 2009.

Prakash (2005), Arun, Admiral, "Future strategies and challenges for the Indian Navy", *RUSI Defence Systems*, 8(2), Autumn 2005.

Athas (2006), Iqbal, "Security implications for Sri Lanka, India and South Asian region", in Raman, B., ed., *Sri Lanka: Peace Without Process*, Samashakti, New Delhi.

"Aviation Week and Space Technology", (August 15, 2005), reproduced in *Strategic Digest*, 35 (10), October 2005.

Ban Ki-Moon (2006), "Conditions that foster terrorism", *Defence Watch*, 7(8), April 2008.

Bangara (2005), Vice-Admiral S.C.S., "Security in the Indian Ocean: A naval perspective", in Nambiar, E.K.G. and Suryanarayan, V., eds, *Lectures in Maritime Studies*, Publications Division, University of Calicut.

Banlaos (2008), Romel C., "Non-traditional security issues in Southeast Asian maritime domain: Implication for the Indian Ocean", in Raghavan V.R. and Prabhakar, W. Lawrence S., eds, *Maritime Security in the Indian Ocean*, Tata McGraw-Hill Pub., New Delhi.

Bateman (2007), Sam, "UNCLOS-III and its limitations in the foundation of a regional maritime security regime", *The Korean Journal of Defence Analysis*, 13(3), Fall 2007.

Beckman (2006), Robert, "The 1988 SUA Convention and the 2005 SUA Protocol: Tools to combat piracy, armed robbery and maritime terrorism", *Maritime Affairs*, 2(2), Winter 2006.

Bingley (2004), Barrett, "Security interests of the influencing states: The complexity of Malacca Straits", *Indonesian Quarterly*, 32(4), 4th Q. 2004.

Biswas (2009), K.P., "Plundering tuna from Indian exclusive economic zone", *(JIOS), Journal of Indian Ocean Studies*, 17(1), April 2009.

Bowbrick (2003), LV. Commander R.C., "Piracy", *Naval Review*, 91(3), August 2003.

Byers (2003), Michael, "Policing the sea and skies: Gunboat Diplomacy" *World Today*, 69 (10), October 2003.

Carneiro (1991), Commodore J.P., "A functional Coast Guard of the 21st century: Some thought", *(USI) Journal of the United Service Institution of India*, October 1991.

Casseset (1989), Antorio, "The international community's legal response to terrorism", *International and Contemporary Law Quarterly*, 38(3), July 1989.

Chalk (2002), Peter, "Piracy reemerges as a modern-day threat", *Jane's Naval Intelligence*, 107 (2), May 2002.

Chitley and Rao (1970-71), Chitley, D.V. and Rao, S. Appu, *The Constitution of India With Exhaustive Analysis and Commentary*, A.I.R. Commentaries, Vol. IV, 2nd ed., The All India Reporter Ltd., Bombay, Nagpur.

The Constitution of India (1977), Government of India, Ministry of Law, Justice and Company Affairs, New Delhi.

The Customs Act, 1962 (2008), as amended by the Finance Act 2007, Universal Law Publishers Pvt. Ltd., Delhi.

Defence News (2004), February 16, reproduced in *Strategic Digest*, 34 (4), April 2004.

Defence Watch (2010), "Introspective time", 9 (5), January 2010.

De Silva (2009), John C., "Environmental Conflict Management and New Trends in Piracy", (*JIOS*), *Journal of Indian Ocean Studies*, 17 (2), August 2009.

Dixit (2006), Sandeep, "New system planned to monitor ships", *The Hindu*, December 1, 2006.

Dixit, (2008), Sandeep, "Pirates, India defends action", *The Hindu*, November 27, 2008.

Donny (2002), Michael, "Maritime search and rescue, and Indian perspective", (*JIOS*), *Journal of Indian Ocean Studies*, 10 (2), August 2002.

Economic Survey, 1988-89, GoI, New Delhi, 1989.

Economic Survey, 1994-95, New Delhi, 1995.

Economic Survey, 2001-02, New Delhi, 2002.

Economic Survey, 2003-04, New Delhi, 2004.

Economic Survey, 2006-07, New Delhi, 2007.

Economic Survey, 2010-11, New Delhi, 2011.

FAO (1987), *Regional Compadium of Fisheries Legislation, Indian Ocean Region, Vol. I,* Food and Agricultural Organisation, UN, Rome,

1987.

Fernandes (2000), George, "Maritime dimensions of India's security", *Indian Defence Review*, 15 (4), October-December 2000.

Fenwick (1965), Charles G., *International Law*, 4th ed., New York,

Flynn (2006), Stephen E., "Port Security is still a house of cards", *Far Eastern Economic Review*, 169 (1), January-February 2006.

Forbes and Rumley (2008), Forbes, Vivian Louis and Rumley, Dennis, "Asymmetric conflict in the maritime dimension: The Indian Ocean basin", in Raghvan, V.R. and Prabhakar, W. Lawrence S., eds., *Maritime Security in Indian Ocean Region*, Tata McGraw-Hill Pub., New Delhi.

Friedman (2005), Benjamin, "Homeland Security", *Foreign Policy*, July-August 2005.

Ghosh (2006), Commander P.K., "The maritime dimensions of India's energy calculus", *Maritime Affairs*, 2 (1), Summer 2002.

Gunaratne (2001), Rohana, "Sea Tiger's success spreads copycat tactics", *Jane's Intelligence Review*, 13 (3), March 2001.

Gupta (2002), Commander Manoj, "India's maritime security",(*USI) United Service Institution of India*, 132 (548) July-September 2002.

Habib (2009), Haroon, "Chittagong arms were for ULFA", *The Hindu*, March 8, 2009.

Halberstam (1988), Malvina, "Terrorism on the high seas: the Achille Laura piracy and IMO Convention on maritime safety", *American Journal of International Law*, 82 (1), January 1988.

The Hindu (2009), "Piracy Menace, a Challenge to India', March 23, 2009.

Hiranandani (2003), Vice-Admiral G.M., *Transition to Eminance, Indian Navy 1976-1990*, Lancer, New Delhi.

Hiranandani (2008) Vice-Admiral G.M., "The Sethusamydram Ship Canal project – defence aspect", *Defence Watch*, 8(1), September 2008.

Holmes and Winner (2004), Holmes, James and Winner, Andrew C., "WMD interdicting, the gravest danger", *Proceedings of US Naval Institute*, February 2004.

India, 2005, Government of India (GOI), Ministry of Information and Broadcasting, New Delhi,

India, 2008, GOI, New Delhi, 2009.

India, 2010, GOI, New Delhi, 2011.

The Indian Penal Code (text), in *The India Code, Vol. III*, (1956), GOI, Ministry of Law, Government Printing Press, Calcutta.

Jane's Defence Weekly (1997), "Thailand seizes illegal arms bound for Manipur", March 26, 1997.

Singh (2008), Jasbir, Lt. General R.K. "Combating terrorism – Indian way", *Defence Watch*, 8(1), September 2008.

Joshi (2008), Sandeep, "Anti-money laundering bill introduced", *The Hindu*, October 18, 2008.

Joengensen (2008), Niels P., "Maritime transportation, port security and technological initiatives in the post-9/11 period", in Raghvan, V.R. and Prabhakar, W. Lawrance S., eds., *Maritime Security in Indian Ocean Region*, Tata McGraw-Hill Pub., New Delhi.

Joyner (1984), Christ C., "Off-shore Maritime Terrorism", *Naval War College Review*, 34 (4), July-August 1983, reproduced in *Strategic Digest, 14(3), March 1984*.

Kamath (1979), Vice-Admiral V.A., "The emergence of the Indian Coast Guard", *(USI) Journal of the United Service Institution of India*, 109 (457), July-September 1979.

Keyuan (2005), Zou, "Seeking effectiveness for the crackdown of piracy at sea", *Journal of International Affairs*, 59 (1), Fall-Winter 2005.

Khurana (2005), Gurpreet S., "Cooperation among maritime security forces, imperative for India and South-East Asia", *Strategic Analysis*, 29 (2), April-June 2005.

Krishna Dev (1995), Rear-Admiral (Retd.), "Indian merchant shipping, an appraisal", *Indian Defence Review*, 10 (1), January-March 1995.

Lehr (2008), Peter, "Asymetric warfare in the Indian Ocean: What kind of threat from which kind of actor?" in Raghavan V.R. and Prabhakar, W. Lawrence S., eds. *Maritime Security in Indian Ocean Region*, Tata McGraw-Hill Pub., New Delhi.

Lele (2006), Ajay, "Technology revolution and maritime security", (*JIOS*) *Journal of Indian Ocean Studies*, 14 (2), August 2006.

MoD (Ministry of Defence), *A.R.* (Annual Report), *1976-77*, GoI (Government of India), New Delhi, 1977.

MoD, *A.R.*, *1980-81*, GoI, New Delhi, 1981.

MoD, *A.R.*, *1981-82*, GoI, New Delhi, 1982.

MoD, *A.R.*, *1986-87*, GoI, New Delhi, 1987.

MoD, *A.R.*, *1987-88*, GoI, New Delhi, 1988.

MoD, *A.R.*, *1994-95*, GoI, New Delhi, 1995.

MoD, *A.R.*, *1996-97*, GoI, New Delhi, 1997.

MOD, *A.R.*, 2001-02, GoI, New Delhi, 2002.

MoD, *A.R.*, *2002-03*, GoI, New Delhi, 2003.

MOD, *A.R.*, *2003-04*, GoI, New Delhi, 2004.

MoD, *A.R.*, *2007-08*, GoI, New Delhi, 2008.

MoD, *A.R.*, *2009-10*, GoI, New Delhi, 2010.

MoD, *A.R.*, *2010-11*, GoI, New Delhi, 2011.

MoF (Ministry of Finance), *A.R.* (Annual Report), *1974-75*, GOI, (Government of India), New Delhi, 1975.

MoF, *A.R.*, *1980-81*, GoI, New Delhi, 1981,

MoF, *A.R.*, *1987-88*, GoI, New Delhi, 1988,

MoF, *A.R., 1993-94*, GoI, New Delhi, 1994,

MHA (Ministry of Home Affairs, Department of Internal Security, States and Home), *A.R.* (Annual Report) *1993-94*, GoI, (Government of India), New Delhi, 1994.

MHA *A.R. 2001-02*, GoI, New Delhi, 2002.

MHA *A.R. 2002-03*, GoI, New Delhi, 2003.

MHA *A.R. 2003-04*, GoI, New Delhi, 2004.

MHA *A.R. 2005-06*, GoI, New Delhi, 2006.

MHA *A.R. 2006-07*, GoI, New Delhi, 2007.

MHA *A.R. 2008-09*, GoI, New Delhi, 2009.

MHA *A.R. 2009-10*, GoI, New Delhi, 2010.

MHA *A.R. 2010-11*, GoI, New Delhi, 2011.

Mahapatra (2010), Dhananjay, "India needs tough law to tackle terrorism, *The Times of India*, May 9, 2010.

Malaviya and Paleri (2000), Malaviya, G. and Paleri, P., "Responses to ocean crimes", (*JIOS*) *Journal of Indian Ocean Studies*, 8 (3), December 2000.

Mani, (2002), V.S., "Needed a law on genocide", *The Hindu*, April 10, 2002.

Manohar and Chitley (1988), Manohar, V.R. and Chitley, W.N. eds., *The AIR Manual, Unrepelled Central Acts*, Vol. 1, 5th edition the A.I.R. Publications, Nagpur. Also, see Manohar and Chitaley (1988), *The AIR Manual, vol. 7, vol. 19, vo. 36, vol. 41, vol. 43 and vol. 45*. A.I.R. Pubs, Nagpur.

Mehta (2007), Admiral Suresh, "Freedom of the seas, a contemporary outlook", *Defence Watch*, 6 (8), April 2007.

Military Balance, 2003-2004, (IISS) International Institute of Strategic Studies, London, 2004.

Murphy (2006), Martin, "Maritime terrorism: the threat in context", *Jane's Intelligence Review*, 18 (2), February 2006.

Nambiar (2006), V.K., "India's national security: the maritime context", in Nambiar, E.K.G. and Singh, K.R., (eds.), *India, 2020: Maritime Perspectives*, Publications Division, Calicut University.

Naravane (2002), Vaiju, "Terrorist outfit owns up attack on tanker", *The Hindu*, October 12, 2002.

Nariman (2002), Fali S., "Why I voted against POTA", *The Hindu*, March 24, 2002.

Nazeer (2008), Mohamed, "Radio becon for fishing crafts mooted", *The Hindu*, December 1, 2006.

O'Connell (1984), D.P., *The International Law of the Sea, vol. II,* ed. By I.A. Shearer, Clarendon Press, Oxford.

Oppenheim (1972), I.L., *International Law: A Treatise, vol. II,* 7th edition (8th impression) ed. by H. Lauterpacht, Longman, London.

Paleri (2004), Prabhakaran, *Role of the Coast Guard in Maritime Security of India*, Knowledge World, New Delhi.

Paleri (2006), Prabhakaran, "Maritime activities in the choke points of Indian Ocean", *(JIOS) Journal of Indian Ocean Studies*, 14 (2), August 2006.

Paleri (2007), Prabhakaran, "Suppression of Unlawful Acts Against Safety of Maritime Navigation and Fixed Platform on the Continental-Shelf", *(JIOS) Journal of Indian Ocean Studies*, December 2007.

Pandit (2010), Rajat, "Intel network planned to keep an eye on sea", *The Times of India*, November 14, 2010.

Pereira (2009), Ignatius, "Electronic I. card for fishermen soon", *The Hindu*, January 10, 2009.

Pon (2008), Anand, "Role of private maritime security on the maritime security domain: Focus on South-East Asia and the Indian Ocean littoral", in Raghvan, V.R., and Prabhakar, W. Lawrance S., eds., *Maritime Security in the Indian Ocean Region,*Tata McGraw-Hill Pub., New Delhi.

Prasad (2009), K.V., "Overall charge for the Navy", *The Hindu*, March 1, 2009.

Qasim (2001), S.Z., "Minerals of the deep seabed (abyssal depth)", *(JIOS) Journal of Indian Ocean Studies*, 9 (1) April 2001.

Raman (2006), B. ed., *Peace Without Process*, Samashakti, New Delhi.

Raman (2007), B., *The Kaoboys of R &W, Down Memory Lane*, Lancer, New Delhi.

Rao (1983), P. Chandrashekhar, *The New Law of Maritime Zones, with Special Reference to India's Maritime Zones*, Milind Pub. Pvt. Ltd., New Delhi.

Report of the Kargil Review Committee, Executive Summary (2002), *(USI) Journal of the United Service Institution of India*, 130 (539), January-March 2000.

Rix (2005), Commodore Anthony, "Maritime security operations in the Arabian Sea", *RUSI Defence Systems*, 8 (2), Autumn 2005.

Ronzitti (1990), Natalino, "The law of the sea and the use of force against terrorist activities", in Ronzitti, Natalino, ed., *Maritime Terrorism and International Law*, Martinus Nijhoff Pub., Dordrech, London.

Roy (2002), Vice-Admiral Mihir K., "Disaster management, Indian Ocean", *(USI) Journal of the United Services Institution of India*, 132 (549), July-September 2002.

Roy-Choudhury (1997), Rahul, "Ocean/marine management in India", *Strategic Analysis*, 20 (5), August 1997.

Roy-Choudhury (1998), Rahul, "India's energy security, CNG and shipping", *(JIOS) Journal of Indian Ocean Studies*, 6 (1) November 1998.

Sakhuja (2002), Vijay, "Shipping containers as Trojan Horses – challenge to maritime security", *(JIOS) Journal of Indian Ocean Studies*, 10 (3) December 2002.

Sakhuja (2005), Vijay, "Maritime order and piracy", *Strategic Analysis*, 24 (5), August, 2005.

Schofield (2003), Clive, "Australia shores up its maritime security", *Jane's Intelligence Review*, 15 (11), November 2003.

Sen (1995), Pulak, "India's Coast Guard comes of age", *Maritime International* (Mumbai), 1 (2), February 1995.

Shankar (2001), S., "Tamil Nadu: patrol boats lying idle for long", *The Hindu*, July 14, 2001.

Sharma (2000), O.P., "Piracy at sea, legal aspects", (*JIOS*) *Journal of Indian Ocean Studies*, 7 (2-3) March 2000.

Sharma (2005), O.P., "Integrated ocean management and UNCLOS-III, 1982", (*JIOS*) *Journal of Indian Ocean Studies*, 13 (3) December 2005.

Shekhawat (2006), V.S., "Approach to sea power", *Seminar* (562), June 2006.

Singh (1990), K.R., *Intra-regional Interventions in South Asia*, USI Paper No. 9, USI, New Delhi.

Singh, (1992), Madhvendra, "Does India really need two maritime services? *Trishul*, 5 (2), December 1992.

Singh (1993), K.R., "International terror from across the seas", *Pioneer* (New Delhi, September 21, 1993.)

Singh (2006), K.R., *New Challenges to Maritime Security: Legality and Legitimacy of Responses*, Publications Division, University of Calicut.

Singh (2008), K.R. *Maritime Security for India: New Challenges and Responses*, New Centuty Pub., New Delhi.

Singh and Seethi (2010), Singh, K.R. and Seethi, K.M., eds., *Coastal Security: Need for a New Look*, K.P.S. Menon, Chair for Diplomatic Studies, School of International Relations and Politics, M.G.U., Kottayam.

Song (2007), Yann-Huei, "The US-led Proliferation Security Initiative and UNCLOS-III, legality, implementation and assessment", *Ocean Development and International Law*, 38 (1-2), 2007.

Starcevic (2002), Feodor, "UN's role in combating terrorism", *The Hindu*,

April 14, 2002.

TERI (2006), *Energy Data Directory and Yearbook, 2004-05*, Tata Energy Research Institute, New Delhi.

Vasan (2006), R.S., "Maritime security in India's security calculus", *Dialogue* 8 (2), October-December 2006.

Velencia (1997), Mark J., "Asia: The law of the sea and international relations", *International Affairs*, 73 (2), 1997.

Venkataraman (2006), K., "Dilemmas of external actors", in Raman, B., ed., *Sri Lanka, Peace Without Process*, Samshakti, New Delhi.

Winner (2005), Andrew C., "The Proliferation Security Initiative: the new face of interdiction", *Washington Quarterly*, 28 0000(2), Spring 2005.

Index